Objectivity
and
Cultural Divergence

ROYAL INSTITUTE OF PHILOSOPHY LECTURE SERIES: 17
SUPPLEMENT TO *PHILOSOPHY* 1984

EDITED BY:

S. C. Brown

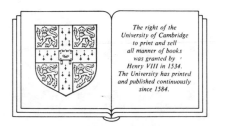
CAMBRIDGE UNIVERSITY PRESS

CAMBRIDGE
LONDON NEW YORK NEW ROCHELLE
MELBOURNE SYDNEY

Published by the Press Syndicate of the University of Cambridge
The Pitt Building, Trumpington Street, Cambridge CB2 1RP
32 East 57th Street, New York, NY 10022, USA
10 Stamford Road, Oakleigh, Melbourne 3166, Australia

Library of Congress catalogue card number: 84–45451

British Library Cataloguing in Publication Data
Brown, Stuart, *1938–*
Objectivity and cultural divergence—(Royal Institute
of Philosophy lecture series; 17)
1. Cultural relativism
I. Title   II. Series
306   GN345.5
ISBN 0 521 26940 7

Printed in Great Britain by Adlard & Son Ltd, Bartholomew Press, Dorking

Contents

Foreword

The existence of significant differences between human cultures has been known since antiquity and has long been the occasion for philosophical reflection. Sceptics, for instance, have almost traditionally pointed to cultural divergence in matters of morality in order to challenge the assumption that such matters can be discussed objectively. On similar grounds they have cast doubt on the pretensions of any particular religion to be the 'true" one. It is a commonplace that much we find natural and necessary to our way of thinking proves on examination to be no more than a local custom. But if cross-cultural comparisons could lead to scepticism they seemed also to lead back from scepticism to be a true science of human nature. For the more striking the points of divergence within a range of cultures the more striking is any feature which is universally to be found among them.

Reflections such as these still find some place in recent philosophical discussions, including those which comprise the present volume. But recent discussions have taken new turnings. In the first place, they have tended to reflect the considerable growth of a variety of culture studies as well as the greater sophisitication which results from pursuing them in a professional way. Classics of social anthropology well illustrate, for example, how easy it is for a researcher to project the values and assumptions of his own society on to that which he claims to be observing. The problem of 'subjectivity' is now acknowledged as a professional hazard for anyone whose business it is to try to understand cultures other than his own. At a philosophical level it can be asked what kind of understanding that would be and whether the kind of understanding sought can be achieved.

These are among the matters discussed in the first group of papers included in this volume. Placed between this group and a third group on ethics is a group of papers concerned with an alleged way of imparting objectivity from one of the natural sciences into culture studies and into ethics. But, if that is how advocates of sociobiology see their enterprise, their critics have not been slow to question its objectivity.

Several contributors to this volume have sought to characterize the natural sciences as possessing a kind of objectivity not attainable in ethics or in cultural and social studies. This is a view partly defended by Bernard Williams. Renford Bambrough, by contrast, seeks to defend a strong form of moral objectivism.

Foreword

The final two papers are both, as their titles indicate, partly sociological in approach. They are both, moreover, concerned with the objectivity of natural science. David Bloor suggests that this objectivity consists in effect in the prevalence of certain social institutions. These encouraged the view that nature was remote and could only be understood by painstaking experiment, the view later advanced in positivism. Dr Bloor's analysis might appear to be implicitly critical of a positivist theory of objectivity. But the terms of his analysis do not seem to leave him room to talk of a correct theory as opposed to one which seems right to us because it is part of our cultural heritage. If relativism seems endemic to Dr Bloor's approach, however, it presents itself to Ernest Gellner as a problem to be overcome. Professor Gellner concedes that there really is a difficulty in comparing radically diverse visions of reality such as the 'positivistic' or the 'Hegelian' so as to assess 'their relative cognitive purchasing power'. None the less Gellner seeks to provide a defence of positivism, albeit an unorthodox one.

I have presented some of these contributions as if they might have been replies to one another. But they were not so. Some of the later lectures were able to take account of what had been said earlier. But this has only marginally affected what is written here. Moreover the lectures were not presented in the order in which they are printed. They were written as self-standing pieces and can be read as such. None the less there are many connections—more perhaps than can be represented by any single ordering of them.

Stuart Brown

Objectivity and Social Anthropology

J. H. M. BEATTIE

This lecture is divided, roughly, into three parts. First, there is a general and perhaps rather simple-minded discussion of what are the 'facts' that social anthropologists study; is there anything special about these 'facts' which makes them different from other kinds of facts? It will be useful to start with the common-sense distinction between two kinds or, better, aspects of social facts; first—though neither is analytically prior to the other—and putting it very crudely, 'what people do', the aspect of social interaction, and second, 'what—and how—people think', the conceptual, classifying, cognitive component of human culture. Now in reality, of course (and perhaps not so 'of course'; people do tend to think of them as separate 'things'), these two aspects are inextricably intertwined. But it is essential to distinguish them analytically, because each aspect gives rise to quite different kinds of problems of understanding for the social anthropologist. We shall see that the problem of how to be 'objective', and so to avoid ethnographic error, arises in both contexts, but in rather different forms in each.

So, in the second part of my lecture, I look, fairly briefly, at the situation from the point of view of *social action*; what are the special snags and snares involved in understanding what people are doing? We shall of course find it difficult to understand what they are doing without trying to understand what they *think* they are doing. But in a sense that is more than trivial, and at least up to a point, the attempt may, I believe, legitimately be made.

Then, thirdly and lastly, I turn to the problem of understanding people's ways of thought, the concepts, beliefs, values, symbols, etc., current in different cultures. In this highly complex field there are two broad dimensions which are not always clearly distinguished. The first gives rise to the question whether, in order to avoid ethnocentricity, a different *kind* of rationality, in some way different from 'ours' (whoever 'we' may be), must be imputed to certain other cultures, so that if their judgment of what is the case appears to differ from 'ours', we have no right to say that our judgment is correct and theirs is mistaken. This position is, or has been represented as being, that taken up by the philosopher Peter Winch some years ago, and it still seems to have its adherents, as we shall see. More complex, perhaps, is the question how far, if at all, we can legitimately use the categories of our own particular culture or cultures (as distinct from the categories of human reason

1

supposedly shared by everybody), in order to make sense of the institutions of other cultures. Here the celebrated French social anthropologist Louis Dumont is (or appears to be) the protagonist of the view, I think plainly untenable, that we can and should eschew *altogether* the question-begging categories of our 'own' culture.

So, *is* ethnocentricity unavoidable? It might seem to be so even in framing problems about it! Or, putting the question in positive terms, is objectivity possible? Well, yes, I shall conclude, at least up to a point. As a foregone conclusion not a very exciting one, perhaps. But, who knows, maybe we shall find something to entertain and interest us along the way.

I

Let me, then, begin by taking a quick look at social or cultural data as 'facts'. Anthropologists are no less aware than other scientists (at least if they are it's not for want of being told) that 'facts' are not 'given', but constructed, with the inevitable help of concepts. This of course has been generally understood since Kant. To quote the sociologist Werner Stark, 'a fact, in both the common and the scientific meaning of the term, is always something already in some way shaped and made concrete by our mental activity. Facts only stand out from the chaos . . . when we put some question to reality'.[1] As Popper puts it, 'the *problem* [or hypothesis] always come first'.[2] All this is old hat, but its implications are often overlooked by social scientists, including social anthropologists, who constantly project their mental constructs or 'models' into 'reality', without always recognizing that they are doing so. What exactly *is* a lineage, for example, or a society, for that matter? How can one know what they are, and how can one go about studying such elusive entities? Whitehead's fallacy of misplaced concreteness is always with us, and no doubt it always will be so long as we use words.

There's a familiar dilemma here for anthropological fieldworkers. If the researcher has no clear idea (or no idea at all) of what he's looking for, it is fair to say that he is unlikely to find it. But if he has *too* precise a notion of what he expects to find, he is all too likely to find it, even, sometimes, if it isn't there. When I first went to the kingdom of Bunyoro, in western Uganda, from Oxford, steeped in lineage theory, Evans-Pritchard's book *The Nuer*, etc., I found, perhaps not surprisingly, lineages all over the place; not until later did I discover that 'lineages', so far as they existed at all, were relatively unimportant.

[1] W. Stark, *The Sociology of Knowledge* (London: Routledge, 1958), 109.
[2] K. R. Popper, *The Poverty of Historicism* (London: Routledge, 1957), 121.

I don't think I was the only social anthropologist to impose, to begin with anyway, my preconceived notions on the data—maybe there's no other way of beginning. One just has to be on one's guard all the time. As Ernest Gellner has remarked, contrasting social anthropology with sociology: 'Sociology can sometimes be a matter of ascertaining facts within an institutional framework which is taken for granted. The anthropologist can virtually never take anything for granted in this way'.[3] It might perhaps be doubted whether the sociologist can, or should, either. But that is another story.

Given, then, that social and cultural facts, like all 'facts', are in some measure constructs, are they in no important way different from other kinds of 'facts', so that no special problems arise in studying them? Some have thought so. The American philosopher of science Ernest Nagel, for example, has claimed[4] that there are 'no methodological difficulties unique to the social sciences'. Much evidently depends on what one means by 'methodological difficulties'. But it is my view, and I think that of most social anthropologists, that what we (as social anthropologists) study and what, say, physicists and even biologists study, do differ in a very important way, and that this difference is bound to affect the very nature of each of the two kinds of enquiry. Put very simply—perhaps over-simply—the question is: can people, as people, be studied simply as 'things', as a natural science might study them or is there something special about 'people' which calls for special methods of investigation?

I suppose the latest example of this 'natural science' approach is the 'Modern Synthesis' of sociobiology, associated especially with the name of E. O. Wilson. The aim is to bring all the social sciences within the scope of genetic biology, a vain hope, according to the critics of this approach. I shall say no more about sociobiology here, other than to quote one of these critics, the anthropologist Marshall Sahlins: ' . . . biology, while it is an absolutely necessary condition for culture, is equally and absolutely insufficient: it is completely unable to specify the cultural properties of human behaviour or their variations from one human group to another' (p. xi).[5]

No doubt a strictly behaviourist social science is at least theoretically conceivable; indeed much of the distinguished social anthropologist Radcliffe-Brown's writing—e.g. about his hoped-for 'natural science of society', and the search for the regularities which he mistakenly identified with 'scientific laws'—pointed clearly in that direction, though I doubt if he would have admitted this. And, like 'functional-

[3] E. Gellner, *Cause and Meaning in the Social Sciences* (London: Routledge, 1973), 18.

[4] E. Nagel, *The Structure of Science* (London: Routledge, 1961), 503.

[5] M. Sahlins, *The Use and Abuse of Biology* (London: Tavistock, 1977), xi.

ism', behaviourism may be, or need be, only a method, not a dogma. But I think the consensus among social anthropologists is that such approaches leave out all that is characteristically human. Let me quote from one of my favourite American anthropologists, Robert Redfield; the woolliness, even discursiveness, of his style is part of its charm:

> We look from our position, that of an anthropological investigator out, to, and inside of those other people, over there, doing things and thinking thoughts that we seek to understand . . . using the sentiments and ideas that we have within us as other human beings. We could not understand those others at all if we did not or could not feel some part of the sentiments and hold the ideas which we come to understand that they feel and hold. We do not observe 'behaviour' in the sense of events that may be described in physical terms, as motion and velocity . . . We observe the overt indications, from which, using imaginative sympathy, we infer the states of mind and feeling of those others that we study . . . So we 'project ourselves' into the mind of that other by means of our own humanity . . .[6]

And so on.

The point, I think, is valid. Isaiah Berlin is saying the same thing when he writes 'except on the assumption that history [and the same applies to social anthropology] must deal with human beings purely as material objects in space—must, in short, be behaviourist—its methods can scarcely be assimilated to the standards of an exact natural science'.[7] Elsewhere Berlin writes (no doubt a little unfairly!) that 'a man who lacks common intelligence can be a physicist of genius, but not even a mediocre historian',[8] presumably because it requires the common intelligence shared by all, or most, human beings, rather than genius, to put oneself in the other fellow's place. The philosopher Antony Flew, in a review of Popper's *The Poverty of Historicism*, put the point even more forcefully; what he says is worth quoting in full. Flew begins:

> Popper writes: 'most of the objects of social science . . . are abstract objects; they are theoretical constructions. Even "the war" or "the army" are abstract concepts . . . What is concrete is the many who are killed; or the men and women in uniform, etc. These objects, these theoretical constructions used to interpret our

[6] R. Redfield, 'The Anthropological Study of Man', *Anthropological Quarterly* **32**, No. 1 (1959), 4.

[7] I. Berlin, *Historical Inevitability* (London: Oxford University Press, 1954), 52.

[8] I. Berlin, 'History and Theory', in *Studies in the Philosophy of History* **1** (1960), 30.

experience, are the result of constructing certain *models* (especially of institutions) in order to explain certain experiences—a familiar theoretical method in the natural sciences . . .'

To say this [Flew goes on] is at least very misleading. For the notions of *the war* and *the army* are quite certainly not explanatory concepts invested by sociologists. Furthermore, and much more importantly, whereas the concepts created by the natural scientists play their parts only in the explanation and description of phenomena, such institutional ideas as Popper is indicating are essentially and inextricably involved in the phenomena themselves. Men *decide to* join the army or to take on a fresh job *because* their country is at war. Their behaviour is guided consciously by the institutional ideas: the ideas are not introduced by external students to explain the non-conscious behaviour of men at war. Unlike things, people often up to a point explain their own behaviour for themselves, while this very understanding in turn frequently determines their behaviour. . . . It is this which makes possible and demands distinctive sorts of explanation, in terms of *having reasons, forming plans*, and *following rules*.[9]

The crux of the matter is that for the most part the behaviour of people in societies only makes sense when we seek to discover what they *think* they are doing, a mode of enquiry which would obviously be inappropriate if we were dealing, as 'natural' scientists, with (say) molecules or, for that matter, with the social life of white ants or bumble-bees.

So much for the 'facts'. Let me now go on to my second and third themes, the consideration of the problem of understanding and (what is part of that problem) of being 'objective', in the context of the two dimensions of our understanding which I distinguished earlier, what people do, and what, and how, they think. As I noted at the beginning, these two dimensions interpenetrate constantly and continuously, and the anthropological fieldworker—like everyone else—operates in both contexts simultaneously. But neither can be reduced to the other. Social and cultural institutions have both consequences and meanings, and the social anthropologist is, or may be, legitimately interested in both. But such is the human craving for unity that some anthropologists, like some philosophers, have stressed one dimension at the expense of, sometimes to the virtual exclusion of, the other. Let us first of all consider some problems of objectivity and ethnocentricity in the context of understanding what people *do*.

[9] A. Flew, review of Popper's *The Poverty of Historicism*, in *Sociological Review* **6**, No. 2 (1958) 283–284.

II

When we are looking at societies and cultures as what Talcott Parsons called 'systems of action', we are explicitly concerned with relationships of cause and effect. Historians, without for the most part bothering about the philosophical difficulties involved in the notion of causality, ask how particular states of affairs came about; what were the causal factors involved? Likewise, social anthropologists who are interested in problems of social change may ask what have been the consequences in paticular contexts of the introduction of a cash economy, say, or literacy, or Christian missionaries (or all three). In studying such questions evidently the anthropologist is playing the historian, the main difference being in the kinds of evidence each uses, the historian depending mostly on documents, the anthropologist primarily on observation and enquiry in the social field itself.

But as well as providing a common ground of understanding with historians, the concern with causes and effects in social contexts lies at the centre of the 'functionalist' or 'structural-functionalist' anthropology of Britain in the 1930s and 1940s. Though 'functionalism' in its various forms has come in for a good deal of in part deserved obloquy during recent years, it is by no means dead. In fact Professor Ioan Lewis of the London School of Economics has roundly declared that 'we are all structural-functionalists today'.[10] Not all social anthropologists would agree with him, however.

Though I have myself recently been described as an 'orthodox functionalist' (from the context I don't *think* this was meant as a compliment), I am not here going either to attack or to defend 'functionalism', however qualified or defined. I only want to point out that in its earlier and more unregenerate days it was concerned—at least in Radcliffe-Brown's version of it—not with unique historical processes but essentially with repetitive cycles in on-going social life, the effects of which were, it was believed, to contribute to 'the functioning of the total social system'.[11] This has long been seen to be a very inadequate and indeed misleading model for anthropological enquiry, if only because it implied that the only way such a 'functionalist' hypothesis could be disproved was by the destruction of the entire society in question.

If, however, we abandon this holistic view, and concern ourselves rather with the implications for *one another*, not for the 'whole', of interacting social institutions, there is still some sense in functionalism.

[10] I. Lewis, *Social Anthropology in Perspective* (Harmondsworth: Penguin Books, 1976), 64.
[11] A. R. Radcliffe-Brown, *Structure and Function in Primitive Society* (London: Cohen and West, 1952), 181.

This is especially so if we follow Gellner in regarding it not as a 'doctrine', but rather as 'an obligation placed upon anthropological enquiry',[12] an obligation, that is, to investigate the causal interconnectedness of events, even—or especially—when the connections are by no means obvious. And it is worth stressing here that the concept of 'cause' in social science does not entail behaviourism; it is closely bound up with beliefs and concepts. Thus in the case of social sanctions it is the *idea* of the results of a possible breach that is effective; if it isn't, the sanction hasn't worked.

As an example of a recent, and I think quite illuminating, 'functional' hypothesis one might cite Mary Douglas's thesis, supported by evidence from the neighbouring Nuer and Dinka peoples of the southern Sudan, that where social, i.e. 'group', control is weak, a concern with physical, i.e. bodily, boundaries (an emphasis on notions of pollution, for example) tends to be diminished, and vice versa.[13] A comparable 'functional' hypothesis, in another African context, is proposed—and I think demonstrated—by Alan Harwood in his study of the Safwa of Tanzania;[14] in disputes *within* lineages accusations of *witchcraft* (the supposed possession of an innate, usually hereditary, power to injure others) predominate; in dealings with affines and other 'outsiders' accusations of *sorcery* (acts of harmful magic deliberately entered into) prevail. The underlying theme is familiar in various guises; it was developed by the anthropologist Fredrik Barth and others as the contrast between *incorporation* (e.g. in a lineage) and *transaction* (a relationhip, voluntarily entered into, between members of different groups). But the distinction traces its ancestry back to Maine and Durkheim.

These illustrations show, I think, the acceptable face of functionalism, not as involving any reference to the maintenance of whole societies or 'total social structures', but rather as concerned with the mutual interdependencies, on the causal level, of the the different institutional complexes which make up a society.

But—and this is the $64,000 question—how are we to identify and describe these institutionalized complexes in an unfamiliar society? Can we really, looking out 'from our position' as Redfield put it, be 'objective'? Or is ethnocentricity unavoidable? For it seems to me obvious that we have, to begin with at any rate, to identify these unfamiliar institutions in *our* terms, by reference to those aspects of social life with which they are, or appear to be, concerned. Thus if a

[12] Op. cit. 136.

[13] M. Douglas, *Natural Symbols: Explorations in Cosmology* (London: Barrie and Rockliffe, 1970), 119–128.

[14] A. Harwood, *Witchcraft, Sorcery and Social Categories among the Safwa* (London: OUP for the International African Institute, 1970).

particular complex of belief and behaviour in a given society seems to be concerned with (no doubt among other things) the exercise of authority and the maintenance of social order, we may refer to it as 'political', in the sense that it has, or appears to have, a political aspect; if it is concerned, again *inter alia*, with the production and distribution of goods and services, we may speak of it as having an economic aspect, and so on. Obviously we must be aware that an institution which at first sight appears to be 'economic' may not in fact be so, and even if it is, it is likely to have many other kinds of significances as well (political, juridical, ritual, etc.). Here the danger of false disjunction, 'if this, then not that', to which social anthropologists are particularly prone, arises. But despite these difficulties, and they are considerable, we have, to begin with, no alternative to labelling, provisionally at least, the institutions of other cultures in terms of the categories of our own. It is an anthropological commonplace that we are engaged from the beginning in an enterprise of *translation*.

This is where the distinguished French anthropologist Louis Dumont comes in. In a discussion some years ago of how anthropologists think, or ought to think, about kinship (the question was whether one could say that a kinship relationship had, or might have, an *economic* content, as opposed to a strictly 'kinship' content), Dumont wrote: 'only our sociocentricism warrants the attribution of a substantial quality to economy by preference to kinship'.[15] I won't go into details of the issue here, but what Dumont is saying is that 'economy' is *our* term, and the concept it denotes is *our* concept, while 'kinship' (though this term is of course 'ours' too, a fact which Dumont does not remark) denotes an idiom, a system of thought, which exists and has meaning in the culture itself. Again, in the same place Dumont writes that when an anthropologist attributes to a kinship relationship 'a "content" of political–economic nature' (Dumont's phrase), what he is doing is applying *'the ideology of his native society* [Dumont's italics] (economy, etc.) to the denomination of happenings which are denoted differently' in the society concerned.

Now all this, if it means what it seems to mean, evidently goes a bit too far. Surely all the anthropologist is saying when he imputes 'economic' or 'political' content to a kinship relationship is that the relationship seems to involve economic co-operation by the kinsmen concerned, in agricultural production, for example, or that it embodies some structure of authority which we may call 'political'. Certainly the danger of ethno- (or socio-) centricity is always with us. But to speak of economics or politics in describing another culture is not necessarily—

[15] L. Dumont, 'A Fundamental Problem in the Sociology of Caste', in *Contributions to Indian Sociology* 9 (1966), 21.

though it may be—to impose an 'ideology'. It is simply to use words as a means of communicating some observed facts about the culture being investigated. Unless we are to write our accounts of other cultures entirely in the language of these cultures themselves (and it must be said that some anthropological monographs look rather as if this was what their authors were attempting) we have no alternative.

There is a further point. Surely it cannot be only the terms 'economic' and 'political' which are so grievously tainted. What about other 'Western' terms in common ethnographic use, like 'marriage', 'family', 'parenthood', 'authority', 'kinship' itself, and even 'hierarchy' (Dumont's own speciality)? Social anthropologists should indeed be constantly aware of the difficulties and dangers of extrapolating the terms and concepts of their 'own' cultures into their representations of other cultures. But these dangers can hardly be confined to only one or two such terms, all others being somehow miraculously exempt. Even though the danger may be greater in the case of some terms than it is in others, all must be tarred with the same 'sociocentric' brush, and all of them need to be handled with the same care and discretion. Ethnography provide many examples of errors arising from the ambiguity of words; Bacon's 'idols of the market-place' are a constant and characteristic concern of social anthropologists. But they are not to be resolved by forswearing altogether the categories of our own thought, whoever 'we' may be. Ernest Gellner once proposed an 'ideal language' for talking about kinship.[16] But this idea never, I think, got off the ground, perhaps partly because for social anthropologists it is of the nature of kinship to be about something else. In fact it was an attempt by me to demonstrate this[17] that provoked Dumont to make the remarks which I have just quoted.

III

I turn now from the problem of understanding systems of social relationships (regarded as systems of action), to the problem of understanding ideal or conceptual systems; from (to put it crudely) 'what people do', to 'what people think', or 'from function to meaning', in Pocock's neat phrase.[18] We may, if we like, look at this (in British social anthropology at least) as a movement from one kind of structure to another; from the 'structural-functionalism' of Radcliffe-Brown and his present-day successors to 'structuralism' in the modern sense, associated for social anthropologists largely (though by no means only)

[16] Op. cit. Ch. 11.
[17] J. Beattie, 'Kinship and Social Anthropology', *Man* **64,** No. 130 (1964).
[18] D. Pocock, *Social Anthropology* (London: Sheed and Ward, 1961) 76.

with the name of Lévi-Strauss. I won't be so rash as to attempt to define 'structuralism' in any of its numerous contemporary senses, but it may perhaps be agreed that it is about the human mind and its proclivity to categorize and classify experience, primarily through language, secondarily (I am quoting here from Peter Caws' useful essay) through the agency of magic, totem and (especially) myth—including, some would add, the modern versions of these agents, as science, art and morality.[19] It is, I think, of interest in considering the relativity of the terms 'structure' and 'structuralism' in social anthropology, that the same classic work, Evans-Pritchard's *The Nuer* (a study of the social importance of descent in a Nilotic tribe) has been interepreted as being about 'structure' in both of the two senses I have distinguished (i.e. as being concerned with both 'social' structure and 'mental' structures). Twelve years ago an anonymous reviewer in the *Times Literary Supplement* (3 December 1971) referred to *The Nuer* as 'the supreme, but characteristic, achievement of the Radcliffe-Brown ['functionalist'] school', while four years later Louis Dumont argued (in his *Introduction* to the French edition of the work) that what Evans-Pritchard was really concerned with were 'conceptual oppositions, oppositions in the structuralist's sense', and he castigated Meyer Fortes for seeing in *The Nuer* 'collective entities, solid and "corporate" unilineal groups'.[20] It is perhaps a measure of the enduring significance of Evans-Pritchard's work that it can plausibly be subjected to two such contrasting interpretations, though in fact they are not as 'contrasting' as they look.

At first sight, understanding people's ideas, the patterns and structures (especially the 'deeper' ones, of which they themselves may be unaware—and here lie many complex problems) of their thought must seem to be an even more difficult matter than understanding their behaviour. After all (and up to a point) we can *see*, or we sometimes think we can, what people are doing, but what and how they think is a different matter, which has to be inferred—if it can be ascertained at all—from what they do and say. Obviously the problem is even more acute in the understanding of people's ritual beliefs, the comprehension of which involves problems which do not arise, or do so only in lesser degree, in the context of people's technical, 'practical' concerns, ideas about which are more readily assimilable to 'Western' models. I am

[19] P. Caws, 'What is Structuralism?', *Claude Lévi-Strauss: the Anthroplogist as Hero*, E. W. and T. Hayes (eds) (Cambridge, Mass. and London: MIT Press, 1970).

[20] Preface to the French edition of E. E. Evans-Pritchard, *The Nuer* (Paris, 1968), trans. M. and J. Douglas in *Studies in Social Anthropology: Essays in memory of E. E. Evans-Pritchard by his former Oxford Colleagues*, J. Beattie and G. Lienhardt (eds) (Oxford: Clarendon Press, 1975), Ch. 14, 335, 341.

aware of the difficulties involved in the concept of 'ritual', and I have tried to say elsewhere what I mean by it.[21] The concept of 'belief' is perhaps even more complex. We may perhaps agree with Professor Rodney Needham that it is 'not a discriminable mode of experience'.[22] But, taken in the broadest possible sense of *assent*, however qualified, it can, I suppose, be said to be either explicit or implicit in any assertion about anything. There are, however, two aspects of belief in particular which should be mentioned here, since failure to distinguish them is, I believe [*sic*], a frequent source of confusion. The first is the degree of *explicitness* a belief must have in order to be a 'belief', and the second is the existential *status* ascribed to whatever it is that is believed in.

First, explicitness. Can we properly speak about 'belief' when the alleged belief is not explicitly formulated by anyone? And, to make the matter more complicated, are there not *degrees* of explicitness, from vague and unspoken assumption to formal and exact assertion? And can one speak of a 'belief' when there is *no* degree of explicitness? Confusion may arise from the failure to distinguish between 'beliefs' that are actually held by people, and those that are not consciously held by anyone, though they may be implicit in beliefs that people do, or may, consciously hold.

Second, what about what it *is* that is believed? I think that there is, or may be, a difference between saying 'I believe that 2 and 2 make 4', or 'I believe it's raining (I'm not concerned here with the difference between *these* two kinds of statements), on the one hand, and saying 'I believe in witchcraft', or 'I believe in ghosts', on the other. In the latter cases, what is believed is not, or need not be, taken absolutely literally, as would-be 'scientific' statements of fact, but rather as essentially metaphorical, i.e. symbolic; as a kind of poetry in fact. As such it has its own kind of truth and its own kind of validity, a validity *different* from so-called 'scientific' or 'practical' statements about what 'is'.[23]

The issue was well put in a letter to *The Listener* some years ago; the writer was William Scammell, and the context was the 'two cultures' disagreement between Leavis and C. P. Snow. I quote:

> The fact is that there *are* two cultures . . . scientists and logicians, on the one hand, and poets and novelists on the other, are describing *different* aspects of reality; they have *different* concepts of 'truth' and 'knowledge'; hence we employ *different* criteria in evaluating the

[21] J. Beattie, 'On Understanding Ritual', *Rationality*, B. R. Wilson (ed.) (Oxford: Blackwell, 1970), 241.

[22] R. Needham, *Belief, Language and Experience* (Oxford: Blackwell, 1972), 206.

[23] This theme is further discussed in J. Beattie, 'On Understanding Ritual', *Rationality*, B. R. Wilson (ed.) (Oxford: Blackwell, 1970), Ch. 12.

thinking that goes into a scientific theory and that which goes into a lyric poem. To apply analytic criteria to intuitive knowledge, or intuitive criteria ('maturity' and the like) to analytic knowledge, is both fruitless and fatuous . . . (*Listener*, 6 February 1969).

It is, in fact, to commit what Winch calls a 'category-mistake'. Add to this the deeply held—or felt—conviction that symbolic, 'expressive' procedures may also be thought to be somehow causally effective, and we have the beginnings of a theory of ritual. Let me give you two examples of the confusion which may result from the failure to distinguish clearly between these two aspects of 'reality'.

First, an example from my own research in Uganda in the 1950s. A woman had just been 'possessed' by the ghost of her dead father, whom the diviners had identified as being responsible for the illness of her son, a boy of about seven. The ghost which was possessing her had just 'eaten', while 'in the head' of the medium, a large bowl of millet porridge and meat, which had been specially prepared for it. My informant's text describes the conclusion of the ceremony, at which he was present; he was then a schoolboy of about twelve. His text begins:

> After my mother's sister had finished being possessed, she came back into the living-room and said to another woman who was there, 'My dear friend, hunger is killing me! Give me some of that millet porridge which is over there! I [that is, my informant] said to her 'But you have just eaten lots of millet porridge and meat!' She answered, 'My child, do you think it was I who was eating?' I said, 'Yes!' She went on to explain: 'No, it was the ghost that was eating, not I. Well', she continued after a pause, 'perhaps it *was* I who was eating, but I don't know where the food has gone . . . These are things of the devil [Shetani].'

The point is that she was putting on an act, a ritual performance, with its own kind of validity, and confusion only arose when she was compelled to apply everyday criteria to her performance.[24]

My second example is from Bernard Levin in *The Times* (26 November 1980). He is talking about 'the extraordinary belief held by listeners to the Archers . . . that the characters in the stories are real people, so that when one of them has a baby the BBC is swamped with gifts of rattles and bootees'. He goes on to say that these listeners 'were suffering from the delusion that [the actors in the plays] were real people, even though there were at the same time characters in a play, and in this somewhat schizophrenic situation they behaved exactly as

[24] See J. Beattie, 'The Ghost Cult in Bunyoro', *Ethnology* **3**, No. 2 (1964), 138.

they would if the things that happened to the imaginary people had happened to their own real neighbours'.

He then mentions a lady who 'ever since she had heard that Sir Mortimer Wheeler was fond of sherry, had put a glass of it on the television set whenever he was appearing, so that he might take a sip whenever he felt like it'.

Now I don't think these people are at all 'schizophrenic'. It is the 'two cultures' distinction again; in each different rules and conventions apply. Perhaps after all this is not so far from what Winch is getting at when he says that to deny the 'truth' of Zande beliefs is to commit a category-mistake (see below). I'm sure that Sir Mortimer's admirer was really (more or less) aware when she 'entered into the act', so to speak, that she was carrying out a ritual, valid as such, and not engaging in a 'real' relationship. Otherwise she (and the hundreds of others like her) would *really* be crazy.

In fact the understanding of unfamiliar rituals and of the symbolic ideas underlying them has appeared to be so difficult that some social anthropologists seem to have given up hope altogether. The anthropologist Jack Goody once wrote that ritual has to be defined in negative terms as 'a category of standardized behaviour (custom) in which the relationship between the means and the end is not intrinsic, i.e. is either irrational or non-rational'.[25] This seems to amount to defining ritual simply by saying we can't understand it, which doesn't seem to take us very much further. More recently Dan Sperber, in his stimulating short book *Rethinking Symbolism,* argues that the search for the *meaning* of symbolic behaviour is vain, for it does not, or may not, have any. He refers to 'the absurd idea that symbols mean',[26] and concludes that 'a representation is symbolic precisely to the extent that it is not entirely explicable, that is to say, expressible by semantic means'.[27] Symbolic behaviour represents a kind of irrationality—'a failure of the conceptual mechanism'.[28]

Sperber makes some good points, for example his argument that the anthropologist's (or the subject's) interpretation of a symbol is itself part of the total phenomenon which calls for explanation, and some of his criticisms of other anthropologists are valid. And of course it is easy to criticize an author unjustly by selective quotation. But one cannot help feeling that Sperber's problem arises at least partly from the fact that the Ethiopian Dorze, among whom he carried out fieldwork, have a

[25] J. Goody, 'Religion and Ritual: the Definitional Problem', *British Journal of Sociology* **12** (1961), 159.

[26] D. Sperber, *Rethinking Symbolism*, Alice I. Morton (trans.) (Cambridge: Cambridge University Press, 1975), 84.

[27] Ibid. 113.

[28] Ibid. 142.

variety of what appear to be symbolic usages, which, it seems, they are quite unable, or unwilling, to 'explain'. For example they sometimes walk around with lumps of butter on their heads, apparently without knowing why they do so. A similar apparent unconcern with and lack of interest in the 'meanings' of what they do seem to be characteristic of other neighbouring peoples, when asked about such things. 'How different from the Dogon!', the anthropologist is tempted to exclaim (the Dogon are a West African people who—or at least one or two of whom—are willing to go on almost indefinitely explaining the complexities of their exceedingly intricate symbolic system). Certainly Sperber would not be the first to construct a general theory on the particularities of his own field research.

Well, can we say anything valid at all about the concepts and belief systems, symbolic or otherwise, current in cultures other than our own? The problem is about relativism. Can the meanings (pace Sperber) of the representations of other cultures, if they are to be understood at all, be adequately understood in 'our', that is in the anthropologist's, terms? Or do they have to be understood entirely in their own contexts, that is, relatively to other aspects of the cultures of which they are a part? Indeed, we may ask, does such a dichotomy make sense?

The first thing to note is that the dilemma faces us on two different levels. First, there is what we can call *epistemological* relativism; are we faced, in so-called 'primitive' cultures, with a totally different way of thinking about, apprehending, experience, a logic of a different order from our own (whoever 'we' may be)? The second level is that of *cultural* relativism. If it be acknowledged that as members of the species *Homo sapiens* all men share a common rationality (however we define this), how far, if at all, are we justified in using the categories particular to our own culture in attempting to understand those of other cultures? This takes us back to Louis Dumont's argument, which I mentioned earlier in the context of our discussion of the understanding of social action. But the first and more radical kind of relativism I have indicated seems still to have some currency among anthropologists, and I now go on to deal with it briefly.

As representatives of this first kind of relativism, which I have called epistemological relativism, I return briefly to the philosopher Peter Winch, usually taken to be its first and most vigorous proponent, and one or two of his recent followers. And as a proponent of an extreme 'cultural' relativism, I shall return to Louis Dumont, who for all his sophistication seriously overstates, in my opinion, a good case. First, then, Peter Winch.

Talking about the Azande (another people of the southern Sudan, also studied by Evans-Pritchard), Winch argues that Zande ideas about witchcraft, magic and so on can only be properly understood in *Zande* terms, and not in terms of the categories of Western thought. If you ask the question 'is Azande's belief in the power of their magic (for example their poison oracle) true or not?' Evans-Pritchard's answer (according to Winch) would be 'no'—or at least 'not in the sense in which they seem to think it is'. On this point, Winch goes on, Evans-Pritchard would wish to add 'and the European is right and the Zande wrong'.[29] I suppose most of us, no doubt choosing our words carefully, would say the same. But as against this Winch, adopting or seeming to adopt a position of extreme, one might almost say absolute, relativism, appears to be claiming that truth is entirely relative to context, and that Evans-Pritchard's, and our, scepticism is inadmissible. The belief is 'true' for the Azande, and we have no right to impose our 'Western' ideas of what constitutes truth and falsehood in the context of Zande beliefs. To do so is to commit a category mistake, and to be guilty of the worst kind of ethnocentricism.[30]

But is this so? Some of Winch's fellow philosophers whose essays are also included in the same volume think otherwise, and I believe we must agree with them. Thus Martin Hollis[31] argues that even the simplest kinds of verbal communication between members of different cultures involve the assumption of 'common perceptions, common ways of referring to things perceived, and a common notion of empirical truth'. Such shared assumptions provide the indispensable 'bridge-head' by means of which cross-cultural communication is possible. Truth and falsity, as qualities of statements about what is, cannot be wholly relative to the cultures or languages in which the statements are made. Even though there is room for discussion as to what the minimum of such indispensable shared assumptions might be, without the 'bridgehead' they provide we should all be inescapably constrained to cultural solipsism.

It would not be necessary to go on about this at such length were it not that some recent writers, including two anthropologists, seem to adopt a comparably extreme, and to my mind unacceptable, relativism. Take, to begin with, a recent book by a young American anthropologist, F. Allan Hanson (1975). His statement of the case seems unambiguous. The 'meaning and truth [of 'all propositions, beliefs and other cultural institutions'] is [sic] to be found in their logical relations with other propositions, beliefs and institutions' in the

---

[29] P.Winch, 'Understanding a Primitive Society', *American Philosophical Quarterly* **1**, No. 4 (October 1964), reprinted in *Rationality*, B. Wilson (ed.) (Oxford: Blackwell, 1970) 87.

[30] Ibid. 93.

[31] M. Hollis, 'Reason and Ritual', *Rationality*, B. Wilson (ed.) (Oxford: Blackwell, 1970), 230–231.

same culture.[32] Thus 'the concepts of truth and meaning . . . can legitimately be applied only *within* systems of thought and institutions', so that 'all cultures . . . must be understood from within, in their own terms'.[33] I do not here attempt a full-scale critique of Hanson's argument.[34] But it will be plain, I think, that he is not very far from what I have taken to be Winch's position. However Hanson does later concede, not altogether consistently, I think, that certain 'purely formal criteria', such as 'the laws of identity and non-contradiction', may after all be granted universality, though he draws the line at admitting to this status 'the concept of "truth" as verifiability (or falsifiability) against experience'.[35] But he has already conceded too much, if only because to admit 'the laws of identity and non-contradiction' is to admit that what they assert is the case. And with members of a culture which lacked any notion of things being 'the case', and of its being possible to check whether they are or not against experience, rational discourse would be impossible.

The second anthropologist to adopt, rather more naively, I think, an extreme relativism is Roy Wagner (*The Invention of Culture*, 1975). Recognizing, no doubt justly, that 'we must give up hope of absolute objectivity', he goes on to the opposite extreme, and suggests, or seems to suggest, that we must give up hope of achieving any degree of objectivity at all. For every culture, including the anthropologist's own, is 'invented'. 'An anthropologist "invents" the culture he believes himself to be studying';[36] 'people *literally* [my emphasis] invent themselves',[37] and so on. Wagner may not mean all this to be taken 'literally', but he certainly implies that he does, and if he does not he certainly gives at least one reader the contrary impression.

My third example of the relativist approach is perhaps a bit 'way out' from the anthropological point of view, but it is none the less worth mentioning in the present context. It is that of the distinguished Ghanaian philosopher Professor Kwasi Wiredu, who in his recent book *Philosophy and an African Culture* (he is writing about Ghana as well as about philosophy) argues with force and lucidity that 'truth is nothing

[32] F. A. Hanson, *Meaning in Culture* (London: Routledge, 1975), 21.
[33] Ibid. 22.
[34] I have reviewed it at a little more length elsewhere. See J. Beattie, review of F. A. Hanson, *Meaning in Culture* (London, 1975) in *Bijdragen tot de Taal-Land- en Volkenkunde* **1333,** No. 1 (1977).
[35] Op. cit. 35.
[36] R. Wagner, *The Invention of Culture* (Englewood Cliffs and London: Prentice Hall, 1975), 4.
[37] Ibid. 105.

but opinion'.[38] He recognizes that this assertion, if true, is itself nothing but opinion, and he has no difficulty in showing that it is impossible to know 'things as they are'. This would seem, in the present context, to put him squarely in the ranks of the epistemological relativists. Professor Wiredu does not tell us how, if all truths are just opinions, we are to tell true opinions from false ones, or how, if 'to be is to be known'[39] we can meaningfully say, for example, that the earth rotated round the sun before anybody knew it did. Perhaps we can't.

These three relativist writers seem to be in danger, at least, of putting themselves in a literally hopeless position: there seems to be no way of escaping from their dilemma, of really getting to know another culture, except by totally abandoning their own, 'Western' criteria of rationality, condemned by Winch as ethnocentric. But as we have seen, this is an impossibility, if only because the thoughts that we think can only be *our* thoughts, not 'theirs'. And even if we could jump over the fence and become *wholly* assimilated to 'their' category systems and world view, we would be no better off, only marooned on their side of the fence instead of on our own.

Though one sympathizes with these authors' uncompromising rejection of a naive philosophical realism, they really, I think, go a good deal too far. Of course the knower contributes something to what he knows, and his culture as well as his human rationality shape what he contributes. But this does not mean, as Wagner seemed to be suggesting, that what we know is just our 'invention'. We may never attain complete or perfect knowledge of another culture, or even of another individual. But evidently we can learn something about it (or him—or, of course, her), maybe a great deal.

Could it not be that the whole argument about rationality rather misses the point? Perhaps the mistake is not so much to suppose that the Azande, or any preliterate people, are any less 'rational' (or somehow *differently* rational) than we (whoever 'we' are), but rather to suppose that their thinking in the context of the symbolic, 'magical' side of their culture can, and must, be assimilated to 'scientific', practical, thinking, either ours or theirs. Bernard Levin's radio audience are not all schizophrenics (though some of them may be), and neither are the Azande, or the Banyoro of Uganda, whose culture I studied many years ago. There *is* a 'confusion of categories' here, but it is more than merely a failure to take account of the context. We are back with Snow's (and Scammell's) 'two cultures', and even though these may be, and are, hopelessly confused in experience, it is, as we have seen, essential to

[38] K. Wiredu, *Philosophy and an African Culture* (Cambridge: Cambridge University Press, 1980), 176.
[39] Ibid. Ch. 9.

17

distinguish them analytically. Reverting once more (and finally!) to the Azande, is not the position rather that if Zande beliefs about witchcraft, etc., *were* taken to be, or to be intended as, 'scientific' statements about reality, *then* it would be fair to describe them as false. Perhaps the error is to think of them as 'scientific', or 'pseudo-scientific' statements at all. There are difficulties in this position, but I do not think that they are insuperable.

Let me turn now to the *second* of the two kinds of relativism which I distinguished earlier, cultural relativism, with which I have, perhaps a little invidiously, saddled Professor Dumont.

Dumont's position is at once more subtle and perhaps—at least to the social anthropologist—more interesting. His problem is not about epistemology but about culture, 'ideology', as he puts it. Granted that understanding between different cultures does require a common basis of shared assumptions, a 'bridgehead' of rationality, what about those assumptions which *are* specific to our own culture (whatever it may be), and which are *not* necessarily the same in other cultures? And the question now is: can we, in the attempt to understand the categories and classifications, the ways of thought, of other cultures, abstain from using the categories of our own culture (once again, whoever 'we' may be)? Dumont, if I have not misunderstood him, seems to think that we not only can but ought to. I discussed earlier, under the rubric of 'social action', his apparent belief that the use of the terms 'economic' and 'political' to characterize people's behaviour outside the contexts of the 'Western' cultures in which these terms originated, is 'sociocentric'.

But now Dumont goes further. It is not only that we misrepresent the alien social reality if we use our vocabulary (or some of it) in our attempts to describe it; Dumont now claims that we can actually *experience* that reality in two quite different ways. He distinguishes 'two quite different manners' in which 'we actually come to a knowledge of social facts in a foreign society', one 'directly', by 'adopting the native modes of thinking and looking at what happens in their terms', the other by 'leaving the native ideology and adopting our own for naming what we observe . . .'.[40] Five years later he reaffirms this distinction even more emphatically: 'The opposition is . . . between what is known directly in the categories of the society studied, and that which is known *indirectly* [Dumont's emphasis] through the intermediation of the categories of the society of the anthropologist himself'.[41]

Now I would suggest that it is seriously misleading to distinguish

[40] L. Dumont, 'A Fundamental Problem in the Sociology of Caste', *Contributions to Indian Sociology* **9** (1966), 21.

[41] L. Dumont, *Introduction à deux théories d'Anthropologie Sociale* (Paris: Mouton, 1971), 32, translation mine.

these two approaches as 'opposites', and so as mutually excluding one another. What they represent are aspects of a single procedure, not two quite different procedures. Both are involved in our gradual approach to understanding, though we may hope that we shall move closer and closer to the 'native' view as our research progresses. But the process of moving over from one set of categories to the other can never be quite complete. Assimilation to 'our' ways of thought is involved in both of Dumont's 'quite different manners' of learning what are the 'facts' in foreign cultures. We cannot jump out of our own cognitive skin (so to speak), and into someone else's. As I suggested above, it is probably just as well that we cannot.

Let me quote from a British social anthropologist, already mentioned, who appears to take a similar view. Rodney Needham, in a discussion of the French philosopher-anthropologist Lucien Lévy-Bruhl's approach to the problem, asks 'how it is that we can apprehend alien thought immediately in its own categories, without influence by our own. There is no doubt that we can in fact do so', he goes on, 'for ethnographers thus reach such a point of understanding that they then have to confess themselves unable to translate the indigenous concepts back [*sic*] into their own languages.'[42]

The use of the word 'back' in this quotation seems significant. Can it, perhaps, have the unconscious implication that the 'indigenous concept' was somehow already 'there' (in some sense and in some part) in the anthropologist's own mind? It is difficult to see how something could be translated 'back' to somewhere if it hadn't already been there. Translation is, as Needham himself emphasizes, a 'dialectic', a two-way road.

So what is our conclusion? There is no short cut to the anthropological understanding of other cultures, especially at the level of their ways of thought, their categories and classifications, of many of which even the members of those cultures themselves may be hardly, if at all, aware. But even if perfect understanding of another culture, or of another person for that matter, is unattainable, we all know that we can get a long way, or at least some way, towards it, and many good ethnographic studies offer evidence of this. Certainly there is room for sudden insights and inspirations. But they are *the anthropologist's* insights and inspirations. They derive from *his* mind, in the face of the culture he is trying to understand. And his growing understanding is not the result of, so to speak, unarmed raids into alien territory, where unfamiliar 'facts' may be picked up like pebbles on a beach. Rather it is, usually at least, painstakingly built up over months and years of patient observation and interaction. And

[42] R. Needham, *Belief, Language and Experience* (Oxford: Blackwell, 1972), 170.

underlying this process are both Redfield's humanism, or humanity—
we deal as human beings with other human beings—and Flew's
insights; even though we cannot discard our own categories of
understanding, it is after all 'their' categories, not 'ours', that we are
attempting to understand.

Let me conclude. It will be fair, I think, to give another French
anthropologist the last word. Roger Bastide, in his book *Applied
Anthropology*, deals, as we have been doing at least in part, with the
inseparability of 'facts' and our notions about them. As he says rather
obscurely, here oddly echoing Wagner, whom I quoted earlier, 'Our
concept of social reality suffices to cause us to change it until we are
re-creating it when we believe we are only examining it'.[43] So ethno-
or sociocentricism is scarcely avoidable, and certainly the problems
posed by our ineluctable subjectivity are formidable. But according to
Bastide we need not despair. The scholar who sets the search for truth
above all other values can sometimes 'fight against his ideologies'.[44]
He may even win the battle, though, as we have seen, his victory is
unlikely to be either clear-cut or complete.

[43] R. Bastide, *Applied Anthropology*, Alice I. Morton (trans.) (London:
Croom Helm, 1973), 6.
[44] Ibid. 155.

Emotions Across Cultures: Objectivity and Cultural Divergence

PAUL HEELAS

One of the themes of this lecture series has to do with the bearing of radical cultural divergencies on the issue of whether or not there is an invariant human nature. Put starkly, the options are between: first, man as a socio-cultural product, which entails that human nature must vary significantly across divergent cultures; second, man as a biological product, which entails (racist theories aside) that human nature is universal and invariant, impervious to cultural influence; and third, man as a mixture or synthesis of these two options.

I concentrate on emotional life, examining the question of whether emotions are under cultural control (thus being culture-specific, the psychic disunity thesis) or whether they are biologically grounded (thus being culture invariant, the psychic unity thesis). My conclusion is that both these theses are in measure correct. In senses to be explored, emotional life is varigated across cultures, and shows constancies.

Arriving at this conclusion involves erecting bulwarks against relativism. Peter Winch has argued that,

> we should not lose sight of the fact that the idea that men's ideas and beliefs must be checkable by reference to something independent— some reality—is an important one. To abandon it is to plunge straight into an extreme Protagorean relativism.[1]

As shall become apparent, men's ideas and beliefs about their emotions diverge considerably across cultures. If indeed there is nothing independent to allow these divergencies to be assessed, one might let the divergencies speak for themselves, this supporting the view of psychic disunity, or one might conclude that since there is no way of assessing the significance of the divergencies (do they indicate real differences in emotional life, or are they adventitious?), it is best to remain sceptical, agnostic, even solipsistic about the emotional life of other cultures.[2]

[1] Peter Winch, 'Understanding a Primitive Society', in *Rationality*, B. Wilson (ed.) (Oxford: Basil Blackwell, 1970), 81 (78–111).

[2] On the first option, see Lucien Lévy-Bruhl, *The Notebooks on Primitive Mentality* (London: Harper, 1978), e.g. p. 189;; for discussion of the second option, see Rodney Needham, 'Inner States as Universals: Sceptical Reflections on Human Nature', in *Indigenous Psychologies*, P. Heelas and A. Lock (eds) (London: Academic Press, 1981), 65–78.

Simply relying on whatever ideas different cultures have arrived at about emotional life in order to infer psychic disunity is not a satisfactory way to proceed. Such ideas might be adventitious, if not mistaken. And neither is retreating into frozen scepticism whatever its safety and appeal, a desirable course of action. It is rather important to introduce objectivity into the cross-cultural study of emotions, if, that is, we want to learn from other cultures. It is important, for example, and to introduce the culture which provides the ethnographic pivot of what follows, to establish whether or not the Chewong of aboriginal Malaysia experience anger. The Chewong are one of the handful of societies which, on good ethnographic grounds, can be said to be non-aggressive. Their ethnographer, Signe Howell, reports that, 'all the time I was there I never witnessed a quarrel, nor an outburst of anger, except among small children'.[3] Chewong culture manages to do what our own so patently does not. It virtually eradicates aggression and violence. How is this effected? Psychological research and our own first-hand experience shows that anger provides an important incentive to aggress. Explanation of Chewong non-aggression must therefore involve exploring the possibility that Chewong culture somehow severely curtails anger. Providing a naturalistic experiment, examination of the relationships between Chewong culture, 'anger', and non-aggression, should help deepen our understanding of a pressing concern in the West.

Given that it is desirable to study the emotional life of other cultures, how is it possible to be objective about them? Is it indeed possible to resist the relativist's claim that, as Lukes puts it, 'there are no theory-independent objects of perception and understanding'?[4] Is it possible, in other words, to develop a strategy for 'getting behind' divergent cross-cultural representations of the emotions in order to assess their significance? We could then decide whether such divergencies favour the psychic disunity thesis, whether psychic unit actually prevails (divergencies being assessed as adventitious or 'erroneous'), or whether they indicate that psychic unit is tempered by disunity.

My strategy for bypassing relativism is twofold. On the one hand I turn to the most objective domain of inquiry into emotional life, that provided by experimental psychology, using findings from this domain to infer the nature of emotional life in other cultures. On the other

---

[3]Signe Howell, *Chewong Modes of Thought,* D.Phil. thesis Oxford, in press (revised) (Oxford: Oxford University Press), 54.

[4]Steven Lukes, 'Relativism: Cognitive and Moral', *Aristotelian Society* Supplementary Volume **XLVIII** (1974) 168 (165–189).

hand, I am as objective as possible in establishing the nature of emotion-talk in other cultures (specifically the Chewong). This second component of the inferential strategy is important because we need to know how to apply experimental findings to real life settings.

Relativism

Before turning to the psychologists' laboratories and to the Chewong, I highlight the problems facing those who want to be objective in the cross-cultural (and intracultural) study of emotions. These are the problems facing those, whether psychologist or anthropologist, who want to establish the nature of emotional life.

The relativist, who raises the problems, argues that objective access to emotions themselves, the independent reality, is impossible. He relies heavily on scepticism.

Emotions, I accept, are inner episodes, experienced as occurring within the self and experienced as meaningful (one is angry about something; one is shy of somebody),[5] As inner episodes, emotions have to be disclosed before they can be identified and compared within or across cultures. This is how the relativist-cum-sceptic can argue that reliable identification, required to compare inner episodes, is impossible.

He begins with his own culture and the fact that emotions can be disclosed linguistically (I feel angry), behaviourally (I express my anger by thumping the table), facially (I snarl), or physiologically (I sometimes go red with anger), and that particular emotions tend to be associated with particular contexts (my friend must have been angry because his wife was rude to him in public). The argument is then advanced that there are in fact no natural signs of anger, both in the sense that none of the displays just introduced need occur when one is angry (one might simply hide one's anger), and in the sense that none of these displays and the angry-seeming context need indicate anger (I might say 'I feel angry' for polemical reasons; I might thump the table to gain attention; my friend might have felt rebuffed when insulted). Emotions, the sceptic concludes, are contingently related to how they are displayed and with what they are associated.

Rodney Needham makes the definitional point that, 'no inner state

---

[5] Certainly most psychologists adopt this view: see, for example, Howard Leventhal, 'The Integration of Emotion and Cognition: A View From the Perceptual-motor Theory of Emotion', in *Affect and Cognition*, M. Clark and S. Fiske (eds) (London: Lawrence Erlbaum, 1982) 122–123 (121–156).

can be expressed socially in a purely natural way'.[6] As we shall see, the absence of clear-cut natural signs of particular emotions raises difficulties for the psychologist studying emotions within our own Western culture. But to make things worse, the relativist-cum-sceptic has a stronger case to make when attention is directed to other cultures.

Imagine, he would say, entering an alien community to try to establish whether or not participants experience anger. For example, what does an apparently angry facial expression observed by the ethnographer actually indicate? It could indicate any number of things, perhaps disgust. So the ethnographer (or psychologist) tries to be more exact, getting participants to say what the expression means and by examining the contexts in which participants use the facial display. But how is one to decide how to translate the participant reply that this expression means 'x'? And on what grounds can one assume that particular contexts are associated with 'angry' responses?

Our relativistic-cum-sceptic points out that there is a strong temptation to translate the term 'x' as 'anger' if it is used in conjunction with contexts, behaviours and facial expressions which we, with our Western conventions, associate with being angry. But, he will argue, this does not guarantee correct translation or, of course, a correct report of the emotional state involved. It might in fact result in illusory, ethnocentric, certitude. That someone in our hypothetical alien culture is, in our terms, 'insulted', walks off in a 'huff', kicks a stone as he does so, and looks 'angry' could imply disgust, perhaps even shame.

'How can one possibly be objective about studying emotional experiences across cultures?' demands our relativist. And, he continues

[6] Needham, op. cit. 76. There is much more to be said about identifying and comparing emotions across or within cultures than can be included here. An obvious point is that it is as difficult to hold that there are no natural signs as it is to hold the opposite view: one requires natural signs to assess the matter. The importance of conventionality, however, is suggested by cases such as the following: Yanomamö wives are often physically hurt by their husbands, but treat this as a sign of endearment (see Paul Heelas, 'Anthropology, Violence and Catharsis', in *Aggression and Violence*, P. Marsh and A. Campbell (eds) (Oxford: Basil Blackwell), 47–61, for further discussion of this and related matters). On the other hand Paul Ekman ((ed.) *Emotion in the Human Face* (Cambridge: Cambridge University Press, 1982)) has argued that certain facial expressions do indeed provide natural signs (for difficulties with his approach see Paul Heelas, 'Anger and Aggression Across Cultures', paper delivered at the Department of Experimental Psychology, Oxford, 1982). Yet another issue is that natural signs of a biological kind, e.g. involving physiological differentiation, tend to be non-specific, do not appear to be directly 'about' emotions but about what I later call 'perturbations', and cannot easily be linked to particular emotions given that these have to be picked up by cultural, not biological, signs.

to say, it is not as though one can avoid circles of mistranslation by pointing to what representations refer to. One can point to the colour spectrum, for example, when translating colour terms; such a strategy cannot be employed when emotion terms are at issue.

Reasonable Inferences

It is perhaps not surprising that anthropologists and psychologists have tended to throw up their hands in horror at the prospect of studying emotions across cultures, and have instead approached the issue of psychic unity by way of more accessible cognitive operations. The problem is finding a way to proceed. After all, here am I, a middle-class, Oxford-educated Englishman, having the temerity to claim that I can make assertions about the emotional life of the alien society on which I concentrate, the Chewong. How can I possibly talk about the emotional life of a small group in the heart of a jungle whom I have not even visited?

There are, however, grounds for optimism. First, the argument of the relativist-cum-sceptic is self-defeating. He argues that the presence of an emotion cannot be read off by means of natural signs (for example a facial expression) or by translating indigenous emotion terms (they cannot be translated). His justification is that there are radical variations in how emotions are displayed. It is this which leads him to his conclusion that displays are embedded in culture specific conventions. But what the relativist-cum-sceptic cannot justify is how he has arrived at the conclusion that there are in fact radical cross-cultural divergencies. How can he translate to arrive at this conclusion?

And second, experimental psychologists have established relatively objective ways of examining and arriving at theories about emotions: findings and theories which provide a 'bridgehead'[7] for exploring the emotional life of other cultures.

I now introduce the two main psychological theories and how they can be employed to make reasonable inferences about other cultures.

According to an increasingly influential psychological theory (or rather cluster of theories), emotions are essentially *endogenous*, that is, grounded in mankind's biological endowment. On such a view, emotions are essentially as impervious to beliefs as are natural phenomena such as the moon. Emotions are basically meaning-independent universals. However the Chewong (or any other culture)

[7] See Martin Hollis, 'Reason and Ritual', in *Rationality*, B. Wilson (ed.) (Oxford: Basil Blackwell), 231 (221–239).

might happen to represent the emotions, emotions are nevertheless operative in their lives. Whether or not anger is identified and acknowledged, it is experienced. This is the reasonable inference or bridgehead: unless one considers racist theories to be reasonable.

Endogenous theorizing, this emphasis on biology, goes back to Charles Darwin and is currently in the hands of Leventhal (who claims that regardless of semantic or conceptual factors, the 'emotions of anger, grief, disgust, fear, shame, joy, interest, should retain a common core in experience as they are based on innate motor scripts'),[8] Ekman (whose list of universals is similar, but who includes surprise),[9] Izard and Tomkins,[10] Zajonc,[11] and others. According to another group of theorists, however, emotions are essentially meaning-dependent or *exogenous*. Emotions are constituted by culturally provided models. On this account, the reasonable inference is that emotions vary cross-culturally in accord with the presence or absence of appropriate cultural models. Emotions are certainly not like the rose in the saying, 'What's in a name? That which we call a rose by any other name would smell just as sweet.'

Associated primarily with the research of Schachter and Singer,[12] this theory is also found in the works of philosophers, cultural historians, and many anthropologists. It is implied by Stuart Hampshire when he writes that, 'The institutions of language are always developing, and the history of their development is the history of the human mind';[13] it is more explicit in Mischel's observation that, 'our descriptions of our experience are, in part, constitutive of what we

---

[8] Howard Leventhal, 'Toward a Comprehensive Theory of Emotion', in *Advances in Experimental Social Psychology*, L. Berkowitz (ed.) (London: Academic Press, 1980), 192 (149–207).

[9] Paul Ekman, 'Biological and Cultural Contributions to Body and Facial Movement', in *The Anthropology of the Body*, John Blacking (ed.) (London: Academic Press, 1971), 72 (39–84).

[10] Carroll Izard and Sylvan Tomkins, 'Affect and Behaviour: Anxiety as a Negative Affect', in *Anxiety and Behaviour*, C. Speilberger (ed.) (New York: Academic Press, 1966), who write that, 'One does not learn to be afraid . . .' (91) (81–125).

[11] R. Zajonc, 'Feeling and Thinking, Preferences Need No Inferences', *American Psychologist* **33** (1980), 151–175.

[12] Stanley Schachter and Jerome Singer, 'Cognitive, Social, and Psychological Determinants of Emotional State', *Psychological Review* **69** (1962), 379–399.

[13] Stuart Hampshire, *Thought and Action* (London: Chatto and Windus, 1965), 13.

experience . . .';[14] and it is yet more explicit in Richard Peters' comment that,

> emotions, such as pride, ambition, guilt and remorse imply a certain view of ourselves. They are probably not felt in cultures in which little importance is attached to individual effort and responsibility;[15]

and it is even more graphically conveyed in C. S. Lewis' claim that, 'French poets, in the eleventh century, discovered or invented, or were the first to express, that romantic species of passion which English poets were still writing about in the nineteenth'.[16] (He later makes it clear that he believes that the earlier poets invented passionate love by providing the appropriate cultural formulations.)

Deciding between these two apparently contradictory theories, the endogenous and the exogenous, is a matter of some consequence. The former tells us that the Chewong experience the same 'core' emotions as ourselves. The latter, on the other hand, tells us that the Chewong only experience those emotions for which they have cultural models. An objective stance is thus required to decide between this divergence in psychological research before we can go on to make inferences about the Chewong.

But an objective stance is also required to characterize the nature of Chewong emotion-talk, that is, to characterize the extent to which it diverges from our own representational system. Characterization is necessary if we want to be in the position to be able to infer from exogenous laboratory findings to the field context. The reason is simple. Schachter's findings show that emotions are meaning-dependent. Emotion-talk must surely provide the most significant constitutive model of emotions. We therefore have to establish the nature of Chewong emotion-talk in order to infer, if we follow Schachter, the nature of Chewong emotional experience. (The application of endogenous theory, it should be obvious, does not depend on characterization of emotion-talk, emotions not being meaning-dependent.)

To summarize, I have suggested that the issue of psychic unity can be tackled by inferring from experimental to field contexts. Objectivity is required to assess divergencies in the experimental setting, and to characterize divergencies in how the emotions are represented across cultures.

---

[14] Theodore Mischel (ed.), *The Self* (Oxford: Basil Blackwell, 1977), 21.

[15] Richard Peters, *Psychology and Ethical Development* (London: George Allan and Unwin, 1974), 402.

[16] C. S. Lewis, *The Allegory of Love* (London: Oxford University Press, 1958), 4.

Paul Heelas

Objective Assessment of the Divergence of Collective Representations: the Case of the Chewong

It is time to enter the jungle, to examine what it is to be objective with regard to how emotions are represented. With a picture of Chewong representations in mind, I then return to the issue of which psychological theory (endogenous or exogenous or both) can be used in conjunction with Chewong culture to infer Chewong emotions.

Discussing the role of convention in the conceptualization of feelings, Hampshire argues that there are only two natural 'resemblances' (non-conventional ways, involving painful and pleasant states) 'that we can expect to find recorded in every vocabulary, *provided that it allows personal disclosures of any kind*' (my emphasis).[17] Hampshire leaves open the possibility of cultures so devising things that personal disclosures, and so talk of the emotions as inner episodes or experiences, are absent.

Examining this possibility involves deciding whether what appears to be talk of the emotions is *actually* about inner emotional episodes. This is because, 'It may be', as Needham puts it, 'that terms for inner states are social more than they are experiential; in other words, that they are useful for the ascription of virtues and demerits to the characters of other individuals rather than as socially contrived instrument by which individuals are enabled to assess their own inner experiencs'.[18] For example, our own distinction between 'guilt' and 'shame' could refer as much if not more so to social affairs than to distinctive inner experiences (cf. 'I plead guilty'). To give another example, this time from a hypothetical alien culture, an expression or action, such as walking away in 'disgust' might appear to indicate 'disgust' to the mentalistically inclined Westerner; but could be about moral and social affairs.

It is not easy to settle such matters. As mentioned earlier, the existence of apparently radical cross-cultural differences in the ways the emotions are represented suggests that there are few—if any—naturally recognized signs of the emotions. Precisely because of this, it is difficult to be objective in establishing whether or not particular representations are about emotions. We cannot claim, for example, that a certain context-action sequence (such as stamping the ground after being insulted) is naturally acknowledged as implying anger, this in turn entailing that when the sequence is found in other cultures, emotion-talk or recognition is present.

In attempting to decide what counts as Chewong emotion-talk, my rule of thumb is that emotion-talk is in evidence *whatever* means are

[17] Hampshire, op. cit. 62.
[18] Needham, op. cit. 77.

28

used for talking about the emotions *so long as* these means are understood, *by participants*, to function (whatever other functions they might have) as ways of discriminating between emotions as *inner episodes or experiences*. Because of translation and accessibility problems, there are no clear rules in applying this rule of thumb objectively. I have to rely on ethnographic pointers.

One thing is relatively clear, the Chewong are little concerned with what could be emotional matters. Their 'emotional' vocabulary is very limited, and the thrust of their culture as a whole emphasizes public activities not the inner self. Concerning their 'emotional' vocabulary, Howell lists a mere handful of 'emotion' terms: *chan* (which she glosses as 'angry'), *hentugn* (glossed as 'fearful', 'frightened'), *punmen* ('like (something)'), *meseq* ('jealous'), *lidva* ('ashamed, shy'), *hanrodn* ('proud'), *imeh* ('want'), and *lon* ('want very much').[19] Even if the Chewong have other, less explicit, ways of talking about their emotions—as by reference to bodily organs (cf. our 'I vented my spleen')—it is surely not without significance that in contrast to their eight or so terms, Malay contains some 230 explicitly emotion terms. Taiwanese, it can be noted, contains over 800 terms; English contains well over 2,000 terms for emotions.[20]

This impoverished language suggests that the Chewong are not concerned with the intricacies of emotional life. Stronger evidence that Chewong culture does not facilitate the acknowledgement of the great majority of emotions which we know in the West is provided by examination of what Howell describes as Chewong 'rules'. Rules are culturally specified sequences linking anti-social behaviour to punishment. They are of fundamental importance to the Chewong: their everyday life is 'largely structured by the all-pervasive presence of them'.[21] To illustrate how they operate, *tola* means that if somebody shows disrespect towards certain categories of affines by behaving too openly, that person becomes ill; *maro* entails that if somebody is 'stingy', not offering food to a visitor, the individual suffers dizziness; *punen* (of seven varieties) can mean the connection between 'speaking badly' (either speaking of an anticipated feast, etc., or exclaiming when an accident occurs) and suffering, or it can mean that someone not given food and the like will themselves be liable to attack from, say, a tiger; and *mali* has to do with the unpleasant consequences of whistling or swinging one's legs (or the like) in an extravagant manner.[22]

[19] Signe Howell, 'Rules Not Words', in *Indigenous Psychologies*, Heelas and Lock (op. cit.), 134 (133–143).

[20] Jerry Boucher, 'Culture and Emotion', in *Perspectives on Cross-cultural Psychology*, A. Marsella *et al.* (eds) (London: Academic Press, 1979), 170.

[21] Howell, ibid. 135.

[22] Howell, ibid. 137; see also Howell, op. cit. 241–280.

What all the rules have in common is that deviant *behaviour*, whether it be acting with disrespect, not sharing food, acting extravagantly (swinging legs), having illicit sex, or, in a more general sense of behaviour, laughing, crying, shouting, 'speaking badly' and whistling, results in punishment. Rules focus on external activities, on the individual as publicly envisaged and as socially or supernaturally accountable. Chewong rules remind us of Skinner-derived behavioural therapy: the 'black box' is left intact in the understanding and management of anti-social behaviour. Thus as regards the activation of rules, *tola* applies when someone shows disrespect (it is not couched in terms of *being* too intimate); *maro* operates if one does not give food (it is not attributed to the inner desire to keep for oneself); one type of *punen* is called into action if one behaves badly in connection with accidents; and *mali* operates because one whistles (not, apparently, because one is, as we would say, 'happy'). And as for the consequences of rule-infringement, Howell makes it plain that attention remains at the behavioural and moral level. As she puts it, 'rather than describe their thoughts and feelings as we would at such times [of punishment or suffering], they describe the cause of the disease or mishap, i.e. they refer to the particular rule that has been broken . . . .'[23]

We in the West turn to emotion-talk when the rational, socialized self goes awry to break rules and conventions. We find it difficult to explain the irrational by reference to the rational. As Jeff Coulter makes the point, 'It is most routinely the case that emotion-concepts function in accounts that explain action that is in some way considered untoward or problematic within a situation, or that explain the absence of some otherwise obligatory or preferred course of action'.[24] As well as employing emotion-talk to explain anti-social behaviour or other forms of deviation, we also use it when suffering from the consequences of rule-transgression (think of 'guilt' and 'shame'), not to mention when we simply find ourselves distressed (think of 'talking out' one's problems) or when we want to express our happiness (think of our 'need' to convey and share good times). That the Chewong appear to resist these apparently natural tendencies, the dominant cultural idiom of rule-talk being called into play by anti-social behaviour and resulting in punishment and the description of the particular rule that has been broken, indicates the extent to which their mode of thought is orientated away from the emotions.

Thus far Howell would probably agree that the evidence presented indicate that the Chewong attach few meanings to 'emotional' life. But

[23] Howell, ibid. (1981), 140.
[24] Jeff Coulter, *The Social Construction of Mind* (London: Macmillan, 1979), 132.

she would then almost certainly point out that there is an alternative to
rule-talk which can more plausibly be held to refer to emotions as inner
episodes. She would point out that the liver (*rus*) appears to provide an
idiom which is based on an interior organ and so appears to provide a
good way of talking about emotions as inner experiences.

She writes,

> The liver, *rus* . . . , is the seat of both what we call 'thoughts' and
> 'feelings', and they do not make any conceptual distinction between
> the two. In fact they have no word for 'think' or 'feel'. Whenever they
> do express verbally emotional and mental states and changes, this is
> done through the medium of the liver. Thus they may say, 'my liver
> is good' (I am feeling fine) or 'my liver was tiny' (I was very
> ashamed), or 'my liver forgot'.[25]

Howell arives at the conclusion that, 'in their concept of the liver as the
seat of all consciousness they have a means, albeit a limited one, for
describing their inner states.'[26] For Howell, liver-talk is about
emotions.

For reasons which are presented elsewhere in greater detail,[27] I am
not convinced that liver-talk performs this descriptive function.
Consider, for example, the fact that it is far from clear why 'my liver is
good' should be glossed as 'I am feeling fine', when, according to the
ethnographer, the Chewong have no word for 'feel'. Does not this
linguistic incapacity suggest that it is more parsimonious to suppose
that 'my liver is good' is a perfectly adequate translation, not standing in
need of additional, possibly ethnocentrically motivated, mentalistic
interpretation? Bearing in mind the public, behavioural orientation of
Chewong rules, is it not parsimonious to assume that 'my liver is good'
means 'my seat of consciousness is behaving well'?

There is little or no positive evidence that the Chewong *know* the
inner episodes which we know of as 'anger', 'jealousy', 'desire' and so
on, let alone *knowing* the differences between, for example, 'anger',
'disgust' and 'irritation'. The Chewong do not pay conceptual attention
to the emotions, except, according to Howell, 'fear' and 'shyness' (I
return to this). Rather than attaching meanings to 'emotional' inner
episodes, their cultural emphasis is on the outside, public world. It is on
regulating behaviour according to the moral code embedded in rules.
Given that the Chewong have been taught not to display whatever

---

[25] Howell, ibid. (1981), 139.
[26] Howell, ibid. 143.
[27] See Paul Heelas, 'Indigenous Representations of the Emotions: the Case
of the Chewong', *Journal of the Anthropological Society of Oxford* **XIV** (1983),
87–103.

'emotions' they might have (with the exceptions of 'fear' and 'shyness'), for display results in punishment, there is no reason for the Chewong to want to acknowledge that they break rules because they have fallen foul of anti-social emotions. The cultural emphasis, as Howell stresses, is on 'controlling and suppressing the self'.[28] Given this emphasis, liver-talk is best understood behaviourally. If someone behaves anti-socially, it is said of him, for example, that his liver is *kenjed*, simply meaning that he is behaving in stingy fashion. The *maro* rule sequence is then activated. There is no reason to add the interpretation 'feeling greedy' to the interpretation of *kenjed* as a form of behaviour.

I think I am justified in claiming that what matters to the Chewong is the social, not the experiential; is behaving appropriately, not attending to (explicitly controlling, satisfying, exploring and communicating) the 'emotions' themselves. Certainly the Chewong emphasis on monitoring and regulating what is occurring in the public world of social activity leaves little room for what is found in many traditional societies, such as the Taita of Kenya, where the 'black box' is broken into, where anti-social behaviour is attributed to inner *sere* ('anger') and then managed by an indigenous psychotherapy.[29]

Applying Exogenous and Endogenous Psychological Theories of the Emotions

The ethnographic facts to be borne in mind are, first, that Chewong rules function as punishment models, second, that the Chewong suppress the self, showing remarkably little 'emotional' display and being extraordinarily non-aggressive, and, third, that they diverge radically from our own society in terms of their paucity of clear formulations of the emotions. I now ask—what are the psychological consequences, on emotional life itself, of the virtual absence of clearly identifiable emotion-talk and of the presence of what we might be inclined to call behavioural rather that psycho therapy?

What has to be explained is the absence of emotional display. In the words of Howell, 'One of the most striking features of Chewong life is the lack of emotional display among adults'.[30] According to exogenous theory, this is due to the fact that Chewong culture does not provide clearly elaborated models teaching participants how to *be* angry and so forth. There is little or no incentive for participants to act in angry

[28] Howell, ibid. 142.

[29] Grace Harris, *Casting Out Anger* (Cambridge: Cambridge University Press, 1978).

[30] Howell, op. cit. (1980), 54.

fashion, all the more so in that the only positive models provided by culture to educate or constitute the emotions are those provided by rule-talk: rules which, when transgressed, result in punishment and so which, it is reasonable to suppose, teach or inculcate 'fear'. Someone who might be inclined to act in 'angry' fashion actually *fears* that display.

Robarchek's explanation of how Semai rules function is of a fully fledged Schachterian variety. Since Semai rules are very similar to those of Chewong culture, I illustrate by introducing his explanation of the *pehunan* rule. This rule is activated when someone is not given food, tobacco and the like, that person becoming open to supernatural attack. According to Robarchek, such a person is 'frustrated'. He cannot get what he 'wants'. Experimental research shows that frustration is a much less specific or cognitively guided state than any particular emotion: frustration can be transformed into various emotions depending on the clutural model present when one is frustrated. Accordingly, Robarchek concludes that, 'in those instances where frustration does occur, the resultant emotion in the frustrated party is not anger but is rather fear of the danger to which he has become vulnerable'.[31]

Howell, in contrast, adopts an endogenous position, claiming that the Chewong experience much the same emotions as we do, but have to suppress them. She claims that 'most emotions commonly acknowledged in the West are suppressed by the Chewong'.[32]

The contrast, then, is between treating Chewong culture as not allowing for the *constitution* of the great majority of emotions, and treating the culture as simply preventing emotional display; it is between the psychic disunity and the psychic unity theses; it is between seeing the Chewong directed to fear (and shyness) but living in other respects a greatly dampened emotional life, and seeing them with a relatively rich but repressed emotionality.

Objective Assessment of 'Divergence' of Experimental Findings: Exogenous and Endogenous Theories and Their Complementarity

I am not entirely happy with either of these alternative accounts. Turning to experimental psychological research, I now argue that since

[31] C. Robarchek, 'Frustration, Aggression, and the Nonviolent Semai', *American Ethnologist* **V** (1978), 769 (762–779).
[32] Howell, op. cit., (1980) 285.

there is sufficient objective evidence to conclude that *both* exogenous and endogenous theories are essentially correct, they *cannot* be divergent but *must* complement one another. Accordingly, Chewong emotional-life must be portrayed in terms of *both* theories.

It is true that the two psychological theories are divergent and contradictory if they are formulated in what might be called 'strong' fashion. Thus if emotions should be entirely bound up with Leventhal's 'innate motor scripts' they cannot be constituted by cultural models, and if emotions should be entirely dependent on Schachter's cultural models, they obviously cannot be due to innate motor scripts. But to emphasize my point, the very fact that experimental evidence supports both positions suggests that the two positions must be formulated in such a (modified) way as to be complementary. And although Leventhal and Schachter differ in their approaches and emphases, both more than leave the door open for this to be done.

Unfortunately, demonstrating this raises too many issues and covers too much territory in the psychological and brain sciences to be more than hinted at here. One would have to cover the evidence which supports modified but not strong versions of the two approaches; one would have to spell out the details of how they can be combined; and, most pertinently for a philosophically minded readership, one would have to examine how psychologists and others handle all those problems which arise from the fact that emotions are inner states. What follows, then, concentrates on the work of two leading researchers (Schachter and Leventhal), and simply hints at some of the evidence which has been uncovered and the kind of problem which must be overcome if the complementarity thesis is to be sustained.

(a) *Schachter's Exogenous Theory*

Schachter's (and Singer's) well-known experiment was designed to test the hypothesis that, 'an emotional state may be . . . a function of a state of physiological arousal and a cognition appropriate to this state of arousal'.[33] An experiment was devised to establish whether or not the same state of physiological arousal is associated with different emotions when that state occurs in connection with different meanings. The conclusion arrived at is that cognitive factors are 'major determinants of emotional states'; that people have emotional experiences—as opposed

[33] Stanley Schachter, *Emotion, Obesity, and Crime* (London: Academic Press, 1971), 2.

to states of physiological arousal or mere cognitions—when they *know* what their physiological arousal is *about*.[34]

I wrote earlier that experimental psychological research is the most objective of ways of studying the emotions. But Schachter himself has raised a problem which appears to cast grave doubt on his conclusion. Bearing in mind that he has to show that experimental subjects *actually* experience different emotions when, injected with epinephrine, they are placed in social milieus meaning euphoria and aggression, what of the problem of access? How can one tell that subjects are experiencing different emotions? As he puts it,

> Are we *really* talking about emotions or are we talking about opinions of emotions? Do the emotions of the subjects in our experiments really vary in the conforming fashion described or is it simply a verbal statement about emotion that varies?[35]

A philosopher, Gordon, has developed this doubt into a radical critique of Schachter's experiment. 'At most', argues Gordon, 'the experiment shows emotional *labelling* to depend on one's belief as to the cause of one's arousal. It doesn't show one's actual emotional *state* to depend on such a belief.'[36] The objection is that subjects turn to the most convenient and plausible explanation (what is going on around them) to handle their arousal, but that this does not show that their arousal has itself changed into an emotion.

Is it credible, as Gordon would have us believe, that a subject, having been injected with epinephrine, '*simply* reports that he is angry'? Is it credible that, 'there is no need to suppose that his belief has somehow wrought a change in the way his arousal feels to him'?[37] It is of course true that the subject reports that he is angry because of what is going on around him. But it is surely less plausible to hold that the subject

---

[34] Schachter, ibid. For additional evidence see Clark and Fiske, op. cit.; H. London and R. Nisbett (eds) *Thought and Feeling, Cognitive alteration of feeling states* (Chicago: Aldine, 1974); Schachter and Singer's 'Comments on the Maslach and Marshall–Zimbardo Experiments', *Journal of Personality and Social Psychology* **37** (1979), 989–995; and work in, e.g. social learning theory and cognitive therapy. I have surveyed much of this evidence— supporting exogenous as well as endogenous theory—in 'Anthropological Perspectives on Violence: Universals and Particulars', *Zygon* Vol. 18, No. 4 (1983) (375–404). Perhaps the most powerful evidence is provided by the fact that rival theorists very rarely deny, *in toto*, the validity of whichever camp they are opposed to.

[35] Stanley Schachter, *The Psychology of Affiliation* (Standford: Stanford University Press, 1959), 123–129.

[36] Robert Gordon, 'Emotion Labelling and Cognition', *Journal for the Theory of Social Behaviour* No. 2 (1979), 130 (125–136).

[37] Gordon, ibid. 130.

reports 'anger' *simply* because he has been exposed to a context of this (meaningful) variety than it is to hold that he has come to experience his arousal (which, all are agreed, stands in need of explanation) as being *about* the context.[38]

If it is taken to be about a distinctive context, the arousal has a meaning—and that is all that Schachter claims is what constitutes the distinctive nature of an emotion. Given the fact that physiological arousal is generally held to be a necessary but not sufficient condition for having an emotion, what, other than meanings, can change the experience of physiological arousal?[39] If indeed physiological arousal is generally bound up with having emotions, why should Gordon (who stresses the meaningful nature of emotions[40]) want to deny that the experience of physiological arousal does not change in the fashion argued by Schachter?

(b) *Leventhal's Endogenous Theory*

Leventhal claims that, 'the appearance of emotion does not require the presence of arousal and cognition as understood in cognition-arousal theory', arguing instead that, 'emotion is generated by some third, independent mechanism'.[41] This 'primary mechanism' must be able to account for 'differences in the quality of emotional life'.[42] 'The expressive motor mechanism', he then argues, 'is the primary generator of emotion'; and that, 'subjective emotional qualities emerge in experience along with the activation of patterned expressive motor reactions'. The conclusion drawn is that, 'the central nervous system contains all the mechanisms necessary for emotional experience'.[43]

It must immediately be said that the body of research findings drawn on to support this conclusion are open to alternative interpretations: again because of the accessibility problem. For example, it is held that a

---

[38] The fact that Schachter reports that 'subjects in the epinephrine ignorant condition are significantly angrier than subjects in the placebo condition' is good evidence that mere exposure to angry contexts does not automatically result in 'anger' reports (Schachter, op. cit. (1981), 19). Arousal is important; cognitive processes are not *so* important as is implied by Gordon.

[39] Necessary but not sufficient because it is generally held that physiological arousal or other forms of physiological activity are too undifferentiated and indeterminate to generate particular emotions (see footnote 51, below), and that cognitions alone do not result in emotions (see Schachter, ibid. 4).

[40] Robert Gordon, 'The Aboutness of Emotions', *American Philosophical Quarterly* **11** (January 1974), 27–36.

[41] Leventhal, op. cit. (1980), 156–157.

[42] Leventhal, ibid. 160.

[43] Leventhal, ibid. 168.

key component of the expressive motor mechanism is that expressive behaviour, in particular facial display, contributes to the generation of distinctive emotions. It is then held that cross-cultural research on the relationship between facial display and emotionality shows that, 'a common set of expressive-motor patterns exists for all people'.[44] As I have discussed elsewhere,[45] at least some of these research findings are questionable. However, the force of the evidence put forward by Leventhal and others does indeed support the claim that a number of 'core or primary emotional experiences' are universal; are given by nature; are differentiated by endogenous processes rather than by culturally triggered learning processes.[46]

(c) *Complementarity*

How can both endogenous and exogenous theories be valid and function in a complementary manner? There is in fact every reason to suppose that emotions are the result of both natural and culture-dependent processes. Is it not inherently plausible that, as evolved beings, we have not entirely shaken off our ancestry (which means that endogenous processes and states are ensured a role), and that, as cultural beings, exogenous processes and states are also important? Emotions, on this account, are influenced and constrained by nature at an elemental level (and so have a life of their own), but also enter into the sphere of culture-dependent processes (and so live with their society).

A crucial consideration in arguing for the complementarity thesis is that Leventhal does not claim that endogenous processes can result in emotions. Discussing young children, he claims that, 'the earliest emotions may be characterized by expressive behaviour without awareness of subjective emotion'. Endogenously given 'emotional

[44] Leventhal, ibid. 162.

[45] See footnote 6.

[46] Leventhal, ibid. 192. More generally, evidence for endogenous theories (bearing on triggering processes, behaviours associated with 'emotions', consequences of 'emotional' activity, brain processes and structures, as well as the issue of differentiation), can be drawn from many domains of inquiry. These include psychosurgery, electroconvulsive therapy and brain stimulation, the use of psychotropic drugs, the study of child development, facial expressions, aggression, anxiety, etc., and investigation of hormonal, limbic, etc., systems. A useful introduction is K. Moyer's (ed.) *Physiology of Aggression and Implications for Control: an Anthology of Readings* (New York: Raven Press, 1976). Or, for a particular emotion, see J. Gray, 'Anxiety as a Paradigm Case of Emotion', *British Medical Bulletin* **37**, No. 2 (1981), 193–197.

elements' are present, but not until the child acquires 'conceptualizations of affect' does it have 'emotional experiences'. The point, in other
words, is that 'some kind of cognition, broadly defined, is intimately
involved in the generation of emotion'.[47]

Leventhal accepts that exogenous processes are important. The
distinction he draws, between endogenously given emotional elements
and exogenously 'enriched'[48] emotional experiences, allows us to hold
that 'emotions' are both universal and culture-specific. This is not
contradictory. What is universal are emotional elements, or, as I prefer
to call them, *emotional perturbations*; what is culture-specific are
perturbations as enriched by meaning systems.

Another crucial consideration in arguing for complementarity is that
just as Leventhal is happy to allow exogenous processes a role, so is
Schachter happy to acknowledge an endogenous component. Physiological arousal, a form of emotional perturbation, is held to be necessary
for emotional experience. Again, and in the same sense as indicated
above, 'emotions' are both universal and culture specific.

Leventhal and Schachter share the basic premise that *emotions are
inner and meaningful episodes, and so must combine the endogenous
and the exogenous*. Perturbations provide the inner or endogenous
basis for what is universal and necessary to get emotional life under
way; meanings, varying across cultures, provide the basis for what is
culture-specific at the level of emotions themselves. Because Leventhal
does not claim that endogenous processes can result in 'true' emotions,
his theory does not contradict Schachter's exogenous theorizing;
because Schachter is prepared to acknowledge the importance of
endogenous processes, his theorizing does not contradict what
Leventhal has to argue. It is true that Leventhal and Schachter do not
agree as to the extent to which emotions are constituted by endogenous
differentiations (Leventhal's emphasis) or by exogenous models
(Schachter's emphasis), but then they are talking about different
endogenous systems (the expressive motor mechanism involving
central nervous system processes, and visceral physiological arousal
involving sympathetic nervous system processes). And there appears to
be no reason why both these two processes cannot be operative.

One final point, before returning to the Chewong. It will be apparent
that my effort to reconcile the '"emotions" are universal' and 'emotions
are culture-specific' theses rests on drawing a distinction between
emotional perturbations and emotions themselves. It is worth pointing
out that that very similar distinctions have been made by a great
number of those who have studied emotions. Philosophers distinguish

[47] Leventhal, ibid. (1980), 191–193.
[48] Leventhal, ibid. 192.

between mere feelings and meaning-infused emotions. Thus Coulter argues that emotions, 'are not mere eruptions independent of appraisals and judgments, beliefs and conceptualizations',[49] and Shibles points out that, 'although most people say it is, anger is not just a feeling. You are angry with *someone* or at *something*.'[50] Apart from Leventhal (emotional elements and experiences) and Schachter (physiological arousal and emotions), psychologists who have made similar distinctions include Berkowitz (frustration *v*. e.g. anger), Marshall and Zimbardo (arousal *v*. true emotions), Leff (somatic experiences *v*. emotions), and, on a more general note, Weimer, who points out that, 'An intuitively reasonable belief held by many emotion theorists is that there are some basic emotions, and other emotions are somehow built from or develop out of these more basic *feelings*' (my emphasis).[51] Allowing the operation of both endogenous and exogenous processes, the fact that such distinctions are so frequently encountered supports the complementarity thesis.

Back to the Chewong

What has to be explained, it will be recalled, is the absence of emotional display among adults. It will also be recalled that I have introduced two explanations of this, to wit, the suppression of endogenous emotions by means of punishment models (Howell), and the moulding of physiological perturbations so that fear (and shyness) are inculcated whilst other emotions are not constituted (Robarchek).

My intermediary position is that biology ensures that the Chewong experience something approaching what we in the West experience, and that Chewong culture ensures that these experiences, excepting fear (and shyness) are considerably dampened. Thus I differ from

[49] Coulter, op. cit. 131.

[50] Warren Shibles, *Emotion* (Wisconsin: The Language Press, 1978), 3.

[51] Lenorad Berkowitz, *A Survey of Social Psychology* (London: Holt, Rinehart and Winston, 1980), 345–346; G. Marshall and P. Zimbardo, 'Affective Consequences of Inadequately Explained Physiological Arousal', *Journal of Personality and Social Psychology* **37** (1979), 923 (970–985); Julian Leff, 'The Cross-cultural Study of Emotions', *Culture, Medicine and Psychiatry* **I** (1977), 324 (317–350); Bernard Weiner, 'The Emotional Consequences of Causal Attributions', in *Affect and Cognition*, op. cit. (footnote 5), 206 (185–209). As George Mandler summarizes the situation, 'The notion that there was something dual about emotional states dates back to Aristotle who, in *De Anima*, distinguished between the matter and the form (or idea) of emotions. Presumably the former could be identified as the visceral component and the latter as the psychological experience' (*Mind and Emotion* (London: John Wiley, 1975), 94.

Howell's endogenous view in that I attach more importance to the absence of constitutive models (she is endogenous to the extent of holding that emotions exist in the absence of such models), and I differ from Robarchek's exogenous view in that I attach more importance to the existence of differentiated perturbations (he is exogenous to the extent of holding that perturbations are entirely open to cultural moulding or channelling).

To the extent that we can objectively decide that Chewong representations are focused away from the emotions (making the Chewong indigenous Ryleians) and that exogenous theory is valid, the doctrine of psychic unit does not apply. The Chewong lack the appropriate cultural models to attach meanings to their perturbations. The culture does not provide the meaning-laden vehicles whereby basic, ill-defined experiences can be clearly differentiated, filled-out and refined. At the very least, and bearing in mind Leff's observation that, 'there is a strong link between the availability of appropriate words for various emotions and the ease with which people distinguish between their experiences', the Chewong have *little knowledge* of distinct emotions.[52]

To the extent that we can objectively decide that endogenous theory is valid, the doctrine of psychic unity does apply. The Chewong experience a flow of perturbations. They are likely to feel 'angry' when thwarted, 'grief' when death occurs, 'fear' when startled, negative affects when aversive stimuli are present, and so on. The fact that endogenous theory holds that such 'emotions' and associated ways of behaving are natural responses to specific triggers[53] ensures that liver and rule-talk is bound up with emotional perturbations and activities (hence one reason for the similarities between Leventhal's list of primary emotions and that provided by Howell). But what culture

[52] Julian Leff, 'Culture and the Differentiation of Emotional States', *British Journal of Psychiatry* **CXXIII** (1973), 304 (299–306). This conclusion has to take a tentative form because the role of Schachterian 'appraisal' or cultural learning models is not easy to establish. My earlier emphasis on the absence or prsence of emotion words only provides a crude approach. In a hypothetical culture, a member could experience anger without knowing that word if another person did something, in terms of a general system of meanings, which unjustifiably affected the member's status (for example, if the other person breaks rules to unfairly put our member down). But the point remains that Chewong emotion-denying rules *are* the rules of that culture's moral code. There is no reason for Chewong to feel angry, other than at the perturbational level, if frustrated by what is culturally imposed. (See Theodore Kemper, *A Social Interactional Theory of Emotions* (Chichester: John Wiley, 1978) for what is probably the most detailed analysis of cultural learning models).

[53] See footnote 46.

does, I have argued, is prevent these culturally resistant perturbations from being elaborated into true emotions. And, I should briefly add, culture might also function to limit the incidence of perturbations. The rules make it less likely that people will be thwarted or that they will be frustrated (remember the emphasis attached to satisfying 'needs') than is the case in the West. And if recent research on the role of facial expression in generating 'emotions' is taken seriously, prohibitions on facial display is also likely to decrease the incidence of potential emotions.[54]

Conclusion

My position lies between psychic unity and disunity; between the endogenous and the exogenous; between biosociology and sociobiology. I have presented ethnographic material which shows radical divergence at the representational level from our own mode of thought and I have made reasonable inferences to suggest, first, that Chewong emotions in general are dampened by the lack of acknowledgment of emotional peturbations and, second, that rules provide models which channel the development and expression of perturbations away from anti-social display (instead of being angry if one is not given food, one is placed in a situation in which *punen* operates, this rule functioning to prevent the constitution of anger, for the model is of fear, although the perturbation of 'anger' remains). So we see why the Chewong are so non-aggressive. They simply are not encouraged to be so inclined.

Robert Burton's *The Anatomy of Melancholy*, published originally in 1621, provides an extract which suits the portrayal I have given of Chewong emotional life. He wrote,

> so we, as long as we are ruled by *reasons*, correct our inordinate *appetite*, and conform ourselves to God's *word*, are as so many saints: but if we give reins to lust, anger, ambition, pride, and follow our own *ways*, we degenerate into beasts, transform ourselves . . . provoke God to anger, and heap upon us this of melancholy, and all kinds of incurable *diseases*, as a just and deserved *punishment* of our *sins* (my italics).[55]

[54] See Ekman (ed.), op. cit. (1982), or, at the popular level, an article in the *Daily Telegraph* (13 September 1983) with the title, 'Let a Smile be Your Umbrella, Say Scientists'.

[55] Richard Burton, *The Anatomy of Melancholy* (London: J. Dent, 1972; original 1621), 137.

This view is appropriate because there is interplay of the endogenous and the exogenous. Culture transforms beast-like perturbations (called 'appetites'). Rules come into play ('reasons' and 'God's word'), as does the punishment of anti-social behaviour ('ways'). Finally, though Burton employs emotion-talk, there is emphasis on an externalized view of man, not amiss for Chewong modes of thought.

Understanding Art and Understanding Persons

FRANCES BERENSON

I have been asked to contribute a paper to the present series of lectures on culture, specifically on whether it is possible to understand the art of other cultures. What I find intriguing is why this question arises; why is such understanding seen as a problem needing discussion?

These are significant questions. How they are answered will be important for any possibility of cross-cultural aesthetic judgments and aesthetic experience. In order to deal with them it is necessary to see how they got purchase, what background they emerged from.

There are at least two recent theories which express doubts about the possibility of cross-cultural understanding. These are relativism, which questions the existence of such understanding in general, and the institutional theory of art from which similar implications follow for aesthetics. I shall discuss these briefly to see whether their claims can be upheld.

First, a point of clarification. Since the concept of culture is notoriously elusive, I wish to specify that I shall use it in its modern sense, as developed in the eighteenth and nineteenth centuries, to mean the whole way of life, material, intellectual, emotional and spiritual, of a given people.

The first important consequence of viewing cultures as somehow isolated in space and time is the modern emphasis on cultural relativism of which there are two main versions: Strong, or what B. Williams calls 'vulgar relativism' and various kinds of weak relativism. The strong relativists argue that the beliefs, social practices and conduct rooted in cultures other than one's own are only understandable and analysable by means of *the concepts* employed within these cultures and thus different conceptual schemes from our own are involved; standards of truth, rationality, right conduct and the expression of these in art are, therefore, inaccessible to members of our culture because they are always relative to particular systems of thought.

B. Williams offers an argument against vulgar relativism in the context of moral judgments which also has analogous implications for aesthetic judgments. The argument takes the following form:

> Vulgar relativism states that 'right' means (can only be coherently understood as meaning) 'right for a given society'; that 'right for a

given society' is to be understood in a functionalist sense; and that (therefore) it is wrong for people in one society to condemn, interfere with, etc., the values of another society.[1]

This thesis, according to Williams, is absurd because:

> Whatever its results, the view is clearly inconsistent, since it makes a claim in its third proposition, about what is right and wrong in one's dealings with other societies, which uses a *non-relative* sense of 'right' not allowed for in the first proposition.[2]

In his later paper 'The Truth of Relativism',[3] Williams gives another version of the argument which results in the possibility of appraisals in cases which he calls 'real options'. Very briefly, he argues that if relativism is taken as a doctrine about *the conditions* under which appraisals can and should take place then appraisals *as such* would be avoided altogether and thus no contradiction would follow, as in the first argument, because we do not appraise; we only examine the conditions under which appraisals could be made in cases of *real options*. Real options are real only for members of a culture who choose between alternatives which are viable for them as a way of life while members of other cultures cannot get a grip on these options; they do not apply to their way of life.

Jack Meiland[4] in a recent discussion of Williams' arguments criticizes his account and suggests that there is a better way of rescuing relativism from the charge of self-contradiction. As relativists typically claim that judgments, knowledge and even truth are relative to conceptual and evaluative frameworks there is no possibility of making any kinds of cross-cultural judgments because we cannot step outside our own conceptual framework to make judgments outside it. Meiland, in stating the relativist claim in this way, shows that the charge of self-contradiction can be avoided altogether because it does not arise.

I do not wish to discuss the respective merits or demerits of the arguments sketched out above; my purpose was to demonstrate the kind of philosophical issues which are raised in this context. My main reaction to these arguments is: Given that they are valid, so what? I find something very artificial in both the above approaches as neither seems to tackle what I take to be the real issue. Why should one be inclined to

[1] B. Williams, *Morality: An Introduction to Ethics* (New York: Harper Torch Books, 1972), 20.
[2] Ibid. 21.
[3] B. Williams, 'The Truth of Relativism', *Proceedings of the Aristotelian Society* **1975** (1974–75), 215–228.
[4] J. Meiland, 'Bernard Williams' Relativism', *Mind* **LXXXVIII**, No. 350, (April 1979), 258–260.

accept any version of relativism which relies on stressing different conceptual frameworks and thus different systems of thought? The obvious philosophical answer is that we must criticize any theory only on its own terms. Fair enough, but why not do so by examining the central thesis? Why not attack head on, as it were? Why not ask whether the postulated different conceptual schemes or frameworks make sense bearing in mind that the temptation, for some, to adhere to certain versions of relativism is a powerful one.

What some[5] find tempting in one kind of relativist thesis is an interesting split which is postulated between the cognitive supremacy of scientific method which stems from universally valid theories embodying truth values, and the non-cognitive status of moral and aesthetic judgments. The vital question which arises is whether it is possible to have partially different conceptual frameworks. If the answer to this question is *no* then it follows that we are confronted with an either/or choice. Either we all, as human beings, share the same form of life, in which case any difficulties arising will be of a different *kind* from those which the relativists raise or no shared knowledge of any kind is possible, whether factual or evaluative; the latter choice resulting in an extreme kind of relativism. On this thesis we are expected to accept that persons from other cultures raise similar problems, regarding the possibility of understanding, that, say, little green creatures from Mars would present to us: that they do not share our form of life, whatever the force of 'our' may be in this context. As a result insurmountable difficulties arise about cross-cultural understanding and thus about the possibility of making any kind of judgments, let alone aesthetic judgments.

Further, our respect for persons from other cultures, on this view, entails never taking up a critical stance and never presuming to judge. What is completely overlooked in this position is that we cannot possibly respect something which we cannot understand. The notion of respect for persons, as invoked in this context, is utterly misconceived. Unless we had shared forms of understanding the notion of respect for persons could not get a grip. The end product of the above view is a kind of isolationism; a moral, intellectual, aesthetic and emotional self-imposed blindness; all of which finally amounts to advocating a course which is not, and never could be, practised.

The step from relativism in general to relativism in art is but a short one. Since all understanding is a social construct, it follows that understanding art is also culture bound as art, most significantly, is the expression of beliefs, feelings and emotions of a given culture. A proper

---

[5]W. Quine, *Word and Object* (New York: Technology Press and Wiley, 1960), 24.

comprehension of art as a mode of experience (a 'reality') and, therefore, of the art of a given culture can only be arrived at through sharing in that experience, in that reality. For the strong relativist this is impossible, for reasons already given. There is, however, a version of weak relativism, postulated by various philosophers and sociologists, which is supposed to be particularly helpful for the understanding of art. The weak relativist, while still assuming the existence of different systems of thought and understanding, tries a kind of compromise by attempting to take into account another person's cultural background with its prescribed norms, shared beliefs, etc. The weak relativist attempts to do this by putting himself in the other's place or empathizing, in his attempts to see what it is that is exercising the other when confronted with an enthusiasm or distaste or indignation or aesthetic appreciation that is *rooted in his own culture*.

This kind of approach can be disposed of fairly easily if, as above, understanding of the art and feelings of members of different cultures is made dependent on empathy. Historically, the concept of empathy stems from the Greek use of 'Empatheia'. One definition is: 'The power of entering into another's personality and imaginatively experiencing his experiences'. The analysis of the Greek word 'Em—pathos' literally translates into 'In—feeling'; so does the German 'Einfühlung'.

Empathy then involves the notion of putting oneself in the other's place. What precisely is meant by this? There are at least two ways in which this could be done:

1. Putting myself in his place could be taken as equivalent to trying to understand how *I* would feel in his place or situation.
2. Putting myself in his place could also be taken as trying to understand how *he* feels in the situation he finds himself in.

The first alternative need not involve any real understanding of the person concerned; at most it need only involve a certain understanding of the situation itself and what my responses or feelings towards it would be like—this allows of the possibility of their being quite different from those of the subject.

The second alternative will not do as a condition for understanding because it presupposes too much. I must already have a real understanding of the person concerned to enable me to become him, as it were. I must already know and understand what it is like to be him, the subject, before I can successfully experience his situation. This is an important ability within an existing personal relationship which enables one to get yet further insights into the other's experiences but it is, without doubt, the end product of already existing understanding, not a condition of it. It presupposes that which it is supposed to achieve.

This leads me to one recent and very influential theory about what it is to understand the art of any culture—the institutional theory of art. The main exponents of this theory are George Dickie[6] and Arthur Danto.[7] The institutional theory of art is concerned very much with procedures *within* a given society, a given culture, which confer the status of an artwork on any artefact. This can be made clearer by an example. Dickie speaks of a painting by Betsy, a chimpanzee, and says that the question whether Betsy's painting is art depends upon what is done with it. Thus, if it should be exhibited in a natural history museum then it is not art but should it be exhibited in an art gallery then it is an artwork because the appropriate institution has conferred the status of artwork on it by exhibiting it.

Works of art become artworks by virtue of given social/cultural conventions including the conventions which govern the use of language in communication and enable us to make judgments about works of art. Art is thus essentially institutional. This does not mean that there are necessarily institution-tokens corresponding to all these labels (some specific institutions such as the Old Vic) but that writing plays and poetry, painting, composing music and sculpturing, etc., are recognized *social* practices; recognized in the sense that there are established institutional procedures for conferring the status of artwork on the products of these practices.

Much has been written about this important theory and several kinds of criticisms have been offered of it. I do not propose to discuss the variety of complex issues arising from the institutional theory of art as such. Instead, I shall concentrate on one influential, later expression of the theory by Joseph Margolis[8] in his important paper 'Works of Art as Physically Embodied and Culturally Emergent Entities'. This paper raises particularly interesting issues pertinent to the possibility of understanding the art of other cultures. I shall state his view briefly and then go on to develop one line of thought which, I hope, will yield an answer to the original question whether such understanding is possible.

Margolis writes that any work of art consists of two related aspects, embodiment and emergence. He writes:

> . . . , I believe that we treat *works of art* and *persons* as entities of a similar sort and speak about them in somewhat similar ways . . . , both works of art and persons . . . are *culturally emergent entities*. . . . Both are accorded a measure of rationality below which they

[6]G. Dickie, 'What is Art', *Culture and Art*, L. Aagaard-Morgensen (ed.) (New York: Eclipse Books, Humanities Press, 1976), 21–32.

[7]A. Danto, 'The Art World', ibid. 9–20.

[8]J. Margolis, 'Works of Art as Physically Embodied and Culturally Emergent Entities', *British Journal of Aesthetics* **14**, No. 3 (Summer 1974), 187–196.

cannot fall, on pain of failing to be works of art or a person. . . .

Works of art and persons, I should say, are *embodied* in physical bodies . . . and as emergent entities exhibit *emergent* properties . . . to be embodied in an object is not to be identical with it.

Margolis gives an example of this distinction:

Thus Michaelangelo's *David* may be identified and referred to as a sculpture embodied in a particular block of marble; . . . Physical objects have the advantage of being identifiable in exclusively extensional terms: the block of marble in which the *David* is embodied may be validly ascribed properties regardless of the description under which it is identified; . . . physical objects have whatever properties they have, *qua* physical objects, independently of any cultural consideration and even independently of the existence of any culture; . . . But this is not true of *culturally* emergent entities . . . hence it is not true of works of art (or of persons or even actions ascribed to persons). . . .[9]

. . . if works of art, as emergent, are *culturally* emergent entities, then they will exhibit culturally significant properties that cannot be ascribed to the merely physical objects in which they are embodied. . . . Stones cannot properly be said to feel anger. . . . And paintings may have expressive qualities, but not the mere physical pigments in which they are embodied.[10]

So reference to physical objects is extensional, in being context-free; and reference to works of art is intensional, in depending on the contextual assumptions of particular cultures.[11]

At this point we get an unequivocal statement asserting institutional relativism:

. . . a work of art can be identified as such *only relative* to a favourable culture with respect to the traditions of which it actually exists[12] (my italics).

. . . works of art are identified intensionally *relative to cultural contexts* in which they may be said to be embodied in a physical medium; . . . characterizations and appraisals of the work are relativized . . .[13] (my italics).

Finally, Margolis says, in passing, that we treat works of art and persons as entities of a similar sort but he is not concerned with working out this analogy. I take the implications of this analogy to be of enormous

[9] Ibid. 187–189.
[10] Ibid. 189–190.
[11] Ibid. 191–192.
[12] Ibid. 193.
[13] Ibid. 194.

importance particularly in areas where the threat of relativism looms large. These implications, therefore, merit a much closer look.

As I see it, two important issues are raised by Margolis' paper which need to be examined in detail:

1. Whether the culture-bound relativity which enters into understanding works of art is of a kind which necessarily precludes understanding? In other words, we need first to answer the question whether cultures are remarkably and fascinatingly diverse or whether truth and logic, i.e. rationality itself, is culture dependent relative to some elusive and mysterious thought system?
2. What exactly is involved in his two levels of understanding: the extensional and the intensional, a distinction which brings in the analogy between persons and works of art. These issues constitute the main aim of my paper.

First, then, let us see what follows from Margolis' statement that 'a work of art can be identified as such *only relative* to a favourable culture. . . .' This statement represents a very extreme form of the institutional theory of art; other, less extreme, forms also maintain that critical appraisals and appreciation make sense only within those societies from which standards and kinds of response stem.

It follows, from all versions of this theory, that we can only understand the art of other cultures from within the aesthetic framework of our own society. This involves observing how members of a given society respond to their works of art and then objectively reaching certain conclusions which will, of course, be limited to the observer's own framework. Alternatively, and absurdly, it follows that if a stranger somehow succeeded in becoming involved in a given society to the extent that, in time, it became his own, he could not express this newly acquired understanding to members of his original culture.

The claims of the institutional theory of art can be interpreted in two ways, as Harold Osborne points out in a review article 'Primitive Art and Society'.[14] If the point is merely that we recognize works of art as such, appreciate them and appraise them, in virtue of the dispositions and standards which we have as members of the society to which we belong, then it is both a truism and a triviality. We are all members of a society and in none of our activities or judgments can we escape from our own skins, allowing, of course, for wide individual differences. But if the institutional theory of art is intended to mean that we are all

[14] H. Osborne, 'Primitive Art and Society', *British Journal of Aesthetics* **14** No. 4 (Autumn 1974), 300.

of us trapped in our aesthetic response acquired exclusively from our own societies, as if in tightly closed boxes of the societies to which we belong, then the theory can be shown to be false because contrary to fact.

This kind of approach to aesthetics completely overlooks important facts such as the general ability of members of remote cultures excelling in Western music; we have only to think of the Leeds piano competition or of performances by Japanese, African, Chinese, Arab or Indian musicians. All of these belie the kind of isolationism mentioned earlier. One might object that we have great difficulties with, e.g., the music of India or the Middle East; so we may have but the difficulties are of the same kind as those which we encounter on first hearing Schönberg or even Alban Berg. One has to work at it in order to understand it with no guarantee of success. One needs to learn something about the twelve tone system and about what such music is trying to achieve, how it differs from classical music, why it is mistaken to listen for melodic lines, and so on. As for other kinds of art the same considerations apply. On first encountering ancient Greek and Arab art in its natural setting, far from experiencing difficulties about our aesthetic response, the impact is so powerful as to almost defy description. The rule in Muslim art that there are to be no representations of living creatures is, similarly, not difficult to understand, neither is the fact that this rule was and is broken occasionally. The answers are to be found in the teaching of the *Qurran*[15] for those who wish to know.

One could again object that there are examples of art, for instance, some African or Brazilian art, where garish colours predominate in combinations which we find vulgar and crude. Apart from the very important considerations of local light, which has dramatic effects on colour combinations, this kind of general criticism just will not do. Gauguin's visit to Martinique resulted in his dramatic use of strong colours in vivid contrast to his post-impressionist period which was prior to his visit to the tropics. The late Shah of Iran's Peacock Throne room is a good counter-example to the above objection. The room has, along both its long walls, cases displaying gifts from various heads of state. Quite indisputably, the ugliest and most vulgar by far is a bronze ship with a clock stuck in its bowels. This gift was presented to the Shah by Queen Victoria. No further comment is necessary.

In as much as we can legitimately speak of knowledge and understanding as in any way culture bound, we can profitably do so in terms of interests of various cultures. By 'interest' I mean simply that

[15] *The Holy Qurran*, M. Ghulám Faríd (ed.) (The London Mosque, 1981): (a) Ch. 57, v. 35 and 55, 1175–1176; (b) Ch. 7, v. 153, 359; (c) Ch. 5, v. 91, 268. All these passages forbid the making of images of living things; the Imáms, in their interpretations, have extended this ban to art.

different cultures will know and understand more about certain things, more about certain particular *areas* of knowledge, than about others. Cultures where technology is highly developed will, quite obviously, be expert in that kind of knowledge stemming from their predominant interests. Cultures which live constantly with the problems of, say, water shortage, will know much about systems of irrigation and their predominant interest, stemming from their particular needs, will encourage the development of knowledge in this particular field. Eskimos, for instance, are said to have over thirty different words to describe qualities of snow which is of great importance in their lives. We could, however, come to understand these fine distinctions if called upon to do so.

These are just very crude examples of the role of interest and its influence on knowledge and understanding. No culture has a single, overriding interest, as my examples may unintentionally imply, but rather a complex, interrelated structure of interests arising from special cultural conditions. Taking knowledge as culture bound in this sense makes 'interest' not 'knowledge' relative and this kind of relativism is quite unexceptionable; it does not require any notion of different conceptual schemes or even anything vaguely similar. The direction which this kind of emphasis points to is to the possibility of learning about other people's conditions, interests and concerns in a way which becomes comparatively unproblematic as opposed to logically impossible for the weak or strong relativist, both of whom deny that knowledge and understanding are objective.

That this last conclusion is, to say the least, grossly misleading is very tellingly shown by Mary Midgley:[16]

> . . . our own society . . . is a fertile jungle of different influences—Greek, Jewish, Roman, Norse, Celtic—into which further influences are still pouring—American, Indian, Japanese, Jamaican, you name it. If we think about this history for a moment, we can see that the . . . picture of separate, unmixable cultures is quite unreal. The world has never been like that; it couldn't be like that. . . . Except for the very smallest and most remote, *all* cultures are formed of many streams. All have the problem of digesting and assimilating things which, at the start, they don't understand. All have the choice of learning something from the challenge, or, alternatively, of refusing to learn, and fighting it mindlessly instead.

Midgley is not by any means alone in voicing this conviction. Several aestheticians also argue along these lines. For instance, E. H.

[16]M.Midgley, 'Trying Out One's New Sword', broadcast on BBC. *The Listener* 15 December 1977.

Gombrich[17] stresses cultural diversity, not cultural isolationism, so does Clive Bell,[18] to mention but two well-known names. Carl Schnaase,[19] a famous art historian, writing as early as 1843, says:

> Thus the art of every period is both the most complete and the most reliable expression of the national spirit in question, it is something like a hieroglyph . . . in which the secret essence of the nation declares itself, concealed, it is true, dark at first sight but completely and unambiguously to those who can read these signs.

Thus, in answer to our first question, we can say that Margolis' claim that understanding is culture dependent relative to some elusive framework of rationality can be shown to be false because it is contrary to fact. Cultural diversity does not imply cultural isolationism.

We can now turn to an analysis of extensional and intensional understanding. For Margolis these focus respectively on *embodiment*, the physical, context-free 'body' (material) which contains the work of art or persons, and *emergence*, which contains expressions of feelings and emotions indigenous to a given culture and so 'emergence' brings in the notion of what a work of art *means* to members of a given culture relative to its institutional or cultural context. This notion brings to light a conceptual relation or dependence of a theory of art on a theory of persons.

I wish to carry this last remark much further and argue that to understand *any* work of art involves, *on a certain level*, understanding something of the persons from whom the work stems. I, therefore, want to enlarge on Margolis' two levels of understanding because I don't think that they are adequate for what is involved. His two levels work fairly well where sculpture, architecture and paintings are concerned but it is not at all obvious what would count as equivalent to the slab of marble, in which *David* is embodied, in the case of music, literature and dance. If, in the case of music, we take embodiment to be marks on paper, as Margolis suggests, then we get the same sort of embodiment for music as for literature. Perhaps that, by itself, is not a serious objection but it is not at all clear that marks on paper are what embodies music because rhythms (time) are an essential part of music. It is very difficult to decide here what the physical body or material is. Similar difficulties arise in the case of dance. It is not *just* the human body which embodies dance because, again, at least rhythm also is involved. Even in the case of the piece of stone, in which *David* is embodied, we

---

[17] E. H. Gombrich, *In Search of Cultural History* (Oxford: Clarendon Press, 1966), sec. 1, p 5.

[18] C. Bell, *Art* (London, 1949), 37.

[19] C. Schnaase, *Geschichte der Bildenden Kunste* 1, (Leipzig, 1843).

cannot say that the identification of the stone is context-free because it is a particular *kind* of marble which was chosen to embody *David*, it was chosen with David in mind. Not just any kind of stone would have done for Michaelangelo; his decision was an aesthetic decision. Margolis says that physical objects have physical properties *qua* physical objects and are, therefore, context-free. But the physical marks on paper have certain physical characteristics (shapes) which are only understandable, identifiable and describable from within the context of music or of the novel. I therefore propose, by looking closely at three examples of understanding, that of music, Greek folk dancing and persons, to illustrate the levels involved.

1. First level—Identification (Embodiment)

On this, basic, level, we can easily identify music by certain marks on paper or by sound recognition, the dance by the universal, though not altogether context-free, bodily movements in time to rhythms and we can pick out persons as opposed to material objects.

2. Second Level—Identification (Particular Embodiment)

The second level invokes the notion of particular identification of a piece of music as a song, a sonata, a symphony, etc.; the dance involves identification of particular bodily movements in response to particular rhythms and patterns which are rule governed and, therefore, identifiable as such. This enables us to identify a given dance as a Greek folk dance as distinct from, say, ballet, a Dervish dance, an Indian temple dance or disco dancing. In the case of persons we employ concepts involving what it is for someone to be a person of a particular kind. My distinction between first and second level concepts is one of generic and specific identification respectively. The two levels stress the logical priority at stake here. The concepts of what it is to be a person, a piece of music or a dance of a particular kind are considered as second level because these concepts and their application presuppose the first level concept of 'person', 'music', and 'dance', i.e. the level of generic identification.

3. Third Level—Subjective Meaning (Emergence)

The third, most complex, level is concerned with understanding what a particular dance or piece of music means to the performer; what its subjective significance consists of. And it is here that a mere analogy between works of art and persons undergoes a dramatic shift and is shown to be inadequate. In order to understand something of what a particular work of art *means* to a person who is a member of a given culture we need to understand something of that person. At this point, instead of a mere analogy, we find a conceptual dependence on understanding *persons* for understanding *particular aesthetic experiences*.

The first and second levels employ what I shall call factual or scientific understanding which presupposes an understanding of basic concepts and their application in identifying something generically followed by concepts of specific identifications. These involve the notion of what a given performer or spectator does or says about a work of art; they involve a degree of knowledge and competence as outlined in the examples given earlier. The third level employs what I shall call personal understanding, an understanding which to a large extent depends on the sort of person one is; this will be decisive to one's appropriate relationship to the work, one's capacity to be aware of the work in a certain way. It is at this point that a very significant change occurs. Apart from aesthetic considerations we now have to enter the area of the philosophy of persons in order to give an account of how this kind of subjective meaning is to be understood; certainly not through empathy, for reasons already given, nor through a mere analogy with persons. It is also clear that the two levels of understanding postulated by Margolis are quite inadequate for the task which they are designed to perform. In a paper of this length I can only give a hint, an outline of one aspect of this kind of understanding which ties in with relativism. I have written more fully on this subject elsewhere.[20]

We need to remember what gives rise to the spectre of cultural relativism. Recent versions of the theory were first put forward by various sociologists[21] whose claims for *the methodology* of sociology are based on observations and interpretations of various practices, this method being insisted on because it is supposed to guarantee objectivity. Now it is precisely this method which creates insurmountable difficulties for understanding persons and how they feel about things which are important to them. This kind of understanding cannot be achieved purely by observation.

[20] F. Berenson, *Understanding Persons* (Brighton: The Harvester Press, 1981).

[21] E. Durkheim, 'Essais sur la conception materialiste de l'histoire', *Revue Philosophique* (December 1897); *Suicide* (London: Routledge and Kegan Paul, 1952); V. Pareto, *The Mind and Society* (New York: Harcourt Brace, 1935), sec. 7.

It is undeniable that practices are always partially, even if to different degrees, constituted by what certain people think and feel about them. In order to discover this we face the difficulty of translation between *the subject's* and *the observer's* respective thoughts and feelings and this is of paramount importance to the kind of understanding of another that one is capable of achieving, either cross-culturally or within one's own culture.

When contemplating a work of art we need to discover what the terms which the natives use in talking about art really mean to them; what is the role played by these terms within their culture or, generally, within their experience. We need to be aware of the danger of ethnocentrism and egocentrism in any form of understanding, in any kind of interpretation, particularly that based on observation only. The experiences of another person recounted, explained or described in an observer's own terms may bear little or no relation to the subject's experience. This point is also related to my earlier discussion of empathy.

We tend to speak in this context about the non-translatability of language of certain cultures but if any culture uses language for communication this presupposes that the language was learned interpersonally. Concepts and thus understanding and meaning are logically dependent for their sense on social interaction. This, in turn, presupposes certain rules which are constitutive of the language. Once we accept the above then it follows that such rules are discoverable, at least in principle, by any other language user.

Art and creativity are a vital part of this because we start from a common, shared ground, from what one might refer to as the human impulse to create and express. Why then should we not also accept the existence of a kind of universal response? Thus, for instance, Ruby Meager writes:

> But if we could draw together the traditional twin concerns of art and beauty, it might be because we could treat art also as a form of human life, as relating to a near-universal human responsive framework within which we can understand the intelligibility, of a non-utilitarian kind, of art as a distinct human activity. . . .[22]
>
> . . . art . . . would have intelligibility born not merely of a local fashionable culture-phase but of a universal mode of communication relating to some universally shared human sensitivity. . . .[23]

[22] R. Meager, 'Art and Beauty', *British Journal of Aesthetics* **14** No. 4 (Spring 1974), 102.
[23] Ibid. 104.

Given this crucial, shared starting point, understanding can develop at various levels; we can now deal with any difficulties arising because:

(a) they cease to be mysteries, and
(b) they are now seen as difficulties of a certain different kind.

Now we can speak in terms of understanding what a particular reality consists in, in terms of what bearing such understanding has on the life of individual persons who are also members of society; what a given activity means to the agent, his emotional response and his perception of special qualities and meanings in the work of art. This understanding just cannot be achieved by observation alone, a method which results from a misguided obsession with objectivity.

Knowledge and understanding based on observation could be described as scientific knowledge, referred to earlier, whereas knowledge and understanding resulting from our standing in some kind of relationship with the person concerned is personal understanding. Personal understanding is achieved as a result of reflections upon our personal dealings with others; in our recognizing them as persons different from each other in important respects. I prefer this contrast to the objective/subjective distinction which is rather misleading for reasons I hope to make clear. Objective knowledge does not necessarily entail viewing people as objects; on the contrary, having the concept 'person' already prevents us from this and in an important way objective knowledge enters very much into personal understanding. Scientific knowledge, however, although valid, is in an important sense abstract knowledge because it precludes the knower from knowing and understanding a whole range of things pertinent to the person concerned. Many things about a person, including what works of art of his culture mean to him, can only be understood through entering into a relationship which enables the development of personal attitudes to take place.

Thus, what is important is that once we stand in any kind of relationship with a person, personal attitudes begin to play a lesser or greater part in our understanding of him. In such cases the knowledge and understanding we begin to acquire is no longer to be equated with scientific knowledge as such; it is no longer abstract because it is no longer disconnected fom personal attitudes.

Each individual has a private life of thoughts, hopes, feelings and emotions which, although largely dependent on others, do not necessarily figure explicitly in his objective life and cannot, therefore, be observed, absorbed or be accessible to others. These aspects are profoundly different in kind from overt aspects and it is at this stage that the distinction between personal knowledge and knowledge gained through observation begins to emerge.

One point needs to be stressed. I do not wish to imply that the distinction between personal and scientific knowledge is one which is more or less equivalent to knowledge based on a person's subjective and overt factors respectively. On the contrary, both kinds of factors are necessary for personal understanding. Conversely, scientific knowledge of a person may include knowledge of how his feelings, thoughts, etc., find expression. Furthermore, knowing someone as a person is not simply tantamount to knowing his subjective side. Having said this, I am not denying in any way the importance of the fact that persons have a subjective life and that without this there would be nothing personal to know and understand. But the subjectivity at stake here is of a harmless kind because all that is meant by it is that a person subjectively selects from within a rich and varied objective framework and this guarantees intelligibility in principle.

Acquiring knowledge of overt characteristics and facts about a person could be said to require, where the person is not known personally, conditions where information is gathered indirectly or by observation, where something like scientific method is employed, where hypotheses which are postulated can be tested by gathering the information necessary for the denial or confirmation of them. This type of information is usually accessible and thus discoverable regardless of the wishes or intentions of the person about whom it is gathered. In cases where we stand in some kind of direct relationship with the person concerned, access to his personal feelings, attitudes, etc., is certainly direct, first-hand access and may or may not also be indirect. What is important here is the manner in which our knowledge of characteristics and facts is acquired.

It can now be seen why the distinction between personal and scientific knowledge cannot be equated with knowledge based on subjective and overt factors respectively. Personal knowledge is and has to be based on both factors. Similarly, scientific knowledge based on observation and gathering of information may result in an understanding of both subjective and overt factors. But *the quality* of the understanding is different. It is only in reciprocal personal relationships that subjective aspects of a person's life have a chance of spontaneously and fully manifesting themselves. Attitudes, purposes and reciprocal responses which manifest themselves *naturally* are of crucial importance here. These are lacking in cases of scientific knowledge. The point is *not* that we cannot come to know a person's subjective side in cases of scientific knowledge but rather that the resulting understanding is limited and qualitatively different. We have no experience of the reciprocal development of understanding nor have we the means of checking whether our understanding is correct. It is only on a personal level, as a result of sustained interaction, shared time and shared activities, that mistaken understanding is exposed and corrected.

It may be objected that, after all, scientific knowledge is precise because uncluttered by personal attitudes and is thus likely to be correct and, therefore, constitutes the only valuable kind of knowledge of persons. To argue in this way is to construe knowledge of persons on the model of knowledge of material objects. Scientific knowledge, acquired mainly by observation, can be most misleading because it is based on the assumption that a man's observed behaviour is the sole or main context in which understanding takes place. But it is precisely in this context where, significantly, checks of correctness or incorrectness of conclusions become very elusive if not absent altogether. If our attempts to understand are inadequate or misguided then they lead to a kind of disintegration which manifests itself in a negative puzzlement, as in relativism, where ultimately any possibility of understanding slips from our grasp.

To understand the music of any culture involves certain capacities for experience which are, in an important sense, *sui generis*. Thus understanding is not the same state of mind in all cases. Here we find a strong relationship with understanding a person, as this involves having a sense of what a given person might do or think, just as one often 'knows' what the music (the composer) might do next. Also, music, on a deeper level of understanding, bears a strong relation to personal understanding in that it involves at least the possibility of the kind of intuitive knowledge of another's feelings. Composing music is a human activity and very much bound up with any particular composer being the sort of person that he is. Fundamental beliefs influence our feelings, perceptions and responses to any work of art. Aesthetics, therefore, has to avoid the cultural bias of the scholar who insists on a purely intellectual approach to a field which does not lend itself to such an approach nor does it, necessarily, result in the desired kind of 'objectivity'.

In conclusion, I have argued that in order to understand the art of any particular culture we need to distinguish between three levels of understanding. The basic two levels demand understanding something of the artistic background from which any work stems, e.g., Duchamp and his anti-art statements, the classical music tradition, twelve tone music or Bach's strong religious commitment. Similarly, as already mentioned, we need to understand why living creatures are not represented in Muslim art and then judge it and appreciate it within the right categories, as above. For instance, as a result of this rule, we find highly developed, intricate and often very delicate *geometric* designs like the Arab design of the arabesque in painting and sculpture which has been transferred to Western music and dance so very successfully.

An important aspect of art is that such transferrence and development are possible.

On the third level of understanding we enter into the area of person understanding in general and what works of art mean to individuals, in particular. This brings in an understanding of the kinds of feelings, emotions and commitments which play a crucial part in aesthetic experience. Thus in our original examples of dance we need to understand something of the religious feelings which are an integral part of the Dervish dance and of the total emotional and intellectual abandonment to prayer and communion with God. Greek folk dancing involves much more than sheer enjoyment. It is a visual, deeply emotional expression of the very complex Greek character which requires a complex understanding of the historical and emotional life of the persons concerned; something that cannot be achieved by observation or detached investigation alone.

The impulse to create and express are exclusively human and universal. So is the appeal which art has. Any difficulties which arise are, therefore, also universal, not specifically cultural, as alleged, in some mysterious way.

One could go on multiplying examples but my main point was to bring out what I take to be a most important phenomenon which tends to occur whenever we talk about cultures other than our own. We seem to be *looking for* mysteries and difficulties instead of using familiar, everyday criteria to assess situations. There is a presupposition about difficulties in understanding which has most adverse consequences more often than not quite unnecessarily. The significant point which emerged from the controversy about the TV documentary *The Death of a Princess* was that, in the discussions between the interviewers and the various Saudi Arabians involved in the case, there was no particular difficulty regarding criteria of rationality, as was amply demonstrated by the justifications offered. The difficulties arose from differing views about suitable punishments for various transgressions, a problem found in our own culture. In other words, the outcome of this particular debate was to show that to understand all does not necessarily mean to forgive all. The criteria used by both parties were familiar, objective criteria; familiar in the sense that they stem from a shared conceptual scheme. Without this precondition the discussions would not have been possible at all. We may find certain attitudes wrong, barbaric, infuriating, frustrating or difficult to accept but these reactions on our part are only possible as a *result* of our understanding what is involved. This applies to all kinds of judgments.

Given that anything intelligible is so by virtue of certain rules then such rules are discoverable, at the very least, in principle, by other cultures who, as language speakers, are also familiar with the notion of 'rule'. This is what guarantees objectivity.

I have, in effect, argued that there exists an important confusion in the area of intercultural understanding because we constantly confuse the understanding of something with the quite different notion of approving of certain practices, often stemming from various institutions which we do not approve of. My last example, above, illustrates exactly this point.

In so far as art is undoubtedly an expression of experience stemming from a way of life and from human emotions, any understanding of it necessarily involves some understanding of that particular way of life; a personal understanding which particular areas from an objective range of areas of knowledge a given society or a given person finds important. Understanding of anything at all, on a deep level, is never easy and requires a certain commitment and hard effort. There are enough problems about understanding persons different from oneself and of understanding the expression of their experiences and emotions in art, whether it be within one's own culture or interculturally, without our adding gratuitous mysteries to this complex field. I have, in this paper, tried to plead that we exorcise this particular ghost.

The Devil's Disguises: Philosophy of Religion, 'Objectivity' and 'Cultural Divergence'

D. Z. PHILLIPS

> Satan himself masquerades as an angle of light
> II Corinthians 11:14

In approaching the topic, 'Objectivity and Cultural Divergence', there is little doubt that certain styles of philosophizing will conceive of the task confronting them as that of devising or at least calling attention to standards of rationality by which distinctions between objectivity and divergence are to be drawn. This mode of philosophizing is marked by the confidence it has in its own methods. It seldom occurs to it to question its own operations; to ask whether the heterogeneity of our culture does not itself create difficulties for the practice of philosophy. It is to such questionings as these, however, that I want to direct attention in this lecture.

The difficulties for the practice of philosophy I want to mention can only be appreciated if we agree that philosophy is interested in clarity. We become confused when certain tendencies in the ways we speak lead us astray. We are led to deny the possibility of knowledge, the possibility of knowing others, the possibility of a difference between right and wrong, the possibility of belief in God. The confusions involved in these expressions of scepticism may be dispelled by reminders of the natural contexts in which the challenged possibilities have their home. We are reminded of what we are tempted to misrepresent. If the reminders are successful, the conceptual possibilities are allowed their proper place. But is the provision of reminders unproblematic? In this lecture I shall show, in relation to the philosophy of religion, why no confident affirmative answer can be given to this question. My conclusions, I believe, have implications for other branches of philosophy, but I shall not elaborate on these.

I

I have referred to a misplaced confidence philosophy may have in conceiving its task as that of devising rational means for distinguishing between objectivity and cultural divergence. To speak of divergence

61

D. Z. Phillips

implies confidence in a norm. Many philosophers have declared, confidently, that religion constitutes a divergence from the norm of rationality. This fact is widely recognized by philosophers whether they are sympathetically or unsympathetically disposed towards religion. Norman Malcolm has said: 'In our Western academic philosophy, religious belief is commonly regarded as unreasonable and is viewed with condescension or even contempt. It is said that religion is a refuge for those who, because of weakness of intellect or character, are unable to confront the stern realities of the world. The objective, mature, *strong* attitude is to hold beliefs solely on the basis of *evidence*.'[1] Kai Nielsen has said in reply: 'Surely the response of intellectuals to religion is more complex and varied than that, but there is enough truth in this exaggeration and in Malcolm's further remark "that by and large religion is to university people an alien form of life" to make it an important sociological datum to keep before our minds when we consider religion. A religious human being, a person who prays and goes to church and all that, is something of an anomaly among present-day Western intellectuals and particularly among philosophers. That form of life does seem very alien to many of us.'[2] The purpose of this lecture may be described as an examination of the implications of what Nielsen acknowledges to be an 'important sociological datum'; the implications for the practice of providing reminders to achieve clarity in philosophy.

The first thing to note is that the situation in which religious belief has come to be alien for many people is a situation with a history. Religious belief is seen as an aberration of the human mind from which enlightenment should rescue us. Religious beliefs have failed to pass the tests of rationality. Hume, having shown how an argument from world to God is logically flawed, bequeathed to the nineteenth and our century the task of explaining how people, despite the enlightenment at hand, can continue to believe what is irrational. Philosophy, aided by anthropology and psychoanalysis, was to be the angel of light which was to bring enlightenment to the dark recesses of the human mind. The confident tone of the intellectual partnership is found in the following remarks by E. B. Tylor: 'To the promoters of what is sound and reformers of what is faulty in modern culture, ethnography has double help to give. To impress men's minds with a doctrine of development will lead them in all honour to their ancestors to continue the progressive work of past ages, to continue it the more vigorously

[1] Norman Malcolm, 'The Groundlessness of Belief', *Thought and Knowledge* (Ithaca: Cornell University Press, 1977), 204.
[2] Kai Nielsen, 'On the Rationality of Groundless Believing', *Idealistic Studies* **XI,** No. 3 (September 1981), 215.

because light has increased in the world, and where barbaric hordes groped blindly, cultured men can often move onward with clear view.'[3]

The cultured, modern man Tylor refers to is described by Flannery O'Connor as one who 'recognizes spirit in himself but who fails to recognize a being outside himself whom he can adore as Creator and Lord; consequently he has become his own ultimate concern. He says with Swinburne, "Glory to man in the highest, for he is the master of things", or with Steinbeck, "In the end was the word and the word was the man". For him, man has his own natural spirit of courage and dignity and pride and must consider it a point of honour to be satisfied with this.'[4] Freud too was anxious to show that courage, dignity and pride are not incompatible with seeing through the other-worldly promises of religion: 'And, as for the great necessities of Fate, against which there is no help, they will learn to endure with resignation. Of what use to them is the mirage of wide acres in the moon, whose harvest no one has ever yet seen? As honest smalholders on this earth they will know how to cultivate their plot in such a way that it supports them.'[5] They learn to endure with resignation because they have come to realize, as primitive man did not, that the forces of nature to which they are subject, winds and rains, come when they do, and that no amount of magic will make any difference. When man dispenses with such magical rites as rain dances, he is coming of age, seeing that there is no causal connection between the dances and the coming of the rain.

Despite the fact that many writers, Tylor and Freud included, insisted that primitive people could not be blamed for thinking as they did, inevitably, it was hard to keep out a congratulatory element from the claim that they were speaking from an intellectually superior vantage point in human development. This intellectual superiority, however, has been challenged from many directions, not least among them being the reminders of philosophy. Such a reminder was Wittgenstein's telling observation that the rain dances were performed when the rains were due anyway.[6] The dance did not cause the rains to come; it celebrated their coming. When we see the dances a part of a celebratory activity, we no longer speak of confusion. We achieve conceptual clarity and are rescued from a condescending misunderstanding.

Yet, many have resisted the kind of reminders Wittgenstein and

[3] E. B. Tylor, *Primitive Culture* (London: John Murray, 1920), 453.

[4] Flannery O'Connor, *Mystery and Manners*, selected and edited by Sally and Robert Fitzgerald (New York: Farrar, Strauss and Giroux, 1969), 159.

[5] Sigmund Freud, *The Future of an Illusion* (London: Hogarth Press, 1962), 46.

[6] Ludwig Wittgenstein, 'Remarks on Frazer's *The Golden Bough*', *The Human World* No. 3 (May 1971).

others have provided. Further, the reminders seemed to have caused a degree of anger and resentment, rare even in philosophy. Why is this so? The answer lies, partly, I believe, in the kind of change needed in a philosopher if he is to accept the philosophical reminder. In order to elucidate the character of this change, I want to compare the task facing a philosopher providing conceptual reminders in the philosophy of religion against the intellectual background I have described, with the task of providing reminders in literature which faces the religious author in a similar context.

Like the philosopher of religion, Flannery O'Connor, as a Catholic writer, faced the problem of how to convey a religious perspective in literature in a pervasively secular American culture. Just as many philosophers regard religious belief as a cultural divergence needing rational enlightenment, so many in the North in the sixties regarded the South with its racial problems and evangelical religion as being in the grip of irrationality. Robert Coles observed of Flannery O'Connor and her South: 'Surely neither she, nor other Georgia writers, nor the black rural field hands of the state, have ever had much say in the matter of what in this nation is and is not considered "appropriate", "seemly", "desirable", let alone "grotesque". The standards come from elsewhere.'[7] Yet, there were voices raised in Georgia which refused to accept the North's version of what was happening. Here is one such voice, which accuses the Northern critics of lacking the very virtues in terms of which they claimed to be making their criticisms. The speaker insists that the distinction between North and South was not a distinction between purity and impurity: 'You think the coloured people don't know who's here to stay, and who's just passing through—looking for a *cause* . . . to find people to look down on, and people who will look up to them as if each and every one of them was Jesus Christ Himself. So they say to each other: let's go South and have us a damn good time down there, with all those dumb crackers. There will come a day when the shoe will be on the other foot, and all the trouble we have down here won't look so bad, when you see what's going on up there. And when that day comes, I'll promise you something: no one from Georgia is going to go up there, pointing his finger at people, and telling them they're no good, and they're ignorant, and they have to change by federal law, or else. It's not our way, down here, to go poking into the business of others, so we can have our fun. If these people would take themselves to church, other than to organize integration rallies, while they're down here staying among us, they

---

[7] Robert Coles, *Flannery O'Connor's South* (Louisiana State University Press, 1980), 6–7.

might learn something—about pride, the worst sin of all. But they'd laugh if I went and told them that—because I didn't go to college.'[8]

We can see why the reminder about pride from the South would be hard to accept. To accept it would be to admit to the very sin one was accusing others of so confidently. Flannery O'Connor's reminders in her stories had a similar effect. They outraged her critics because they took the form of using the secularist's perspective as a testimony to the reality of the religion it attacked. She realized that in a pervasively secular culture she could not give her reminders in a straightforward way. Flannery O'Connor said that she, 'instead of reflecting the image at the heart of things . . . has only reflected our broken condition and, through it, the face of the devil we are possessed by. This is a modest achievement, but perhaps a necessary one.'[9] In the Georgian censure of Northern attitudes, the sting came, as we saw, in the location of pride and condescension in the very attitudes which prided themselves on being those of concern and fellow-feeling. So in Flannery O'Connor's short stories, the very age which prides itself on freedom from superstitions such as belief in the devil, is accused of demon possession. Flannery O'Connor observes, 'Probably the devil plays the greatest role in the production of that fiction from which he himself is absent as an actor'.[10] These considerations are embodied in Flannery O'Connor's short story, *The Lame Shall Enter First*.

In the story, Sheppard, a part-time social worker, befriends a lame delinquent called Johnson. He compares his own son, Norton, unfavourably with him. Norton's mother has died, but Sheppard believes his son's grief is excessive, and that instead of moping he should build for the future. Sheppard sees more spirit in the delinquent, despite all his disadvantages. Johnson is brought into the house. Sheppard is appalled to find that the delinquent attributes his deviance to the fact that he is in the Devil's power. He promises to explain his devil to him. Johnson is bought a telescope to encourage his interest in astronomy. Yet, when Johnson is alone with Norton he reveals his contempt for the attention of the social worker, '"God, kid", Johnson said in a cracked voice, "how do you stand it?" His face was stiff with outrage. "He thinks he's Jesus Christ."'[11] He feeds the young son with crude pictures of heaven and hell. He tells him that if his mother was a good woman she is in heaven, but that he would have to die to reach her. Norton is convinced that through the telescope he can

[8] Ibid. 10–11.
[9] Op. cit. 168.
[10] Ibid. 189.
[11] Flannery O'Connor, 'The Lame Shall Enter First' in *Everything That Rises Must Converge* (London: Faber, 1965), 161.

see his mother waving at him. Sheppard tells him that all he can see are star clusters, but to no avail. The story ends with Sheppard's discovery that the delinquent has misled him all along; has used his trust as a cover for committing further crimes. Johnson is led away compounding lies and it is at this point that revelation comes to Sheppard:

'"I have nothing to reproach myself with", he began again. "I did more for him than I did for my own child." He heard his voice as if it were the voice of his accuser. He repeated the sentence silently.

'Slowly his face drained of colour. It became almost grey beneath the white halo of his hair. The sentence echoed in his mind, each syllable like a dull blow . . . He had stuffed his own emptiness with good works like a glutton. He had ignored his own child to feed his vision of himself. He saw the clear-eyed Devil, the sounder of hearts, leering at him from the eyes of Johnson . . .'[12] He rushes back to his son, to ask for his forgiveness, to tell him he loved him. He finds him in the attic: 'The tripod had fallen and the telescope lay on the floor. A few feet over it, the child hung in the jungle of shadows, just below the beam from which he had launched his flight into space.'[13]

The social worker had promised to explain away Johnson's devil. Flannery O'Connor's reminder shows how, from a religious perspective, the social worker's confidence in his explanatory categories is an aspect of the Devil's victory. Johnson wanted to be caught by the police. When asked why, he replies, referring to the social worker, 'To show up that big tin Jesus! . . . He thinks he's God. I'd rather be in the reformatory than in his house. I'd rather be in the pen! The Devil has him in his power.'[14] The irony is that the social worker is seen as possessed by the very devil he set out to explain away.

Philosophers may call attention to the kind of criticism from Georgia I quoted or to a story from Flannery O'Connor, as I have done, in order to show that there are perspectives from which matters can be seen in ways which the secular rationalist cannot account for. While the secularist may not embrace these perspectives, he cannot explain them away, as he thinks, in terms of their irrationality. Yet, that is not my main reason for using these examples. I have used them to show how moral criticism and Flannery O'Connor's story, in their different ways, accuse certain attitudes of possessing a character they prided themselves on being free of. This is why both caused so much anger and controversy. It is in this respect that they throw light on the earlier question we posed: Why should the reminders of the philosopher of religion cause so much agitation among those who deny that religious beliefs can mean anything? Is it not because they too, if accepted, would

[12] Ibid. 189–190.
[13] Ibid.
[14] Ibid. 187.

involve the philosophical sceptic in recognizing that he was possessed by that very thing he prided himself on being free of? While we do not object to saying that we are blind to science, we do object to saying that we are blind to religion. Why? We must remember that for many philosophy is supposed to be an angel of light ministering to the darkness of superstition. But in being reminded of the character of certain religious beliefs, philosophers are being asked to accept that they may be in the grip of the very superstition they take themselves to be attacking. Consider the following gloss given by Tylor on the ritual among the Seminoles of Florida of holding a newborn infant over a mother's face to receive her parting breath if she was dying after child-birth. Speaking of the notion of the soul involved in the ritual he says, 'It is a thin unsubstantial human image, in its nature a sort of vapour, film or shadow; the cause of life and thought in the individual it animates; independently possessing the personal consciousness and volition of its corporeal owner, past or present; capable of leaving the body far behind to flash swiftly from place to place; mostly impalpable and invisible, yet also manifesting physical power, and especially appearing to man working or asleep as a phantasm separate from the body of which it bears the likeness; able to enter into, possess, and act in the bodies of other men, of animals, and even of things.'[15] Commenting on Tylor's conception of the soul I said: 'Tylor thinks that the meaning of his examples are unequivocal and that it is accounted for in his analysis. As a matter of fact, his analysis is more influenced by a philosophical dualism concerning soul and body than by the examples under consideration. . . . What Tylor fails to take account of is the significance these gestures have in the relationship between a dying mother and the child she is giving birth to . . . A mother has given her life for her child and this is expressed in the ritual by the child receiving her parting breath. What more needs to be said? . . . these acts are not based on hypotheses or opinions concerning strange invisible substances which, by mysterious means, are transferred from one person to another. On the contrary, the gestures are expressions of something. What they express can be indicated in the ways we have just noted. Ironically, it is Tylor, the rational critic, who is in the grip of the very conception of the soul he sets out to criticize. It is precisely because for him there would have to be a strange substance called the soul in order for the notion to have any meaning that he finds the examples he discusses unintelligible. It is his own positivistic conception of the soul which prevents him from appreciating what the notion may mean in its natural setting.'[16]

[15] Op.cit. 429.

[16] D. Z. Phillips, *Religion Without Explanation* (Oxford: Basil Blackwell, 1976), 40–41.

We can appreciate why a philosopher would find it hard to accept these criticisms. He is accused of being in the grip of the very superstition he prides himself on exposing. In the same way it is a shock to hear Wittgenstein saying, 'Frazer is much more savage than most of his savages, for these savages will not be so far from any understanding of spiritual matters as an Englishman of the twentieth century. His explanations of the primitive observances are much cruder than the sense of the observances themselves.'[17] The words are a shock because, once again, the rational enquirer is said to be possessed by the very savagery and crudity he claims to be exposing.

Little wonder, then, that certain philosophical reminders have aroused controversy among philosophical critics, for in accepting the reminders it is as though they were accepting a philosophical version of the admonition, 'If therefore the light that is in thee be darkness, how great is the darkness!' (*Matt.* 6:23), which might be rendered, 'If therefore your very conception of rationality is confused, how great is the confusion!' Philosophers are being asked to re-open a road on which they have put a 'no through road' sign. Their irritation at this is compounded by the fact that they are not told that they have not investigated the road thoroughly enough. Rather, they are told that they should not have turned down their particular road in the first place. Yet, the irritation may go deeper. Philosophers may not appreciate the force of the reminders presented to them. For them to accept this possibility would be for them to recognize not only that they had gone down a wrong road, but that there is a road, a flourishing neighbourhood even, which they know little about. Their ignorance would have been a direct result of too narrow a conception of the character of human activities. If a philosopher is rescued from this narrowness he may begin to appreciate the genuine diversity to be found in a culture.

II

It would be rash to assume that no confusions concerning religious belief remain once we cease speaking of it as a cultural divergence from the norm of rationality. On the contrary, the very readiness to add religion to an ever-growing list of diverse human activities may lead to confused ways of discussing them all. In this section of the lecture I shall comment on two of these.

First, it may seem that the recognition of diverse movements, perspectives and attitudes within a culture, makes an external,

[17] Wittgenstein, 'Remarks on Frazer's *The Golden Bough*', *The Human World* No. 3 (May 1971), 34.

relativistic assessment the only rational response to them. So far from regarding anything as a divergence from a norm, the opposite tendency prevails. Given the plurality of movements and perspectives within a culture, there is said to be no norms from which one can diverge. One man's norm is another man's divergence. A pseudo-objectivity is achieved by treating everything as if it were on the same level. Flannery O'Connor observes, 'It is popular to believe that in order to see clearly one must believe nothing . . . For the fiction writer, to believe nothing is to see nothing".[18] When Flannery O'Connor spoke at a Catholic university in the South 'a gentleman arose and said that the concept *Catholic novel* was a limiting one and that the novelist, like Whitman, should be alien to nothing'. She replied, 'Well, I'm alien to a great deal'.[19]

If someone believes in nothing, he can only give external accounts of various perspectives in human life. If these external accounts come to be what people mean by objective accounts, it will be extremely difficult to give a conceptual reminder of what it would be like to see things from a particular perspective. A person who gives a purely external account simply parades second-hand opinions. All he could say would be, 'Some people see things like this' and 'Other people see things differently', but if you asked him how he saw things, no answer would be forthcoming. He is a slave to conventions. *What* is said has no importance for him apart from the *fact* of its being said.

Judgment formed on such external relations to movements and perspectives are themselves external judgments. Morality is reduced to statistics. Flannery O'Connor, commenting from her point of view as a writer says, 'The story teller is concerned with what is; but if what is can be determined by survey, then the disciples of Dr Kinsey and Dr Gallup are sufficient for the day thereof'.[20] She has little doubt what effect such judgments would have on our understanding of the values and insights of various perspectives: '. . . when we are invited to represent the country according to survey, what we are asked to do is to separate mystery from manners[21] and judgments from vision, in order to produce something a little more palatable to the modern temper. We are asked to form our consciences in the light of statistics, which is to establish the relative as absolute. For many this may be a convenience, since we don't live in an age of settled belief; but it cannot be a

[18] *Letters of Flannery O'Connor: The Habit of Being*, selected and edited by Sally Fitzgerald (New York, Vintage Books, 1980) 147.

[19] *Mystery and Manners*, 193.

[20] Ibid. 31.

[21] For a discussion of these issues see my paper 'Mystery and Mediation', in *Images in Belief and Literature*, David Jasper (ed.) (London: Macmillan, forthcoming).

convenience, it cannot even be possible, for the writer who is a Catholic. He will feel that any long-continued service to it will produce a soggy, formless and sentimental literature, one that will provide a sense of spiritual purpose for those who connect the spirit with romanticism and a sense of joy for those who confuse that virtue with satisfaction.'[22]

Having noted that recognizing diversity within a culture may lead to external accounts and judgments of the diverse movements and perspectives involved, we may also note, in the second place, that such recognition may lead to the distortion of the characters of such movements and perspectives. If someone thinks that what is worthwhile can be determined simply by surveying what various groups think is worthwhile, he is likely to distort the conceptions of worth to be found there. He never considers the question of why these conceptions of worth exist at all. They obviously do not do so because some group consensus said they should. The external judgments are parasitic on the existence of movements and traditions within which genuine commitments to values can be found. Because external judgments have no interest in the *content* or *character* of the various values to be found in a culture, they attempt to account for them in terms of their *function*. Beliefs and values, it is said, have the function of serving individual or social stability. Beliefs and values become the means by which an organizational equilibrium is achieved.

From a certain psychological perspective, beliefs and values are seen as the means by which an individual achieves the integration of his personality. According to a popular psychological ethic, personal integration, being comfortable with oneself and others, is what is of primary importance. Of course, the elements of this ethic are satisfied by the well-integrated rogue and mediocrity of many kinds. There is no room in such a context for the notion of a goodness which is out of reach or of a grace one might stand in need of. Flannery O'Connor's reaction to such an ethic is predictable: 'There is a question whether faith can or is supposed to be emotionally satisfying. I must say that the thought of everyone lolling about in an emotionally satisfying faith is repugnant to me. I believe that we are ultimately directed Godward but that the journey is often impeded by emotion.'[23] Religion does not have the function of integrating the emotions. On the contrary, the emotions are to be subject to the demands of faith.

Similar difficulties arise, if, from a sociological perspective, we say that beliefs and values are means by which social solidarity is achieved. No concern with good and evil can give primacy to rules of association as such. Writing to John Hawkes, Flannery O'Connor says, 'You say

[22] *Mystery and Manners*, 30–31.
[23] *The Habit of Being*, 100.

one becomes "evil" when one leaves the herd. I say that depends on what the herd is doing. The herd has been known to be right, in which case the one who leaves it is doing evil. When the herd is wrong, the one who leaves it is not doing evil but the right thing. If I remember rightly, you put that word, evil, in quotation marks which means the standards you judge it by there are relative; in fact you would be looking at it there with the eyes of the herd.'[24]

In a situation in which a recognition of religious values is becoming increasingly problematic, and where even the recognition of diverse values in a culture leads to external accounts of these values, relativistic judgments, and analyses of values in terms of their functions, it becomes increasingly difficult to give telling conceptual reminders of the character of the beliefs and values which are being distorted in this way. Flannery O'Connor sums up these intellectual obstacles, it seems to me, in the following remarks: 'I don't believe that our present society is one whose basic beliefs are religious, except in the South.[25] In any case, you can't have effective allegory in times when people are swept this way and that by momentary convictions, because everyone will read it differently. You can't indicate moral values when morality changes with what is being done, because there is no accepted basis of judgment. And you cannot show the operation of grace when grace is cut off from nature or when the very possibility of grace is denied, because no one will have the least idea of what you are about.'[26]

III

Enough has been said in this lecture by now to show why philosophy's confidence in the efficacy of its own methods cannot be taken for granted. Wanting to give reminders of the character of religious beliefs to those who distort them philosophically, the philosopher finds that he cannot appeal to their acquaintance with those beliefs in their natural settings. On the contrary, he finds himself in a culture where those settings are looked at, increasingly, as cultural divergences, marginal phenomena. The philosopher's audience may only be acquainted with these beliefs *in their distorted forms*. The philosopher's task then becomes one of awaking, possibly for the first time, an awareness of these beliefs in their natural contexts.[27] Flannery O'Connor describes

[24] Ibid. 456.
[25] Whether this could be said with the same conviction now is another matter.
[26] *Mystery and Manners*, 166.
[27] For a discussion of some of these issues see my, 'Alienation and the Sociologizing of Meaning' (symposium with A. R. Manser), *Proc. Aristotelian Society*, Suppl. Volume **LIII** (1979).

the enormity of the similar task with which she was faced: 'The novelist with Christian concerns will find in modern life distortions which are repugnant to him, and his problem will be to make these appear as distortions to an audience which is used to seeing them as natural; and he may well be forced to take ever more violent means to get his vision across to his hostile audience. When you can assume that your audience holds the same beliefs as you do, you can relax a little and use more normal means of talking to it; when you have to assume that it does not then you have to make your vision apparent by shock—to the hard of hearing you shout, and for the almost-blind you draw large and startling figures.[28]

Faced with the task of assembling reminders in a similar context, the philosopher, unless he is blessed with a genius for examples, as Wittgenstein was, may well turn to literature, as I have done, and see there reminders of perspectives he wants his audience and himself to be clear about. The philosopher of religion's audience today is not going to be different from the audience to which Flannery O'Connor addressed herself. She was under no illusions about it: 'My audience are the people who think God is dead. At least these are the people I am conscious of writing for.'[29] The philosopher may hope that her genius for reminders may come to his aid too. We find this genius at work in her short story, *A Good Man is Hard to Find*.

The story is about a family setting out from Georgia for a holiday in Florida. In the car are a husband and wife, their baby and two other young children and their grandmother who has hidden her cat in her basket. The grandmother is there on sufferance. She did not want to go to Florida because she had heard that someone called the Misfit had escaped from the federal penitentiary. In the course of the journey she persuades the father, with the aid of tantrums from the children, to turn down a dirt road which, she thinks, will lead to a fine house which once dominated a large plantation. As they proceed, the grandmother realizes that the house she wanted to see is in another state. The car has difficulty in negotiating the dirt track, and when the cat causes chaos in escaping from the basket, it overturns. While they assess the damage another car approaches. Three men get out. The grandmother recognizes one of them as the Misfit and by telling him so condemns them all. First, the father and son, then the mother and her daughters, are taken into the woods and shot. The grandmother keeps talking to the Misfit until she too is shot.

Thus presented, the reaction of an audience to the story is straightforward. It is read as simply one more example of the tales of

[28] *Mystery and Manners*, 33–34.
[29] Quoted in, Robert Coles, *Flannery O'Connor's South*, 154.

violence to which we have become accustomed. Flannery O'Connor, on the other hand, says that 'in this story you should be on the lookout for such things as the action of grace in the grandmother's soul, and not for dead bodies'.[30] The difficulty is that we concentrate on the dead bodies almost as a matter of course. That this should be so is not surprising. Our recent past is not a distinguished one. The American essayist, Joan Didion, says of the sixties: 'There were rumours. There were stories. Everything was unmentionable but nothing was unimaginable. The mystical flirtation with the idea of "sin"—this sense that it was possible to go "too far", and that many people were doing it—was very much with us in Los Angeles in 1968 and 1969 . . . On 9 August 1969, I was sitting in the shallow end of my sister-in-law's swimming pool in Beverley Hills when I received a telephone call from a friend who had just heard about the murders at Sharon Tate Polanski's house in Cielo Drive. The phone rang many times during the next hour. One caller would say hoods, the next would say chains. There were twenty dead, no, twelve, ten, eighteen. Black masses were imagined and bad trips blamed. I can remember all of the day's misinformation very clearly, and I also remember this, and wish I did not: *I remember that no one was surprised.*'[31]

For Flannery O'Connor's audience, the bodies are realistic, whereas for her they are grotesque. What she sees as realistic, the kind of talk she puts in the mounth of the Misfit, they thought grotesque. The Misfit does not blame bad trips, something the audience would have accepted immediately. He blames Jesus for throwing everything off balance by dying for no crime and raising the dead. These different reactions are startling illustrations of how different perspectives within the culture determine the readings we give of the situations which confront us. Flannery O'Connor says, 'I have found that anything that comes out of the South is going to be called grotesque by the Northern reader, unless it is grotesque, in which case it is going to be called realistic.'[32] When I gave this lecture at Georgia College and the University of Georgia, this quotation provoked amused assent. Yet, what was happening was an assent to judgment from within a common perspective. In these cases, the phenomenon in question does not, independent of any perspective, force acceptance of its character upon us. From the perspective of her critics, the Misfit is an abnormality whose condition is to be explained by reference to drugs, bad trips, etc. His encounter with the grandmother would have been characterized in Joan Didion's Los Angeles in terms of a flirtation with sin. Flannery O'Connor shows us a

---

[30] *Mystery and Manners*, 113.
[31] Joan Didion, *The White Album* (London, Penguin Books, 1981), 41–42.
[32] Quoted in Robert Coles, *Flannery O'Connor's South*, xxviii.

very different perspective. She wants to show how we are not forced in the direction her detractors would have her take. She says boldly, 'I am not interested in abnormal psychology',[33] The grotesque, for her, is found in the way in which the Misfit has distorted religious truths. Some of her critics accused her of wallowing in the grotesque. Yet, her use of distortion is like Kafka's. She says of his *Metamorphosis*, 'a story about a man who wakes up one morning to find that he has turned into a cockroach overnight, while not discarding his human nature . . . The truth is not distorted here, but rather, a certain distortion is used to get at the truth.'[34] The truth she is interested in revealing is how the notion of grace can inform even such distortions. She says she is interested in the kind of fiction that will be always pushing 'its own limits outward towards the limits of mystery . . . Such a writer will be interested in what we don't understand rather than in what we do. He will be interested in possibility rather than in probability. He will be interested in characters who are forced out to meet evil and grace and who act on a trust beyond themselves—whether they know very clearly what it is they act upon or not.'[35]

A pushing to the limits in order to allow mystery to come in at the right place is seen in the grandmother's final encounter with the Misfit. Before facing death, she was simply one of the old ladies 'who reflect the banalities of the society and the effect is of the comical rather than the seriously evil'.[36] Through her encounter with the Misfit we see how such banalities may be transformed by the action of grace. Having seen her family killed, she makes her final response as the Misfit complains about Jesus: 'She saw the man's face twisted close to her own as if he were going to cry and she murmured, "Why, you're one of my babies. You're one of my children!" She reached out and touched him on the shoulder. The Misfit sprang back as if a snake had bitten him and shot her three times through the chest.'[37] Commenting on the scene, Flannery O'Connor says, 'The grandmother is at last alone, facing the Misfit. Her head clears for an instant and she realizes, even in her limited way, that she is responsible for the man before her and joined to him by ties of kinship she has been merely prattling about so far. And at this point she does the right thing, she makes the right gesture.'[38] In this scene, Flannery O'Connor wanted to show that 'Grace, to the Catholic way of thinking can and does use as its medium the imperfect purely

[33] *The Habit of Being*, 437.

[34] *Mystery and Manners*, 97–98.

[35] Ibid. 41–42.

[36] *The Habit of Being*, 389.

[37] Flannery O'Connor, 'A Good Man is Hard to Find' in her collection of the same title (London, Faber, 1968), 29.

[38] *Mystery and Manners*, 111–112.

human, and even hypocritical . . . The Misfit is touched by the Grace that comes through the old lady when she recognizes him as her child, as she has been touched by the Grace that comes through him in his particular suffering. His shooting her is a recoil, a horror at her humanness, but after he has done it and cleaned his glasses, the Grace has worked in him and he pronounces his judgment: she would have been a good woman if *he* had been there every moment of her life. True enough. In the Protestant view, I think Grace and nature don't have much to do with each other. The old lady, because of her hypocrisy and humanness and banality couldn't be a medium for Grace. In the sense that I see things the other way, I'm a Catholic writer.'[39]

In her story, Flannery O'Connor places the action of grace at the heart of the violence for which prestigious movements in our culture seek explanations. She says, 'The story has been called grotesque, but I prefer to call it literal'.[40] In relation to contemporary philosophy of religion in our culture her work may well be dismissed as a grotesque divergence. I have been endeavouring to show how her work can also serve as a disturbing reminder to the over-hasty confidence of philosophers in determining the parameters of the literal.

IV

This lecture should not end without an important qualification being made with respect to the comparison between Flannery O'Connor's literary reminders and the conceptual reminders of the philosopher. First, it must be made clear that she did not regard literature as a means of conveying a Catholic message. Flannery O'Connor insisted, 'Your beliefs will be the light by which you see, but they will not be what you see and they will not be a substitute for seeing'.[41] When this is forgotten, 'the result is another addition to the large body of pious trash for which we have so long been famous'.[42] Nevertheless, although she insists that the Catholic perspective owes all others the duty of truth, it is from that perspective that the others are to be judged. By comparison, the philosopher's reminders of the character of religious belief would be judgments made from a religious perspective which he embraces. But this would be a misunderstanding. The philosopher of religion need not embrace the perspective he reminds us of. Philosophy is not one commitment, on the same level as others, fighting for victory. In reminding us of possibilities of thought which we are tempted to ignore

[39] *The Habit of Being*, 389–390.
[40] *Mystery and Manners*, 113.
[41] Ibid. 91.
[42] Ibid. 180.

or distort, the philosopher is reflecting *on* the various perspectives in human life, but not *from* any of them. This is why Wittgenstein was able to say, 'The philosopher is not a citizen of any community of ideas; that is what makes him a philosopher'.[43] Does not Wittgenstein want to show us language as a city with no main road; to show us the many differences in human life we are tempted to ignore? Perhaps there is something akin to this in literature too. Flannery O'Connor called herself a Catholic writer. Could any such adjective be applied to Shakespeare?

In concluding, let us return to the theme I have wanted to emphasize throughout the lecture: the reasons why neither the literary artist nor the philosopher can be complacently confident of their methods of providing us with reminders of certain perspectives in human life. They cannot take their audiences for granted. Flannery O'Connor was aware of how dependent she was on the Biblical traditions of the South, and how precarious these traditions were: 'It will be ironical indeed if the Southern writer has discovered he can live in the South and the Southern audience has become aware of its literature just in time to discover that being Southern is relatively meaningless, and that soon there is going to be precious little difference in the end-product whether you are a writer from Georgia or a writer from Hollywood California'.[44] Flannery O'Connor knew too that attempting to establish a common language for discussion is often hopeless. On hearing that a university review had given a homosexual interpretation of her novel, *The Violent Bear it Away*, she wrote, 'When you have a generation of students who are being taught to think like that, there's nothing to do but wait for another generation to come along and hope it won't be worse'.[45]

Should the philosopher of religion be more confident of his audience? On the contrary, he has reason to be less confident. Flannery O'Connor was confident about where she stood: 'Let me make no bones about it: I write from the standpoint of Christian orthodoxy . . . I write with a solid belief in *all* the Christian dogmas'.[46] She could be equally confident in locating her audience: 'I have . . . found that what I write is read by an audience which puts little stock either in grace or the devil. You discover your audience at the same time and in the same way that you discover your subject; but it is an added blow.'[47] No doubt there are times when the philosopher of religion may be tempted to speak in the same way. What prevents him from doing so is that there

[43] Wittgenstein, *Zettel*, G. E. M. Anscombe (trans.) (Oxford: Basil Blackwell, 1965), 455.
[44] *Mystery and Manners*, 57.
[45] *The Habit of Being*, 457.
[46] Ibid. 147.
[47] *Mystery and Manners*, 118.

are times when he feels part of this audience himself. In contending with the various angels of light which try to explain religion away, which try to subject religion to external or relativistic judgments, or which try to give functional analyses of religious belief, he does not always think they are confused. On the contrary, at times he has to fight against the attraction of what they say. There will be constant temptations for the philosopher to be either a sceptic or an apologist. It will always be difficult not to present theses or answers; difficult to leave everything where it is. For all these reasons, when a philosopher talks of an audience for whom he provides conceptual reminders, there is always the likelihood that, quite often, he is talking about himself.

On Being Terrestrial

MARY MIDGLEY

We will start with a fable—

There was once a creator who wanted to create free beings.

The other creators, it seems, didn't share this ambition, indeed they thought his project was philosophically confused. They were well satisfied with their own worlds. But our creator (we will call him C) sat down to work it out.

'How will you even start?' asked his friend D, the Doubter.

'Well, I know what I won't do', answered C. 'I won't just give them an empty faculty named Desire, and tell them to invent values and want what they choose. Unless they want something definite for a start, they won't even be able to start choosing.'

'Exactly', said D.

'So what I think I must do,' C went on, 'is to give them a lot of desires which conflict, and make them bright enough to see they have got to do something about it.'

'If that means giving them a desire to drink and also a desire not to drink, it sounds like a good way to deadlock everybody', D objected.

'That's right', replied C. 'So what I propose, instead, is to give them the sort of quite numerous desires which animals usually have, which don't clash all the time, but are bound to clash sometimes. Then the clashes won't be between *drink* and *don't drink* but perhaps between *drink* and *finish building the house*, or between *drink* and *carry drink to your child*. That won't deadlock them, but they'll have to think about it.'

'Are you going to make their thoughts affect their actions, then?' enquired D, somewhat alarmed.

'Well, I believe I am', said C. 'You know how, when they don't, creatures are inclined to get lazy, and not to bother with thinking at all? Somebody has pointed out that, when reason is imparted to favoured creatures on top of their infallible instincts, it only serves them for contemplating the happy disposition of their natures, for admiring it, for enjoying it, and for being grateful to its beneficent cause.[1] And, nice though that is, it somehow doesn't seem to make for a very active intellect. This is a thing (he added) which has bothered me about a number of worlds.'

'I can see that your lot will be kept busy', said D thoughtfully. 'They will have all sorts of reasons for making all kinds of choices. No doubt

---

[1] See Kant, *The Moral Law*, H. J. Paton (trans.) (London: Hutchinson University Library, 1948) Ch. 1, Sect. 5, 61.

they won't be deadlocked, but can you stop them all having breakdowns from trying to do too many things at once?'.

'I mean to leave a lot of animal nature in them as ballast', answered C. 'They will all be fairly similar for a start. They will be instinctively affectionate and sociable. This will give them some steady, lasting purposes in life. It will tend to keep each of them from being carried away by ideals which mean nothing to the others. Then, they can consult each other, which should help choice. And the intelligence which they develop will not be mere abstract calculation. It will be an imaginative activity. Other people's feelings and responses will constantly figure in it.'

'Is that necessary?' asked D. 'Won't they be a sufficiently standard product, so that what is sauce for one of them will always be sauce for the others?'

'No', said C. 'I thought this would surprise you. I'm not going to standardize them, and I'm not even going to integrate them completely intellectually. As I see it, freedom demands that individuals should be genuinely different, so that they really do have to think for themselves. I mean to leave them the individual differences which animals have, and even the wide temperamental differences produced by sex and age. Each one will find itself not only, in a way, alone among aliens, but also a member of a number of distinct tribes, all of which have other, irremediably different tribes to deal with.

'What will you do about disagreement?' asked D.

'Well you see, this is my real problem', C replied. 'There are two extremes. On the one hand, I could make them so harmonious, underneath it all, that in spite of their differences they would never really be in opposition, beause they would feel themselves to be parts of one vast whole. Their swarm or hive would be their real individuality. Or, on the other, I could have them feeling so individual that they didn't give a damn for each other. The first sort might indeed evolve a real way of thinking, but it would be a corporate one. The second sort couldn't evolve one at all, because they couldn't communicate; their lives would be far too fragmentary. I want the best of both worlds. I want real individuality to the extent that, if one gets its way and another does not, the second has really lost something. But I want them to understand this situation, and be able to choose it. I'm not satisfied with the simple, harmonious, corporate solution, because I don't think it allows freedom. I think each being needs to face real conflicts, both within itself and with those around it. And in both sorts of conflict, whoever loses must really have lost something.'

'And *how* did you say were going to make them settle for that?' asked D.

'Well', replied C hesitantly, 'I thought that the best way of doing difficult things is often the crudest and most obvious. It's no good giving them an intellectual proof that they really prefer harmony to getting their own way. That just leads back to the corporate solution. I thought I would simply land them in this mess from the start and let them get used to it. They get born into a group of others on whom they are emotionally dependent, but with whom they are bound to disagree. Quarrels arise, and they have just got to deal with them.

'Quarrels?' said D. 'Are you going to make them, not just different, but naturally aggressive as well?'

'That's right', said C. 'For freedom they will need these real disagreements, and that struck me as a good way to make sure of providing them.'

'No doubt about that', replied D. 'Well, well it's your world. Has it struck you, by the way that with all these problems on their hands, your beings may get the idea that they are creators themselves?

'Yes indeed', replied C. 'Will they be wrong? I'm really not sure. But I think it's time I got started. Do you think you could pass me those compasses?'

At this point, plainly, we must quickly leave the language of myth, before anybody has time to complain that the transaction just described is a highly irresponsible one. From now on, we will speak like good children of the Enlightenment. We will say that it was not C or D, but E for evolution that did all this, and insist, too, that evolution has a small e, and is not some kind of deity. To avoid dogmatic atheism, let us add too that, if a creator was in fact present, then he, she or it seems to have worked through evolution, largely by natural selection. If not, then that process of evolution did the job on its own. I am not suggesting that that process had in any sense the purpose of producing beings who would be free in the way in which we are so. That would be monstrously narrow and anthropocentric, as well as mythical. What I am trying to do is to explore the meaning of that kind of freedom, now that we have got it. I am sure that we shall find there is no clash between this human freedom and our evolutionary origin. More interesting still, I think we can go beyond that and say that it is just the kind which is to be expected in evolved beings. Evolution not only accords with it, but can help to explain it. An evolved being is not one made like a machine. Machines typically have a single, fixed purpose. Evolved organisms have a plurality of purposes, held together in a complex but versatile system. And it is only this second, complex arrangement which could give us our kind of freedom.

What, then, is the central feature of human freedom? People often seem to assume that its core is unpredictability, and that it chiefly consists in an indefiniteness, a vagueness of the will which is sufficient to baffle prediction. This seems a strangely negative idea. I believe it misses the point. In our ordinary thinking, I am not sure that we even think it objectionable to be able to predict the behaviour of a free person. What matters, I suggest, is that we must be able to predict it in a suitable way, not in the way in which we predict the behaviour of things. It is only the unsuitable style of prediction, the thingbound style, which insults freedom. For instance—when somebody whom we know to be heroic (Lech Walesa, say) does exactly the heroic thing which we expect of him, we have no sense of disappointment, no suspicion of automatism. He is *more* free, not less free, than someone who is unpredictable by being disorganized. This whole approach centring on prediction has been thoroughly explored, and I don't think it has ever given much satisfaction. What I suggest is that, for the moment, we try moving right away from it, and look at the suggestion just made—that human freedom centres on being a creature capable of dealing with conflicting desires. This may sound odd, because freedom sounds like an advantage, and having conflicting desires certainly does not. But the conflicting desires themselves are of course not the whole story. They must belong to a being which owns both of them, and which can do something about reconciling them. The more clearly that being is aware of the clash, and the more it can, on occasion, distance itself from any one of its impulses, the freer it becomes.

You may ask, is the objectionable conflict itself even a necessary condition of freedom? To throw light on this, we had better try contrasting this alarming condition with some possible alternatives. The first useful contrast is with the imagined condition of a paradisal being which never experiences a clash at all, because its impulses are always and inevitably in harmony with each other and with what its situation demands This is the supposed situation of God or of angels, approached, but not quite reached, by that of humanity before the Fall. This condition drops a paradox at our feet. It seems plainly better than our present state. But it is surely one which we could not accept if it were offered to us. In order to become paradisal, we would, it seems, have to stop being what we are to so profound an extent that the change becomes quite inconceivable. Even those who are most cross with their creator for making them as they now are do not usually complain of this feature of his work. They want to eat of the tree of knowledge of good and evil, and you can hardly do that if evil means nothing to you, if it has no hold on you at all. This at least seems to be the human situation. The point has been made imaginatively in many stories, of which *Brave New World* is still one of the best.

No doubt if we leave the human problem and speak of God and angels, things become different. But we have great difficulty anyway in imagining their condition, and in using language to describe it—which is not surprising. The word *free* is only one of many terms of praise which are hard to apply to God, as theologians have pointed out. Language, after all, has primarily been developed to apply to our own species. And here, full freedom does seem to presuppose conflict. Paradisal beings are free only in the weaker sense that they are doing what they want. As Hume pointed out, this is an enormously important advantage. But it does not measure up to what is usually claimed for human free will, which is that it distinguishes men from other animals. We have better look at this point next.

What about the motivation of non-human animals? Here the clashes of desire are present, often in forms which seem very similar to those we experience ourselves. The traditional wisdom, however, regards this likeness as deceptive. According to it, the processes are really quite different, and animals have really no self-awareness, so that they cannot be said to know that they have a clash at all. Indeed, from this angle it can scarcely be said that a clash even takes place. There is held to be no conscious being which owns both desires, no self-consciousness, and therefore no conflict. One desire simply replaces another, like successive waves on a beach. There is no fixed scene, within which they can figure as competing. The drama cannot take place, because there is never more than one character on stage at a time.

This seems a strangely exaggerated story, a story which would surely not have occurred to anybody merely from watching the behaviour of animals, or indeed from any other reason except a determination to preserve human distinctness at all costs. Conflict behaviour is in fact quite common in animals, and the more advanced they are, the more sophisticated it grows, and the more it looks like that of humans similarly placed. It can be quite prolonged, involving much hesitation, oscillation, intention movements and displacement activity, with every evidence of stress and strain, including gastric ulcers. It is really not very like the succession of waves on a beach. Not to get embroiled in too much detail, I suggest that we can do justice to both sides of this issue by accepting that freedom is a matter of degree. People are simply much *more* free than other animals. As I have just put it, the *more* aware any being is of its internal conflicts, and the more it can, on occasion, distance itself from any one of its desires, the more free it becomes. If we consider the development of a human baby, this way of thinking cannot be avoided. There is no sudden transition. It also seems highly suitable to advanced social animals. As for the simpler ones, the difficulty we have in applying it there seems more a difficulty about being sure what is happening than a flat certainty that they are in no sense 'free'. After all, they seem to have freedom in the lesser sense; they are apparently doing what they want. They are not slaves, which is the clearest known contrast to freedom.

Mary Midgley

Are they perhaps machines? This is the alternative most likely to occur to people today. But it really is not a clear one. It is a metaphor, and its application is a lot less simple than it seemed to be when Hobbes and Descartes triumphantly produced their clockwork in the seventeenth century. Machines, after all, seem to need a designer in the background. If we write him off, is the point of the machine model that they are actually unconscious? That satisfied Descartes, but it no longer seems reasonable today. The neurological evidence makes such an idea look extraordinary. A more plausible and modest notion is that lower animals at least, though not actually unconscious, cannot really experience conflict because they lack a continuous shaping personality, an enclosing theatre to stage the drama of choice. It should be noticed that this does not mean the complete lack of a character. Distinct characters or dispositions have been observed in most kinds of animal which have been observed at all. But no doubt what we have in mind when we talk of self-awareness is indeed this retaining of a constant framework of decision, a framework which expresses that character, the consciousness of lasting policies with which incoming impulses can conflict. This does call for a fairly sophisticated memory, giving a good sense of the past and future, and of alternative possible pasts and futures. Within this lasting framework, motivation begins to look more like the interaction of currents in the bed of a river than the succession of waves on a beach, and we begin to move towards the idea that the river bed can to some extent contort itself, changing its shape somewhat and altering the way the currents flow. Things are now much more complex, and more intelligence is needed to handle them. The hapless subject must be much more conscious, both of what is happening and of what it is trying to do.

This change, must, I am suggesting, be a gradual one. It cannot be a thunderclap, occurring, along with the instant invention of language, at the moment of the sudden and final emergence of the human race. The idea that language alone did the trick is particularly bizarre. It does not make much sense to suggest that there might be two successive points in the development of a species, one when it has not developed language and the other when it has and that between these two points it would have made the whole journey to self-awareness and free will. The change has to be much more gradual and general, a change with many other aspects and many roots. It is important to be realistic about this, because the comparison of our free state with that of other animals is not going to help us much if we still look at it in the lurid, melodramatic light of the Cartesian tradition. That tradition placed a yawning metaphysical gulf between people and other animals. It saw people as subjects, animals just as objects. Part of its reason for calling animals machines was to contrast them with people as the beings which design machines.

To be more realistic, then, we must move on from Descartes to Darwin. I suggest that we use, for a start, two quotations from *The Descent of Man*. We notice, first, Darwin's general view that 'the difference in mind between man and the higher animals, great as it is, is certainly one of degree and not of kind' (p. 105).[2] We then ask what that means on the topic now before us. Darwin, in his careful way, replies like this—

> The following proposition seems to be in a high degree probable— namely, that any animal whatever, endowed with well-marked social instincts, would inevitably acquire a moral sense or conscience, as soon as its intellectual powers had become as well developed, or anything like as well developed, as in man (p. 72).

The reason why this must happen, he explains, is that the zigzags and anomalies of conduct which successive motives produce cannot fail to bring great distress and remorse once an agent has become clearly conscious of them. The example he gives is that of migratory birds like swallows, which feed their broods with unceasing devotion all the summer, and then desert them suddenly and finally when the moment comes to fly south. As Darwin says,

> the instinct which is more persistent gains the victory, and at last, at a moment when her young ones are not in sight (the mother bird) takes flight and deserts them. When arrived at the end of her long journey, and the migratory instinct ceases to act, what an agony of remorse each bird would feel, if, from being endowed with great mental activity, she could not prevent the image continually passing before her mind of her young ones perishing in the bleak north from cold and hunger (p. 91).

As it is, she apparently does not feel it, or at least we don't know that she feels it. If she does, it is a momentary and passing spasm, which does not affect conduct. The image does not 'continually pass before her mind'. But with a more developed intelligence, says Darwin, it inevitably would do so. His insistence on this greater imaginative activity as a necessary mark of a higher intellect is very interesting. It is not the sort of thing we are accustomed to hear stressed about intelligence at present, but surely he is right. As he puts it,

> As soon as the mental faculties had become highly developed, images

[2] All page references for *The Descent of Man* are given for the first edition, reprinted by Princeton University Press in 1981 (paperback). Later editions vary the arrangement a good deal because Darwin continued to work on his argument, but in all 'the development of the Intellectual and Moral Faculties' figures prominently and may be found in the index.

of all past actions and motives would be incessantly passing through the brain of each individual; and that feeling of dissatisfaction which inevitably results . . . from any unsatisfied instinct, would arise, as often as it was perceived that the enduring and always present social instinct had yielded to some other instinct, at the time stronger, but neither enduring in its nature nor leaving behind a very vivid impression (p. 72).

Darwin's picture is striking, and not at all familiar. It shows light being brought into a dark place, where work has long been carried on here and there by the glimmer of a few scattered candles. The light shows with terrible clarity the relations between enterprises which nobody had ever thought of connecting before. Before we look at the details of this picture, we need to relate it to another, which at first looks rather similar. It may remind us of Plato's cave. But the moral is going to be very different. With Darwin, we are not going to be able to dismiss everything in this alarming workplace as illusion, and follow the light elsewhere into a different and better world. This workplace is our home, our own mind. The conflicts are not illusory; they are real. Our freedom will lie in becoming aware of them and able to arbitrate them, not in preventing them from arising.

Of course the idea of an essentially divided and distracted soul is not new either. Plato expressed that too in the Phaedrus myth, where the human soul's chariot is drawn by an evil black horse as well as a good white one, so that the charioteer cannot keep up with the gods and their well-matched teams of white horses. And of course it is central to Christian thought. 'The flesh lusteth against the spirit and the spirit against the flesh, so that ye cannot do the thing which ye would'. But both Plato and St Paul see this as a straightforward contest between good and evil, with the roles already allotted. Darwin is not saying this; he just points out that the conflict is there. Deciding what side to take in it, as well as how hard to fight, is our task, not his. He is not telling us which side to take. He is doing something much more basic than this—insisting that no creature with inner conflicts of this gravity could avoid taking sides, and that *this* is what makes morality necessary. There is no semi-paradisal option of simply letting things take their course. Once you realize that you are wrecking your own schemes in the sort of way that the swallow does, you are forced to evolve some sort of priority system and make yourself stick to it. That means having a morality. And if 'immoralism' is taken to mean that moralities are unnecessary, it is mistaken.

This view of Darwin's seems to me very interesting and fertile, but it has received remarkably little attention—indeed, people often don't seem to know that he wrote anything about ethics at all. The reasons for this are plain enough. In our tradition, the idea of deep inner conflict has been closely linked with religious thinking, and many intellectuals have associated religion with obscurantism, asceticism and political oppression. The rationalistic tradition of the Enlightenment therefore distrusted the idea of a deep, irremovable inner conflict. Since the seventeenth century, the main course of our psychological thinking has proceeded on the opposite assumption, that the human mind—though of course not a machine—is a well-designed, monistic device for supplying a single product, probably pleasure, happiness or individual survival. All motives are therefore really wishes for this one end, however they may be disguised. Enormous efforts have been made to reduce all motivation tidily to one of these ends. (The fact that they are not actually the *same* end has worried people, but not enough, because they often overlook it). In Hobbesian egoism and its descendant social contract theories, the aim is self-preservation. In Utilitarianism it is pleasure or happiness. Even Freud, who in some ways did lead back to a more realistic recognition of conflict and complexity, thought that reason always demanded the reduction of many motives to one wherever possible, and used both hedonism and egoism vigorously in desperate attempts to achieve this.

The idea that rationality demands this streamlining is a strange one, whose basis is not too clear. The question how many basic motives we have seems to be an empirical one. We have no *a priori* ground for expecting a neat, monistic system. The reason for assuming that we do seems to be largely a historical one. Monism was brought in as a protest against the damage done by the ascetic and other-worldly element in Christian thinking. And it went on being seen as the only way to make sure that people got some satisfaction in this world, rather than just waiting for the next.

This seems to be the background which, when the theory of evolution arrived, produced so much confusion about its bearing on psychology. Since metaphysical disputes were constantly polarized as battles between Religion and Rationalism, it is not surprising that rationalists assumed that evolution was on their side. Science, they hoped, had now delivered its verdict, and revealed the guiding purpose of the human mechanism. What was it? Herbert Spencer, with his tag about 'the survival of the fittest' was ready at once with a simple version of its answer, as he was over every other difficult question. No doubt what Spencer said was more subtle than what the public heard, but not much, and the public seems not to have misunderstood his practical message. Evolution, said Spencer, called for the freest of free enterprise. Cut-throat competition was the law of life, and would thus ensure the general happiness. Accordingly, the raw, burgeoning capitalism of the United States was an example—and not just an

Mary Midgley

instructive example, but a wholly admirable one—of this basic law of life.[3]

Right from the start, the fallacies of this 'social Darwinist' story were denounced by biologists, and by plenty of other people as well. But it has continued to flourish like a green bay tree, like cheese mould, like poison ivy. Some of it is woven into the way we all think about evolution. The very words 'evolution' and 'survival of the fittest' are Spencer's and their apparent implications about value have given continual trouble. Spencer's simple approach to a complex problem still has enormous influence for a host of obvious reasons, political, economic and emotional, as well as because it saves the trouble of further thinking. What concerns us now however is simply the biological objection to it, its factual errors about the actual working of natural selection.

Briefly and obviously, natural selection cannot work simply by competition between individuals, because the most successful and long-lived individuals do not necessarily leave the most offspring. They could even be sterile, or they could fail altogether to nurture their young. Short of this, they could do all kinds of things which would damage the prospects of their descendants, and which could wipe out in the next generation the advantage gained in their life-time. The time-scale of evolution is entirely different from that of the money-market, or even of civil war. In its perspective, the hardest-headed tycoons are mere fruit-flies like the rest of us. Individuals can spread their traits through a population by helping relatives and descendants, even if their traits shorten their own lives. What is needed is only a rough balance of advantage between each individual, its young and its other relatives. This balance is not struck once for all by a central designer. It is kept going on a hit-or-miss basis by mutation, natural selection, and probably a fair amount of sheer chance, known as genetic drift. It is not designed at all to produce a long, harmonious or comfortable life for each individual, and it will normally set him grave problems. As Edward O. Wilson says, in one of his more helpful moments—

> (The emotional centers) tax the conscious mind with ambivalences whenever the organisms encounter stressful situations. Love joins hate; aggression, fear; expansiveness, withdrawal; and so on, in

[3] Richard Hofstadter's fascinating book *Social Darwinism in American Thought* (Boston: Beacon Press, 1955) documents the story, tracing Spencer's enormous influence (he outsold every other philosopher in the United States at that time) and describing the pains which he took—especially on his lecture tour in the 1880s—to leave no doubt about his approval of paticular tycoons and their methods. The effect has been profound and lasting.

blends designed not to promote the happiness and survival of the individual, but to favour the maximum transmission of the controlling genes. . . . What is good for the individual can be destructive to the family; what preserves the family can be harsh on both the individual and the tribe to which its family belongs; what promotes the tribe can weaken the family and destroy the individual; and so on upward through the permutations of levels of organization. Counteracting selection on these different units will result in certain genes being multiplied and fixed, others lost, and combinations of still others held in static proportions (*Sociobiology, the New Synthesis*, p. 4).[4]

That this actually does occur is a matter of experience. Darwin's problem of the migrating birds illustrates it, and endless other examples of the same kind can be found from other social species. We ourselves are not, on the face of it, free of them. Not all these conflicts are equally dramatic, but many are very serious. Once a creature develops enough intelligence to become conscious of them at all, it has to think hard to solve them. Indeed, no complete solution is possible. Intelligence has not enabled our species to spring-clean its vast cavern, to root out the whole pre-existing emotional structure and start again. And this is just as well, since intelligence alone would certainly not be able to generate a whole new set of emotions. What it does is to help us to build a culture—a set of customs expressing a priority system, which will direct us to settle these conflicts in certain agreed ways, so as to make the stresses of decision more or less bearable. It is because there is no pre-set single priority system available that cultures differ so much, and because their basic problems are the same that they are, none the less, so similar. Language is no doubt a necessary tool in this culture-building, but it is not the whole of it. The psychologist Nick Humphrey has an interesting idea which treats this proceeding very much in the spirit of Darwin.[5] He suggests that the whole flowering of intelligence in our species was not primarily a response to practical needs, not directly a matter of tool-making, but rather a response to the difficulties of handling personal relations in communities which were getting more enterprising and co-operative. This might explain the distressing fact that we go on seeing the problems of our lives so much in personal terms, and that personal feelings tend still to take precedence with us over even the most elementary prudence.

[4] Harvard University Press, 1975.
[5] See his paper 'The Social Function of Intellect', in *Growing Points in Ethology*, P. P. G. Bateson and R. A. Hinde (eds) (Cambridge University Press, 1976).

The main point, however, which I think we ought to accept from Darwin and Wilson is that, on evolutionary grounds, we should not expect the psychology of motive to be monistic, and should not go on letting theorists streamline it unrealistically, under the delusion that they are serving Reason. Classical Utilitarianism, for instance, with its emphasis on the whole community, had hold of an important part of the truth, and one badly needed to correct individualism. But neither of them has found the Holy Grail. Nor is there any need to 'reduce' Utilitarianism to egoism in order to make it intellectually respectable. We are beings that naturally care directly for others, as well as for ourselves. There is no single aim for human life. That does not mean, of course, that our aims have no sort of relation and that no principles can be found for reconciling them. They are not a job lot picked up off the street; they have been developed as parts or aspects of a particular kind of life, namely a human one. We can find many principles to help us. There is nothing reductive, either, about Darwin's suggestion here that, when remorse arises, it will usually be because a quiet, persistent, central social motive has been violated at the instance of another which was strong but passing. The point is not the strength, nor merely the continuousness, but that what is quietly continuous is central. Its demands at any time may be slight, but over a whole life their effect can be transforming. This steady, basic sociality is so strong, says Darwin, that it not only determines the direction of remorse, but will be finally satisfied with nothing less than the Golden Rule—

> The social instincts—the prime principle of man's moral constitution—with the aid of active intellectual powers and effect of habit, naturally lead to the golden rule—'As ye would that men should do to you, do ye to them likewise', and this lies at the foundation of morality (p. 106).

What Darwin understands by these persistent social instincts, is, in fact, not just one more set of impulses among others, but a whole way of regarding those around us, based on sympathy, which involves imagining them as subjects like oneself, experiencing life in the same way, and not essentially different in status. There are echoes here both of Hume and Kant, and Darwin quotes both of them with understanding. This is, I repeat, not just one more philistine piece of reductivism. It is an attempt to make sense of morality as it actually is, while regarding it as something which has evolved, and to explain the oddities of its actual working from its evolutionary history.

A word more seems called for in concluding, about why sociobiology, which promises so well in remarks like the one I have just quoted, does not on the whole deliver on the same level. Briefly and brutally, this is a Jekyll and Hyde phenomenon. The central insight of sociobiology is kin-selection, the process just mentioned whereby traits are transmitted by benefiting others as well as their owner. The language in which this process is described, however, obscures this insight continually, because the word 'selfish' is used for all conduct which increases an individual's genetic representation in later generations, and the word 'altruistic' for conduct which diminishes it. This results, not just in confusion, but in an apparent expounding of psychological egoism; since only 'selfish' conduct can succeed in evolution. The writers deny that this is what they mean, no doubt sincerely, but it repeatedly emerges that they themselves have been misled by their language, and indeed that the language was probably chosen in the first place because of strong underlying social Darwinist convictions. At a deep level, sociobiologists seem to be convinced, as so many other people are, that all motivation must really be selfish, and that evolution shows this at a deeper level, even if it refutes it at the obvious one. If it doesn't look that way in the agent's lifetime, it is only because the wily fellow is pursuing his 'inclusive fitness'—planning to maximize his gene representation at some rather uncertain future date. There is also a very unsatisfactory controversy about what are called 'units of selection' which seems to be a desperate attempt to find *some* entity of which it will be true that everything has been designed for its benefit—perhaps the gene, perhaps the population, perhaps even the species? (which has been back in fashion again lately after a period of total disgrace). Sensible biologists point out that this dispute is merely a muddle, that the parts played by different groupings in selection will be different, and that there is no need to find a universal beneficiary. But the dispute goes on. In conclusion, I make the scandalous suggestion that we should regard such disputes chiefly as a displacement activity, produced by a prospect which really does fill the human soul with conflict—namely, the idea of admitting just how much conflict there inevitably is in the human soul, and how many of our troubles come from within it, rather than from outside difficulties in the physical world. To admit this upsetting truth seems to me the first condition of staving off disaster from our species.

The Sociobiological View of Man

ROGER TRIGG

I

What is the relation of the biological to the social sciences? Fierce battles are being currently fought over this question and much hangs on the answer. If society (or culture) is taken as an irreducible category which can only be understood in its own terms, the social sciences can feel safe from the sinister designs of other disciplines. Yet it is a commonplace that cultures vary, and we humans are prone to look at the differences rather than the similarities between them. The result can be a thoroughgoing relativism. If culture cannot be understood by means of any non-cultural categories, cultural differences themselves can be accepted as the ultimate truth about man. When everything is cultural, even the notion of a non-cultural category can seem to be a ludicrous contradiction in terms. The categories with which we think are the product of our culture, or so we are told. Instead of our being able to understand culture in terms of anything beyond itself, our understanding appears totally moulded by the society to which we belong. Any theory can thus be seen as merely the expression of the beliefs of a particular society.

Sociobiology has been defined by E. O. Wilson, one of its leading proponents, as 'the systematic study of the biological basis of all social behaviour'.[1] As such, it challenges at its roots the view that everything is cultural.[2] Yet it is equally possible for the discipline's opponents to argue that it is only the product of the concepts of a particular society at a particular time. Perhaps sociobiologists are merely projecting the norms of their own American capitalist society on to human society at large, and indeed even on to animal and insect society. Sociobiology, combining the insights of modern population genetics with the Darwinian theory of natural selection, has placed great importance on the evolutionary importance of conflict between individuals. Those prone to self-sacrifice, for instance, will not be likely to have as many descendants as those who ruthlessly pursue their own genuine interests. Genes encouraging such self-sacrifice are not likely to spread. Indeed they will die out, as the families of more selfish individuals prosper.

[1] E. O. Wilson, *Sociobiology: the New Synthesis* (Cambridge, Mass.: Harvard University Press, 1975), 4.

[2] See my book, *The Shaping of Man: Philosophical Aspects of Sociobiology* (Oxford: Blackwell, 1982).

93

Some have argued that this is merely the selfishness endemic in the Western economic system writ large. The concepts of one society are given a universal application, which no concepts can ever have. The concepts of one society cannot be applied to others without the risk of grave misrepresentation.

This approach can soon induce paralysis. The sociology of knowledge, relating concepts to culture, is itself a cultural product with a validity which cannot, it seems, be applied beyond the frontiers of the society producing it. It can soon appear that nothing is ever stated objectively *about* societies. Everything is merely the cultural expression of a particular society. The possibility of any social theory, whether allied to or opposed to biology, is thereby removed. Yet once we step back from this conclusion, it must become an open question how far, if at all, society and biology are related. If everything is not automatically social, we are at liberty to examine how much is.

The extremism of some sociology of knowledge can be matched by that of some sociobiology. The discipline is exceedingly young, and it has been very tempting for some to claim that everything social can be reduced to the biological. In a quest for the genetic basis of social behaviour, the connection between genes and social phenomena can be made far too close. Accusations of 'genetic determinism' have often been made. So far from sociobiology being irrelevant to the social sciences or even explicable in terms of them, it can make claim to take over from them. Edward Wilson suggested in his first book on the subject that the social sciences should in effect be superseded by biology. He wrote:

> Let us now consider man in the free spirit of natural history, as though we were zoologists from another planet completing a catalog of social species on Earth. In this macroscopic view, the humanities and social sciences shrink to specialized branches of biology.[3]

This position carries implications about the nature of man. Differences between him and other creatures are thought of little account. Biology can then hope to explain human behaviour as well as it tries to explain that of insects or of birds. Man may be more complicated, but he is not different in kind from other animals. This view can reject mind, consciousness and culture as uninteresting epiphenomena playing no significant part in the evolutionary process. When it is stressed that there is a real connection between genes and behaviour, sociobiologists often explain it in ways which make mind redundant. One sociobiologist, David Barash, says:

> A guiding principle of sociobiology is that individuals tend to behave in a manner that maximizes their fitness. The result is a very strange

[3] Op. cit. 547.

sort of purposefulness, in which a goal—maximization of fitness—appears to be sought, but without any of the participants necessarily having awareness of what they are doing, or why.[4]

The notion of a goal in this context is illusory, although it is very hard even for sociobiologists not to slip into talking of purpose. According to strict sociobiological theory, there can be no goal. Some genes are readily passed on and spread through the 'gene pool'. Others die out. Genes encouraging self-preservation are more likely to spread than those prompting their carriers into dangerous situations. It has therefore been very tempting for sociobiologists to exclude everything else in their search for links between genes and behaviour. They have often argued that we do not need to be conscious of the reasons for our natural inclinations. We may even be programmed to delude ourselves as to the real reasons. Morality, for instance, may be an elaborate system for furthering our own self-interest. We are each out for ourselves, but sometimes we do better through co-operating with others. Yet the system may work better if we do not realize this, but delude ourselves into thinking that we are in fact concerned with other people' interests. Once explicit calculation of personal interest enters into the system it may not work as efficiently. Short-term interests may be pursued at the expense of long-term ones. So consciousness is not only conceived to be ineffective. It actually blinds us to what is actually going on.

This onslaught on consciousness and its cultural products can produce a parallel problem to that incurred by the sociology of knowledge. It claims too much. If the products of the human mind are merely by-products of the attempt by individuals to maximize their biological fitness, what is the status of sociobiological theory itself? Is it an uninteresting epiphenomenon? Through showing us our real motives, it might even change our behaviour and make us less fit biologically. Ultimately sociobiologists as a breed might even die out. A consistent sociobiologist may deny that a theory could ever change behaviour, but few sociobiologists are ready to proclaim the ultimate irrelevance of their discipline. Most seem to imagine that a greater understanding of human nature may somehow enable us to improve it in some way. Yet there is a fundamental confusion here. They want both to insist on a fixed genetic basis for human nature and to hold out the possibility of controlling our natural inclinations more effectively.

Wilson provides a clear illustration when he points out[5] that 'the

[4] D. Barash, *Sociobiology: the Whisperings Within* (London: Souvenir Press, 1980), 25.
[5] E. O. Wilson, *On Human Nature* (Cambridge, Mass.: Harvard University Press, 1978), 208.

culture of each society travels along one or the other of a set of evolutionary trajectories whose full array is constrained by the genetic rules of human nature'. He maintains that this cultural divergence is strictly limited since it 'still represents only a tiny subset of all the trajectories that would be possible in the absence of the genetic constraints'. He continues:

> As our knowledge of human nature grows and we start to elect a system of values on a more objective basis, and our minds at last align with our hearts, the set of trajectories will narrow still more.

Wilson seems to assume that knowledge will bring with it the ability to change culture. Yet if the 'genetic rules of human nature' already govern the way we behave, it is hard to see how understanding them will enable us to behave any differently. Understanding the genetic basis of our inclinations will not remove them. Fear of snakes may have a genetic basis but that piece of knowledge will not remove the fear. There seems in fact to be an admission in what Wilson says that some human cultures can be less well aligned to the 'genetic rules of human nature' than others. A culture encouraging our 'mind' to go against our 'heart' should be changed. Yet why should it be? An extreme sociobiology would deny that such a culture was possible. A rigorous gene to behaviour model finds great difficulty in explaining many of the cultural variations which exist. Some are doubtless the result of the impact of a different environment. It is obvious, for instance, that differences in climate have great influence on ways of life. Yet there ought to be an underlying similarity between cultures, if all humans share the same genetic make-up and if that directly governs their behaviour. The very existence of different cultures appears to be a problem for a crude sociobiology, especially if it took no account of normal interaction between genes and environment.

Wilson's view that greater knowledge of human nature will enable us to bring cultures more in line with it seems odd. It seems remarkable that cultures have gone against our genes, if the latter govern culture. Similarly, if Wilson operates with the simple gene to behaviour model, it will be equally remarkable that mere knowledge can somehow obtain the power to do for the genes what they have proved unable to do for themselves. One answer to this is that Wilson allows for a certain divergence of culture from the interests of genes. He puts forward the view that when cultures develop too far against genetic interests, they are pulled back sharply. A society forbidding sexual intercourse, for example, would soon die out. In his latest book, written with C. J. Lumsden, Wilson amplifies this in a significant way. They write:

> Genetic natural selection operates in such a way as to keep culture on a leash. The leash symbolizes genetically prescribed tendencies to

use culturgens bearing certain key features that contribute to genetic fitness.[6]

'Culturgens' are defined as 'the basic units of culture', and it is doubtless highly questionable how far cultures can be split up into atoms in this way. Nevertheless their introduction marks an important step for sociobiology. The theory at last recognizes that *human* sociobiology cannot operate in precisely the same way as the study of insects. Even the latter has to take account of interaction between genes and environment. Culture is seen as part of the normal environment for humans. It provides the context in which human genes are passed on, and the mutual interplay of genes and culture must be recognized as crucial. Indeed Lumsden and Wilson talk of 'gene-culture co-evolution'. Even here though, the place of consciousness and knowledge is none too clear. The 'leash principle' does not seem to imply any deliberate, rational choice. Wilson may believe that sociobiology enables us consciously to plan our cultures so that they are in accord with 'human nature', but the genes are also supposed to exercise their own influence.

II

Cultures may appear to differ, but they are all rooted in the same soil. A cardinal belief of sociobiology must be that human nature is not so malleable by culture that it can only be explained in terms appropriate to whichever culture formed it. Human nature precedes culture and explains many of its features. The fact of our common humanity gives us a strong foundation for understanding what is occurring in other cultures. This is the positive point which follows from the sociobiological emphasis on genetic influence on behaviour. Yet the introduction of the concept of culture into the theory produces complications. Sociobiology can no longer make bold and simple claims about the origins of human behaviour. Any form of genetic determinism has to under-rate the importance of interaction with the environment, and to ignore completely the active role of human consciousness. Once this is repudiated, the sociobiologist has to talk of mere tendencies and influences, inclinations and felt needs.

'Gene-culture co-evolution' suggests that human culture is a predominant part of the environment in which human genes find themselves. The genes may have prompted man originally to have constructed cultures, and it is an important part of the sociobiological

[6]C. J. Lumsden and E. O. Wilson, *Genes, Mind and Culture* (Cambridge, Mass.: Harvard University Press, 1981), 13.

case that this is so. Once this happened, however, culture itself may begin to play an independent role. Any investigation of the respective importance of biological theory and the social sciences must start from this point. Now that sociobiology accepts that culture is important and cannot be ignored, controversy must concentrate on how closely genes control its content. There is also the further question of how far culture might actually have an impact on genes, encouraging some to flourish and others to disappear.

The 'leash' principle states that there are limits beyond which human culture cannot stray. A range of cultural expression is possible within them, but some cultures further genetic fitness more than others. A good example is the human need for food. A range of diet is possible, and different cultures prefer different foods, or the same food prepared differently. Yet this cannot be a totally arbitrary matter, since some foods are more nutritious than others. Putting the point at its most extreme, a culture encouraging the eating of poisonous toadstools would not do as well as one preferring harmless mushrooms. Even some kinds of ordinary food will be more nutritious than others. Some cultures will inevitably produce people who are better fed and healthier than members of other cultures. The sociobiologist could claim that it requires no great imagination or research to see that as a result of diet the members of one tribe may become biologically fitter and reproduce to the detriment of its weaker neighbours. The one culture will flourish while competitors may gradually die out or even be annihilated. Thus Wilson's leash principle will in the long run keep cultures from relying on diets which lack necessary nutrition. Genetic constraints will ensure not that everyone eats the same kind of food, but that divergence between cultures is kept within limits, set by what is biologically desirable. The genes demand that in the last resort their interests are served.

The leash principle also means that it is not just a question of culture suddenly being tugged back when permissible limits are reached. Strains and stresses will be set up before that when the culture thwarts or frustrates what is biologically desirable. Such stresses may not be the result of conscious reflection, and even here the sociobiological bias against consciousness is perhaps demonstrated. Yet the thesis is that social behaviour has been shaped by natural selection, and behaviour producing what Lumsden and Wilson term[7] 'the highest replacement rate in successive generations' becomes encouraged by genetic processes. Going against such implanted tendencies will only be possible at a cost. This will not just be in biological fitness, although *ex hypothesi* that must be so. There will also be a cost to the individual who

[7] Op. cit. 79.

is straining against a strong inclination to do something. Doing what comes naturally is always easier than going against nature.

Needless to say, all this is highly controversial. Many social scientists concede that man's basic ability to create cultures, think, learn and so on may have been shaped through natural selection. Through them he obtained a clear advantage over less well-endowed mammals. Nevertheless, the sugggestion that the particular form of culture and the actual content of thought is somehow dictated by genes seems repugnant to many. Yet the consequence of resisting the sociobiologist is to refuse to accept limits on the forms which human culture could take. As a result, another culture could have as little point of contact with our own as that of some form of alien life from outer space. We might well have difficulty in recognizing it as a culture. Unintelligibility, or at least degrees of it, may be unavoidable, but it is significant that sociobiology can provide an empirical theory why humans from different cultures *can* find each other comprehensible.

A major problem which has confronted sociobiology is whether it can explain cultural diversity, or merely cultural similarity. It may seem as if 'cross-cultural universals' might be the most encouraging sign that sociobiology is right. For example, the fact (if it is one) that incest is widely regarded with abhorrence would seem to support a sociobiological approach. Incest will lower genetic fitness, and natural impulses towards it would soon die out. Societies practising it on any scale would incur an inevitable penalty. Even this example can be controversial, but the leash principle implies that cultural diversity is also explicable by sociobiology. Diversity will be limited and is still under ultimate genetic control. For this reason, even the existence of societies practising incest would not be a counter-example. What would really create a problem would be if such societies continued to flourish over a long period of time, even at the expense of societies rigorously banning it.

The role of consciousness in these processes is again left vague by sociobiology. Genetic control in such matters as incest seems fairly mechanistic. Presumably genes normally ensure that we just do not want sexual relations with near relatives or those assumed to be relatives. Yet many societies have explicit taboos and even elaborate moral codes about such matters. Why should this be? We do not need to be prohibited from doing what we do not wish to do. What is the relationship of the moral code to the inbuilt mechanism, genetically transmitted? Fear of thunderstorms could well have a genetic basis but there is no corresponding moral prohibition concerning them. Why should some cultures feel the need to reinforce some natural repugnances with explicit taboos? Perhaps this is an example where the quest for genetic fitness has actually taken two simultaneous routes, the direct one through personal inclination, and the indirect one through the demands of society.

The mere existence of inclinations may not be enough to ensure the biologically desirable result. Conscious reinforcement by social rules of what genes are also inclining men to do may be more effective. Cultures where this occurred may well be more successful from a biological point of view than those merely relying on impulses stemming from genes. Sociobiologists, however, are not talking of a competition between cultures as such. They place their emphasis on the individual, or indeed even on the gene,[8] as the unit of selection. An individual is the vehicle of genes, so these two views are not as far apart as they might appear. Group selection, whereby some groups, such as cultures, survive at the expense of others, is much more controversial. The reason is simply that individuals reproduce, and although cultural circumstances may make it easier or harder for them to do so, the success of a culture depends entirely on how far it enables its members to flourish. A culture in which individuals achieve greater genetic fitness will expand while another sapping individual fitness may not.

Sociobiologists are very cautious in envisaging individuals sacrificing themselves or otherwise becoming less fit biologically for the sake of unrelated members of the group. Even if the group as a whole flourished, how could an inclination to such behaviour be transmitted genetically? It is often argued that those acting like this would inevitably be replaced by more ruthless competitors. What is at issue is the status of morality. Does it merely provide a framework in which enlightened self-interest is pursued, or can it continually encourage people to ignore their own genuine interests in favour of others? A society in which there are such altruists may well do better as a whole than one in which no one is ultimately concerned with the general good. The snag is that the altruist and his family will suffer if he is concentrating on promoting the general good. It is inevitable that altruists will gradually die out, if altruism is passed on genetically.

This is a classic argument in sociobiology, but it again raises the question of the nature of morality and of the culture of which it is part. The sociobiologist is always tempted to explain them away because they are social and he is only interested in the individual. Yet, as we have seen, society does affect the individual. Individuals living in some cultures are going to be healthier than in others. Similarly, some forms of morality may prove more beneficial than others. Even here, though, the point is that culture works through individuals. The idea of a culture succeeding in any sense, even though it fails to provide an

[8] See R. Dawkins, *The Extended Phenotype: the Gene as the Unit of Selection* (Oxford: Freeman, 1982).

environment in which its members can flourish , must be dismissed. Sociobiology began by considering that this emphasis on individuals made reference to culture redundant. It now recognizes that culture is not the irrelevant by-product of individual competition. Having created culture, individuals can themselves be influenced by it. It is thus a most important part of the general environment with which the genes of an individual interact.

Culture and genetic processes interact. In other words, the social sciences cannot claim that they are concerned with what occurs at the social and cultural level, and have no need to be concerned with the biological level. Just as human biology has produced culture, culture may in turn have an effect on human genetic constitution. This marks a major step forward from the crude reductionism of some sociobiology. Culture is at last taken seriously, and seen as a formative influence.

III

The apparent compromise between the claims of social science and those of biology will fail to satisfy many on either side. There will still be those who deny the relevance of biology to social science. Kenneth Bock, for instance, is one of those who feel that problems about cultural differences and cultural change cannot be illuminated by biological research. He says[9] of 'humanists' (contrasted with scientists) that they 'take biological man as given and proceed with explanations of sociocultural things in sociocultural terms'. This is not, he argues, because biological factors in human history are insignificant, but 'exactly what they have been and how they might be conceived to account for the variety of human experience has not been made evident'. His advice to humanists is that 'they proceed to see what can be done by tending their own garden'. This is explicitly an argument from ignorance, leaving open the possibility that biological knowledge may advance. More threatening for the sociobiologist is the total refusal to accept the relevance of biology for the social sciences. Bock himself is tempted by the thesis 'that human society and culture are *sui generis*'. In other words, present knowledge in biology is not just insufficient to cast light on them. It never could be relevant.

Like Bock, many social scientists take human biology as 'given'. When pressed, they might admit that human society develops within limits imposed by biology, but they concentrate on the myriad differences within the limits, rather than on the nature of the limits

[9] K. Bock, *Human Nature and History: a Response to Sociobiology* (New York: Columbia University Press, 1980), 194.

themselves. No one could actually deny that human society is influenced by the physical characteristics of mankind. The length of time it takes to grow to maturity, human physical strength, how far it is possible to walk in a day, the amount of food needed to live, the kind of climate humans can tolerate—this is purely a random list of factors that we all take for granted in studying human society. Yet if they were very different, so would be the nature of human society. It is perhaps too easy for social scientists to dismiss all of this. Because of their interest in the nature of society within the limits, they are quite happy to leave study of the limits to others. Yet the theory of 'gene-culture co-evolution' stresses that what happens within the limits is also susceptible to biological explanation.

Many social scientists feel threatened as a result. They have some justification when confronted with more extreme versions of sociobiology arguing for the primacy of the biological. These versions would object to 'gene-culture co-evolution', on the grounds that it gives too great a role to culture. Just as the interaction of genes and culture is anathema to those who only want to study culture, it is also unacceptable to those pursuing a policy of unrelenting reductionism. Culture will seem to them to be an irrelvant excrescence, pushed up by the workings of underlying forces. Genuine science, they will feel, must only study the latter. Alexander Rosenberg, for example, has argued that sociobiology should 'pre-empt', or supersede conventional social science. He maintains that the social sciences can never discover laws since these must be searched for at the biological level. Any expectations which the anthropologist and the historian may have that a study of particular cultures would help provide a more general understanding of culture and history are denounced by Rosenberg as 'equally vain'.[10] Scientific laws cannot, he holds, be concerned with a particular species, but can only deal with man as a biological organism. The more the autonomy of culture from biology is upheld, the more, so Rosenberg considers, it is being proclaimed that culture is irrelevant to science.

A doctrine of the autonomy of culture thus joins battle with reductionists who believe that what cannot be expressed in biological (and ultimately chemical and physical) terms is of no scientific interest. Each side gains some plausibility from the existence of the other. If the findings of, say, anthropology cannot be connected with the rest of the language of science, this may lead some to conclude it is a bogus science. Similarly an extreme reductionism, jettisoning all intentional notions, such as belief, desire and action, along with anything distinctively

[10] A. Rosenberg, *Sociobiology and the Pre-emption of Social Science* (Oxford: Blackwell, 1981), 179.

cultural, can easily provoke the reaction that culture is an independent entity to be studied in its own terms. One side sweeps aside as of no account how men understand themselves and what they consciously think. It is understandable that in retaliation it is held that in fact these are the only things that do matter in the study of man.

The sociobiological theory of gene-culture co-evolution attempts to avoid the trap of either extreme. It at last accepts that human consciousness and its cultural products are of paramount importance. Yet it tries to preserve the essential insights of the discipline by keeping a link between genes and behaviour. This time, however, it is made explicitly through consciousness. Although this avoids crude mechanism, there is more than a suspicion that the theory is still in the grip of one form of reductionism, namely a simple-minded materialism. The curious notion of a culturgen is explicated with the aid of reference to structures in the brain. We are told: 'Culturgens can be mapped into node-link structures in long term memory, and in many instances can be treated as identical with them'.[11] Such 'node-link structures' are envisaged as being neurophysiological, and so it is easy for Lumsden and Wilson to begin by talking of culture and end by talking of the individual brain, without realizing that they have changed the subject.

Nevertheless, the fact that an attempt is being made to demonstrate a link between human culture and genetic origins is of immense importance. While culture is accepted as a formative influence on man, it is not allowed to float free from scientific understanding. Many social scientists, though, will be reluctant to accept that the theory of evolution can be relevant to the explanation of the content of culture. That culture as such was an aid to survival will surprise no one. Scepticism sets in for many when sociobiology tries to explain the vagaries of human history and even the differences between contemporary cultures. Yet refusing to do so may seem to cut human behaviour off from the realm of scientific explanation. The social sciences may be sciences in their own eyes, but they have a different concept of science from that of the physicist if no connection can be established between them and the physical sciences. The fear of reductionism clearly prompts many to resist the suggestion that biology may help in the explanation of culture. There are those with a vision of the unity of science who wish to reduce everything to the propositions of physics. Unfortunately what cannot be so reduced is thought irrelevant. Yet the opposite vice is just as bad. The social sciences must not be allowed to exist in a vacuum, understanding cultures merely as they are understood by their participants. Man is a biological organism

[11] Lumsden and Wilson, op. cit. 368.

(even if he is also more than that), and the social sciences neglect the fact at their peril.

Can due weight be given to the findings of biology without destroying all that is distinctive of human culture? The notion that culture can shape the environment in which genes are selected, just as genetic make-up can influence culture, is very radical. Culture is at last recognized as 'something in itself', with definite biological effects. The leash principle shows how cultures failing to satisfy biological needs will be replaced by those which do. This replacement is not a result of conscious choice, but stems from the fact that one culture will increase its members' biological fitness while another will sap it.

The picture which emerges is one of cultures which are better or worse at dealing with a static range of biological demands. Yet this cannot be the whole story, if genes and cultures genuinely interact. A big part of the theory put forward by Lumsden and Wilson is that the genetic constitution of individuals will change over time. They assert[12] that genetic mutants will gradually arise biasing individuals towards specific 'culturgens', even if man was originally in a 'tabula rasa' state with no inclination to favour one form of culture rather than another. Those biased towards deleterious ones will lose fitness and those biased towards benficial ones will gain it. The population will thus inevitably change from the initial state to one biased towards beneficial elements of culture. It will be no accident if humans tend to like what is good for them and dislike what is bad.

Now if culture itself forms part of the environment in which genetic selection takes place, the conclusion could be that different cultures will each have an effect on the genetic constitution of their members. There will be no biological reason why different cultural practices should not persist, as long as they are equally beneficial for the given genetic constitution of individuals. There is considerable scope for variety within the limits set by the leash principle. Yet it one so-called 'culturgen' proved especially beneficial, a genetic mutation especially inclining individuals towards it could spread quickly through the population. Not only would the particular 'culturgen' have given members of that culture a biological advantage. It would in the course of time have inclined them genetically towards itself, and thus have made them slightly different from those of other cultures.

This is the line of argument followed by Lumsden and Wilson, despite its controversial implications. They write:

We suggest the existence of a rough fifty-generation rule for populations able to exploit highly efficient new culturgens. For

[12] Op. cit. 13.

mankind in particular, this amounts to a *thousand-year* rule: during a period of this length substantial genetic evolution can occur . . . resulting in such effects as the genetic assimilation of culturgen preference and the assimilation of bias towards specific decision heuristics.[13]

Such a genetic change could only occur in a stable environment, but even so the suggestion is very radical. Even amongst biologists, the tendency is to assume that genetic evolution is sufficiently slow for cultural change to be irrelevant for genetic questions. It is usually thought that human genetic constitution has not significantly changed during the period of recorded history. It is an empirical question whether this is so or whether Lumsden and Wilson are right and different cultures could have a distinctive effect on human genes. What is of particular interest is the impact of their suggestion on the question of understanding those in other cultures. If human nature is constant, we have an undeniable base for understanding the participants in different ways of life. It is no accident that genuine cultural relativism can get a grip if the concept of human nature is rejected or attenuated to the point where it lacks any precise content. The strength of sociobiology seemed to be that it related culture to the unchangeable base shared by all societies. The thousand-year rule might seem to complicate and even undermine this. The very existence of different societies with different cultural practices might over a period of time produce new differences.

Could this provide ammunition for the cultural relativist? It has previously looked as if giving empirical content to the notion of human nature is a powerful antidote to relativism. Yet those emphasizing the primacy of culture might be vindicated if different cultures could provide different contexts for genetic evolution. Unless human nature can be assumed to be the same everywhere, it seems useless demanding that social sciences take account of it. Genetic difference might well *follow* cultural difference. There would be a temptation for the social scientist to hold that genes are an irrelevance in explaining cultural divergence if they can vary with culture. Genetic difference would at least in part appear to be there because of the state of the culture, and be useless as an explanation for it. 'Gene-culture co-evolution' could once again encourage social scientists to ignore the biological base.

The retort from the sociobiologist could be that the genetic variations envisaged between cultures are minor. A predisposition in a culture to any particular form of behaviour need involve no greater variation than exists between individuals in the same society. Once again this is an

---

[13] Ibid. 295.

empirical matter but it shows that a viable concept of human nature never did depend on any idea of genetic identity. Natural selection could never have operated without considerable genetic variation. What sociobiology does need to assume is that genes give man a distinctive nature *before* his interaction with culture, and that this stems from his membership of a biological species. The genetic constitution of the species is far more important as a behavioural constraint than any minor, local variations.

IV

Sociobiology must prove an unrelenting opponent of any form of cultural relativism. The latter must uphold the utter distinctiveness of different cultures, coupled with the primacy of culture as a formative influence. Otherwise it reduces to uninteresting platitudes about people behaving differently in different circumstances. The bite of a relativist doctrine must lie in the view that different cultures shape man so differently that it is misleading to talk of any human nature common to them all. The cultural expression of such a nature differs so widely, it may be held, that there is no way we can continue to posit it. There is no difference, it seems, between referring to radically different expressions in culture of the same human nature and denying that there is any common nature underlying human divergences. Both positions can be so obsessed with the undoubted differences between human cultures that any connection is either forgotten or deliberately repudiated. As a result we are left with a series of unrelated cultures which can only be understood in their own terms.

Sociobiology must be opposed to all this since its whole purpose is to examine what it believes is the same starting-point for all cultures. Human biology is taken to be the major influence on the moulding of culture. All cultures develop within the limits imposed by it and so they cannot be viewed as utterly distinct from each other. Studying culture in its own terms only leaves out what is for the sociobiologist the key factor. Biology is seen as not only creating the possibility of culture but as profoundly influencing its content. Thus any human culture must always possess some fundamental similarities with other cultures. The same needs have to be catered for. At times the link between culture and the biological base will be less straightforward. Nevertheless the fact that, according to sociobiologists, the link is there, provides a challenge to those who take cultural divergence at face value.

Treating culture as unconnected with biology can all too easily lead to relativism. The reason is that anyone faced with the multiplicity of human cultures is bound to be tempted by the view that their divergence is their most striking feature. Non-relativist explanations of divergence are harder to find once appeals to an underlying human nature are ruled out. This is one reason why social science does itself little good by ignoring the relevance of biology. Social scientists are clearly eager to preserve their territory from unwelcome encroachment, by limiting biology to talk about the general pre-conditions of culture. For example, human societies all use language and the ability to speak has a biological origin. How they use this ability together may be thought a matter for social science rather than biology. Talk of 'human nature', if it takes place at all may then seem to be merely concerned with what makes culture possible. Different forms of culture are deemed irrelevant to biological research. This is, however, a very attenuated idea of human nature which can explain little of interest. It certainly has nothing to do with the question why we ever behave in one way rather than another. The latter can be regarded as an internal issue for whichever society is concerned. Society can then only be explained in social terms, and the concepts appropriate to one society may well be inappropriate to another. Losing our grip on the notion of human nature can easily lead us in this way into the paths of relativism.

Sociobiology does of course insist that human nature is a matter of *biological* concern. Many may agree that a social scientist jettisons the concept of human nature at his peril, but wonder whether that entails accepting a biological view of man. The emphasis on human society and man's social nature has often been made in order to avoid man being treated as a *mere* animal. Early sociobiology certainly seemed to reject anything distinctively human, which could not be assimilated to a recognizable type of animal behaviour. Even if it is accepted that some animals can possess elementary forms of culture, passed on through teaching, human culture is obviously far more complicated. It is crucial for the understanding of human behaviour in a way that animal 'culture' could never be for the understanding of animals. Lumsden and Wilson have at last recognized this by allowing that *human* sociobiology is a subject in its own right. Humans are not merely one animal species amongst many. Account has to be taken of the positive role of culture and of human understanding. The idea of the zoologist from another planet, able to treat man as one social species amongst many, has had to be modified. Lumsden and Wilson now concede[14] that reference to the 'canalization' of cultural evolution as a biological process need not involve treating it on a par with animal behaviour. Concept formation itself, they say, may be controlled in the last resort by biologically based 'epigenetic rules'. They go on, though, to say:[15]

[14] Op. cit. 344.
[15] Ibid. 345.

Such learning can be analyzed by gene-culture, theory, but not by direct comparison with animal species. The inseverable linkage between genes and culture does not also chain mankind to an animal level.

Reformed sociobiology can in fact join forces with social science rather than simply replace it. There will still be social scientists who will want nothing to do with biology, but this attitude cuts social science off totally from the rest of science and is bound to make its explanations seem suspect to many. In the end, indeed, social science can be made to appear a product of society rather than a dispassionate study of it. The choice can now be seen as less stark. It does not lie between physical science, including biology, and social science as competing modes of explanation. Each can illuminate the other. Social science cannot dismiss the insights of biology, if human society depends in any way on individual human nature. Lumsden and Wilson themselves say: 'When cultural behaviour is treated as an ultimate product of biology instead of an independent stratigraphic layer above it, the social sciences can be connected more readily into a continuous explanatory system'.[16] If this could be done without destroying the subject-matter of social science, the resulting integration of physical and social science would be of enormous importance.

The alternatives until now have often seemed to be a (literally) mindless reductionism and a refusal to allow that the social could be seen in any other than its own terms. This involved a very schizophrenic view of humanity. It could be seen in physical and chemical terms or in social ones. As a result of this split, man's 'social essence' could appear to be something mysterious. Man becomes what he is through his participation in society, and his biological make-up is irrelevant. This doctrine can reach the conclusion that man cannot have any desires that are not social in origin. It trades on the undoubted fact that all human tendencies and inclinations have to be expressed in the context of society. They can certainly be inhibited or even thwarted by a particular culture, but, according to sociobiology, this must always be at a cost. In the long run human nature will re-assert itself. To take again the example of incest, humans may have inbuilt tendencies to avoid it, but it can still occur. What sociobiology denies is that incest could become a cultural norm, without inevitable and disastrous consequences, on individuals, and through them on their culture. The biological effects of culture cannot be ignored, any more than the biological origins of culture should be discounted.

Cultural divergence is no bar, in principle, to the attempt to explain society in a scientific way. In the tug between human biology and

[16] Op. cit. 350.

human culture, both elements have to be given weight. Humanity expresses itself in culture, but sociobiology points out that culture is not an arbitrary phenomenon. The demands of our biology give culture much of its point. There is a danger, though, in dealing with biology and culture in this way. There are not two competing types of explanation, biological and social. It is not a matter of one beating the other into submission. Much controversy is generated merely because of the false opposition of physical and social science. Human society will never be adequately understood as long as biologists and social scientists are in competition with each other. Each side has given credence to this idea by appealing to biological and environmental factors respectively. The emphasis was on either a 'given' human nature or the myriad forms of human culture. The old battle between 'physis' and 'nomos' has been continually refought. This must be a false antithesis, since if human nature is expressed in a cultural context, we can never refer to it without bringing in the question of culture. Sociobiologists now, for the most part, see this.

The opposite danger, of studying culture without recognizing the underlying biological factors, is perhaps more seductive. It is a commonplace that the more similar people are to each other the more the differences between them seem to matter Some of the fiercest battles are fought not between those with radically different ideologies but between those who have what would appear to the outsider to be very marginal differences. Different branches of Christianity or of Marxism find it harder to tolerate similar, but distinctive, views than a totally different outlook. So it is with human culture in general. We all notice and care about the differences, while taking for granted the similarities. Social science can become so obsessed with cultural divergence that it often takes it to be a basic fact about man, incapable of further explanation.

Sebastiano Timpanaro has attacked Marxists in particular for ignoring the biological underpinning of culture. He says:

> Marxists put themselves in a scientifically and polemically weak position if, after rejecting the idealist arguments which claim to show that the only reality is that of the Spirit and that cultural facts are in no way dependent on economic structures, they then borrow the same arguments to deny the dependence of man on nature.[17]

He likens the position of the contemporary Marxist to that of a person living on the first floor of a house who tells the tenant of the second floor

[17] S. Timpanaro, *On Materialism*, L. Garner (trans.) (London: New Left Books, 1975), 44.

that he is wrong if he thinks he is independent with no support from below. Yet at the same time he himself denies that the ground floor supports him, or rather says that the real ground floor is the first floor. In other words economic structures may underpin societies but they must themselves rest on biological facts about man. Non-Marxists, too, must recognize the biological basis of human society. Together the biological and social sciences can vastly increase our knowledge of man. Whether even in co-operation they can tell the whole story is another question.

Biological Ideas and Their Cultural Uses

TED BENTON

'Do you think', said Candide, 'that men have always massacred each other as they do today, always been liars, cheats, faith-breakers, ingrates, brigands, weaklings, rovers, cowards, enviers, gluttons, drunkards, misers, self-seekers, carnivores, caluminators, debauchees, fanatics, hypocrites, and fools?'

'Do you think', said Martin, 'that sparrowhawks have always eaten pigeons when they found any?'[1]

I

The topic of my talk is a very ancient one indeed. It bears upon the place of humankind in nature, and upon the place of nature in ourselves. I shall, however, be discussing this range of questions in terms which have not always been available to the philosophers of the past when they have asked them. When we ask these questions today we do so with hindsight of some two centuries of endeavour in the 'human sciences', and some one and a half centuries of attempts to situate the human species within a theory of biological evolution. And these ways of thinking about ourselves and our relation to nature have not been confined to professional intellectuals, nor have they been without practical consequences. Social movements and political organizations have fought for and sometimes achieved the power to give practical shape to their theoretical visions. On the one hand, are diverse projects aimed at changing society through a planned modification of the social environment of the individual. On the other hand, are equally diverse projects for pulling society back into conformity with the requirements of race and heredity. At first sight, the two types of project appear to be, and often are, deeply opposed, both intellectually and politically.

In their contemporary forms, these issues and struggles have engendered what now appear to be more or less stable alignments of intellectual and political forces. Attempts to think of human beings and

[1] Voltaire, *Candide, Zadig and Selected Stories*, D. M. Frame (trans.) (New York, Scarborough (Ontario) and London: Signet paperback edition, 1961) 68.

their social relationship in terms of biological analogies and metaphors, to assign positive value to actually or supposedly biological human attributes or dispositions, or to directly apply biological ideas and theories in the explanation of human conduct are all quite different intellectual activities which may have diverse and mutually contradictory outcomes. None the less, such 'biologically rooted' ways of thinking generally tend to find favour in politically conservative quarters, and to be treated with suspicion if not outright hostility across the spectrum of the political left—whether feminist, libertarian or socialist. Similarly, in scholarly circles, the leading exponents of biological views of humankind have tended to come from a background in a life-science specialism, whereas the general hostility and suspicion shown by the political left is generally shared by social scientists. This, it seems to me, is not because of any inner connection between leftist politics and the human sciences (though there will always be tensions between such disciplines and the established order) but is rather related to the obvious professional interests at stake. The contemporary sociobiologist aims to 'pre-empt' or absorb the social sciences, whereas the social scientists, in their turn, make it a point of principle to argue the specificity and autonomy of their disciplines.

In the remainder of this part of my talk I want to argue that there is something understandable, yet at the same time paradoxical, about this pattern of alignments. First, an attempt to understand and explain the contemporary alliance of the left and social scientists against 'biologism'. For most of the left, the more popular forms of social Darwinism are little more than conservative ideology covered by a thin pseudo-scientific veneer. This is demonstrably true, for example, of a popular genre of social commentary which works through the naive application of broad categories drawn from animal ethology to the human case: institutions and practices of contemporary society (usually ones ethically abhorrent to the left, and favoured by the right) are presented as natural and (presumably) unalterable, as mere particular instances of biologically governed tendencies (territoriality, aggression, hierarchy, male dominance, egoism, and so on) which we share with other animals.

A second area in which intellectual and political controversy intersect to produce the same pattern of alliance is educational psychology and sociology. If certain types of socially valued performance, linked demonstrably with differential 'life-chances' and social inequalities, can be shown to be wholly or largely biologically determined, then the kinds of egalitarian interventionist strategies widely favoured by the left are without rational foundation. The left has an apparent interest in showing that the types of performance in question are autonomous *vis-à-vis* genetic constitution, though subject to determinate social and cultural influences. But probably more significant than either of these considerations as an influence on left-wing thinking since World War II is the stark object-lesson of the Nazi project of racial purification. Here, epitomized in a single, nightmarish historical paroxysm is the inner unity of biologism and the deepest political reaction.

No doubt, for many social scientists, the political identification of biologism and reaction has been a formative influence. But there is also an intellectual and professional interest in establishing the autonomy of the human from the natural sciences. The *raison d'être* of any would-be science of humanity rests on the identification and demarcation of a field of phenomena, a complex of problems and questions distinct from and irreducible to those encompassed by the intellectual division of labour established in the natural sciences. Methodologically, the human sciences have historically been divided between those traditions of thought which, while asserting the specific autonomy of human social and cultural life, have nevertheless persisted in the attempt to extend the *methods* of the natural sciences to this new domain ('methodological naturalism') and those whose commitment to a radical ontological division between the human and the natural is taken to imply a correspondingly deep methodological gulf ('methodological humanism'). The differences between these traditions run very deep indeed, and I have no wish to obscure their significance. The historical fact remains that both are committed to the idea of the domain of the human and the social as a radically autonomous domain *vis-à-vis* (the rest of) nature. And, just as contemporary social scientists, more or less independently of political standpoint, are disposed to assert their professional status and autonomy and argue the specificity of their subject-matter in terms of opposition to the claims of sociobiology, so the sociobiologists reciprocate in the form of a territorial claim which would dispossess the social scientists.

The considerations, then, which dispose both contemporary social scientists and more or less the whole spectrum of the political left against biological ways of thinking about human nature and behaviour are both diverse and powerful. But they are not, for all that, decisive, and nor are they without paradoxical implications for either partner in the alliance. The conservatism of much of the literature deriving from animal ethology, for example, is often a double-edged or unstable kind. Undoubtedly this literature affects to sustain the 'naturalness' of institutional forms and practices disapproved by the left, but much of it is also committed to a form of 'social pathology' in which contemporary social forms are rendered problematic as obstructing the fulfilment of supposedly natural needs, and overriding natural dispositions. Now the policy-prescriptions engendered by arguments of this type often (though not always) run counter to those favoured by the left, but their very existence poses serious problems for any unqualified rejection of 'biologism' on the left.

These problems are of three main kinds. First, biologistic social pathologies cannot be written off as mere legitimations of the *status quo*. They often express real and fundamental dissent which, whilst it may not be leftist in direction, is important as a sociological indicator, and may have significant implications of a strategic political kind. Moreover, from the standpoint of the social scientists, and not withstanding the crudity and sociological vulgarity of much of this literature, it cannot be ruled out that its perspectives may pick out and identify questions of sociological importance to which the non-naturalistic categories of the orthodox sociologies are blind. Secondly, any argument which deduces a social pathology from the hypothesis that specific cultural forms override or frustrate natural tendencies can no longer be written off as an unqualified biological determinism. At the very least it must be regarded as a 'within-limits' or 'in the last instance' determinism, which recognizes the at least *relative* autonomy of cultural forms as a causal order with determinate effects on the expression/non-expression of biological tendencies. In so far as biologisms take this form, it follows that the standard philosophical arguments of both political leftists and social scientists which rely on the categorial distinction between nature and culture are insufficient to deal with them. Such a distinction is, I shall show in part II, quite compatible with 'last-instance' biological determinism. The third difficulty, posed by works like Desmond Morris's *Human Zoo*, for leftist opponents of biologism is that aside from its specific contents, some features of the *structure* of Morris's argument have a wide currency in sustaining leftist moral critiques of contemporary society. The ideas that specific social and cultural forms may stunt and frustrate human potentials, may fail to satisfy real needs or even manipulate into existence 'false' ones are a commonplace of radical moral and political critique. But a presupposition of their intelligible use is that human beings have dispositions, potentials and needs which are, so to speak, anchored transcendentally with respect to any specific culture. They rely, in other words, on some notion of a non-culturally specific human nature, which can then served as the comparative moral measure of the various cultures which shape its expressions. Since the rational defence of each and every such idea of a culture-transcendent human nature has proved to be inordinately difficult, then the problems faced by what we might call 'moral naturalisms' in their effort to tie such an idea to human biological constitution appear to be no more intractable.

To turn, now, to biologistic theories of human performance and the controversies they have provoked amongst educationalists. Here again, though it would be a tall order to demonstrate this point in detail, it seems that although the 'culturalist' opponents of biological determinism have won important specific battles they have as yet no strategic victory. The probably fraudulent character of much of the most important body of evidence (twin-studies) on which the genetic determinists have based their case has certainly been a valuable 'coup' for the culturalist case. But it remains arguable that the recurrent fashionability of genetic determinism is related to correlative weaknesses in anti-reductionist social theory. The quite specially problematic character of, for example, social inequalities related to race and gender can be shown to derive from the general tendency in each of the main traditions of sociology to assimilate these specific social forms to 'biologically blind' categories such as class and status.[2] I am merely suggesting here what I shall try to argue more systematically for later: that, whilst avoiding any crude reductionism, the social sciences must find ways of theoretically comprehending the incorporation of biological differences within cultural forms. This is indispensable if the human sciences, not to mention the political movements for the emancipation of women and oppressed racial groups, are not to be left intellectually disarmed in the face of the renewed efforts of biological determinism.

Even the 'demonstration-effect' of the Nazi project of racial eugenics is limited in its force. Profoundly abhorrent as this episode in European history is, it would be a grave mistake to see in it only the delirious attempt to implement a racial theory. But even if we focus on this aspect of the phenomenon, we shall not find in it the required demonstration of an inner link between political reaction and biologistic thinking. For one thing, the very idea of a eugenic programme presupposes that human biology is subject to planned intervention and modification. Unless social action, working from cultural assumptions, is supposed capable of determinate effects of genetic constitution, eugenics is not just morally, but also conceptually, unthinkable. Eugenics, no less than the dominant traditions in the social sciences, and the broad consensus of the left, is committed to the idea of human culture as an autonomous causal order *vis-à-vis* human biology. But it is also worth remembering that the eugenic idea—that the human biological constitution might be modified in a planned and intended direction—has also played a part in social and political life independently of the noxious racial valuations and authoritarian political forms with which it has been invested in the Nazi movement. In an earlier historical period it was possible to view the project as a natural extension of the Enlightenment idea of human progress, and few would condemn the contemporary practice of genetic

[2]See D. Lockwood, 'Race, Conflict and Plural Society' in *Race and Racialism*, S. Zubaida (ed.) (London: Tavistock, 1970).

counselling for those with a family history of inherited disease, despite its eugenic rationale.

There are, I think three quite general arguments which can be drawn from what I have said so far, and which 'point up' the paradoxical character of the contemporary alignment of the social sciences and the political left against 'biologism'. First, many, if not all, 'biologistic' theories do implicitly or explicitly recognize the autonomy of culture *vis-à-vis* human biology. What one might call 'strong biological determinism' is hardly ever consistently or seriously advocated, so that the mere incantation of the autonomy of culture is largely ineffective against the diverse array of 'last instance' biological determinisms and 'normative naturalisms' which are commonly confused with it. This is true, for example, of Marshall Sahlins' very influential critique of sociobiology.[3] The main weight of Sahlins' case is carried by his deployment of anthropological evidence to show that the kinship patterns and practices actually found in a wide range of human cultures never distribute human genetic material in the way that would be required if the sociobiologists' model of human actors as egoistic genetic calculators were true. Against this, Alexander Rosenberg, a leading advocate of sociobiology[4] argues that the kind of absolute biological determinism which would be vulnerable to Sahlins' evidence is hardly ever seriously advocated by sociobiologists. Rosenberg himself concedes that 'culture does constitute a crucial indeterminacy in the causal chain from genes to institutions'.[5] But if this much is conceded, then what, now, separates the opponent and the advocate of sociobiology? In large part this turns out to be a matter of their different evaluation of the *significance* of the agreed 'limits' within which culture is autonomous and variable. For Rosenberg these limits define the boundaries of the possibility of genuine scientific explanation, whereas, for Sahlins, 'a limit is only a negative determination': 'Within the void left by biology lies the whole of anthropology'.[6] As I shall argue later, the weak, 'within-limits', biological determinism implicitly conceded by Sahlins is by no means such a trivial matter as he seems to suppose.

Secondly, no effective moral critique (that is to say, no moral critique which is either intellectually cogent, or has any prospect of practical success) can do without standards of evaluation of cultures which are anchored transculturally. Given the predominantly secular orientation

[3] M. D. Sahlins, *The Use and Abuse of Biology* (London: Tavistock, 1977).

[4] A. Rosenberg, *Sociobiology and the Preemption of Social Science* (Oxford: Blackwell, 1981).

[5] Ibid. 189.

[6] Op. cit. 64 and 16.

of modern political radicalism, it is hard to see how this anchorage can be provided without some view of a positive general human nature independent of its specific cultural manifestations. The idea of human nature as an empty and infinitely flexible vessel into which may be poured any cultural content we choose is, like its philosophical partner, the empiricist 'tabula rasa' conception of the human mind, not only quite intellectually indefensible, but also absolutely hopeless as a vehicle for radical critics of specific cultural forms. If human individuals may be satisfactorily and indifferently socialized into any of a whole range of actual or possible cultures, what grounds are there for morally or rationally preferring some of these alternatives to others? And if socialization works upon such inert and malleable human material, where, in the established social order, are to be found the frustrated ambitions, privations and social frictions to motivate any practical movement for change?

The third general conclusion that can be drawn from the foregoing considerations has to do with the widespread opposition amongst social scientists to 'biologism'. For the thorough-going 'anti-naturalists' among them there is certainly no paradox in this opposition, but, as we have seen, there is reason to suspect that important and persistent areas of explanatory weakness in the human sciences can be linked precisely to this thorough-going anti-naturalism. For the naturalistic traditions within the human and social sciences, on the other hand, there *is* a paradox in their opposition to 'biologism'. The characteristic position of social scientific naturalism is to assert on the one hand the existence of an autonomous domain of social and cultural facts as an *ontological* presupposition of the autonomy of the social sciences from biology. At the same time, it is maintained as a *methodological* presupposition of the scientific status of their discipline, that the broad principles of scientific method are applicable in this distinct object-domain. There is, of course, no contradiction here, but it is very difficult to give a rationale for this combination of methodological naturalism with ontological anti-naturalism without some form of commitment to the pertinence of biological concepts and explanations in the human sciences. For one thing, it is difficult to see why human societies and cultures act as causal orders in a way that is sufficiently like the functioning of natural systems to ground the possibility of an application of natural-science methodologies to them. Furthermore, it is difficult to see how the methodological naturalist in the human sciences can avoid recognizing the parallels between the human science/biology relationship and, for example, the biology/chemistry relationship. Biological processes certainly constitute an autonomous causal order *vis-à-vis* chemical processes, but the pertinence of chemistry to scientific biology could hardly be seriously denied. Methodological naturalism in other disciplines has generally been taken to be vindicated by the achievement of theoretical integration ('entrenchment') and explanatory links with other fields of science. Why should not methodological naturalists in the human sciences take a similar view? I think it can be shown that the philosophical priority of establishing the autonomy of the social sciences has so effectively governed concept-construction in even the main methodological naturalist tradition in the social sciences that *relations*, as opposed to *differences* between the natural and the cultural have become literally unthinkable. This can be very well illustrated by the differences between the *conclusions* which Durkheim draws from his arguments in Book 1 of his methodological classic, *Suicide*, and what those arguments actually show.

Finally, in this section of my talk, I want to suggest that the non-necessity, even paradoxically, of our contemporary cultural alignments *vis-à-vis* biologism is underlined by their very historical specificity. I've already suggested that the eugenic project, for example, has had its leftist and 'progressive' advocates as well as its reactionary ones. The same is more generally true of the political receptions and uses of Darwinism. As a biological doctrine it was intially received with suspicion or hostility in conservative circles, and was widely welcomed by anti-clerical reformers, radicals and revolutionaries. Marx and Engels, especially, welcomed Darwinism because it appeared to take a whole domain of nature out of the grip of teleological and hence idealist forms of thought: it was a major step in the triumph of the materialist world-view. But they also welcomed it because it showed in a peculiarly striking way the existence of history, process, change, innovation in the natural world. Naturalism and materialism could now no longer be employed to 'eternalize' the social *status quo*. If dialectics and change were principles of nature, and humanity itself a part of nature, then how could it be denied that dialectics and change were also principles of human society? In the third quarter of the nineteenth century, as I have shown elsewhere, German liberals such as Ernst Haeckel were able to employ Darwinism as a specific *social* doctrine of change and progress against an authoritarian state and clerical reaction. Later on in the century, it is true, racist and sexist uses of Darwinism tended to predominate, but there remained important radical uses of Darwinian and other evolutionary ideas. This was especially true as the credibility of natural selection is the principal mechanism of evolution declined. Adaptation through use and the inheritance of acquired characteristics made possible theoretical fusions of cultural and biological evolution in which the provision of morally acceptable and 'progressive' cultural environments could be argued on biological grounds. Bebel's vastly influential *Women and Socialism* made extensive use of arguments of this type.

I have argued elsewhere[7] against advocates of a historical view of science as internally related to, and more or less directly homogeneous with, ruling class interest and perspectives. Much of our contemporary leftist opposition to 'biologism' works, either explicitly or implicitly, with some such historical view of the place of scientific ideas in culture. Against that view, I have sketched an alternative view of science as a more or less autonomous cultural process, appropriating and transforming the cultural resources of its time, but also itself serving as a cultural resource for competing social groupings, popular movements, social classes and other political forces.

The relative openness in the availability of scientific ideas, including biological ideas, to appropriation by diverse and often contradictory movements is a function of at least three levels of contingency which intervene between a scientific idea and its cultural use. First, it has to be recognized that the conceptual position in any scientific discipline at any historical moment is unlikely to be wholly stable or concensual. Particular, competing versions of evolutionary biology, for example, may present quite radically different prospects for cultural or political exploitation. In the historical episode just mentioned, the evolutionary mechanisms of natural selection and the inheritance of acquired characteristics have radically different political histories. The second level of contingency, or source of possible variation in cultural appropriations of scientific ideas concerns the *intellectual means* of appropriation. To make, say, biological ideas yield conclusions about human history and society, some intellectual work has to be done. Either explicitly or implicitly, theoretical assumptions—usually philosophical—are needed to establish a bridge between biological theories and the doctrines of a particular cultural or political movement. Metaphysical naturalism or materialism, for instance, in some version or other, is a necessary assumption for *any* such use of biological ideas. The precise *nature* of such metaphysical naturalisms (reductionist, non-reductionist, historical emergentist, dialectical materialist or whatever) will make a considerable difference to which social or political interests are served by the resulting doctrine. I have elsewhere introduced the idea of 'mediating discourses' as a way of conceptualizing the metaphysical, moral and other presuppositions which are involved in any cultural appropriation of scientific ideas.

There is, to conclude, a third source of variation in cultural or political uses of scientific ideas. This is that one and the same

[7] T. Benton, 'Natural Science and Cultural Struggles' in *Issues in Marxist Philosophy*, II, Ruben and Mepham (eds) (Hassocks: Harvester, 1979), and T. Benton, 'Social Darwinism and Socialist Darwinism in Germany 1860–1900', *Rivista di Filosofia* **22–23** (giugno 1982), 79–121.

intellectual formation may be the instrument of quite diverse political interventions in different historical conjunctures, or with respect to different fields of cultural or political struggle. Whereas, for example, a liberal individualist form of social Darwinism could play a radical, progressive role against an authoritarian state in the hands of a semi-feudal landowning class, the same set of ideas could play a reactionary role *vis-à-vis* the colonial domination of ethnically distinct peoples. In a subsequent conjuncture more or less indistinguishable ideas could be used to the favour a now predominantly capitalist social order against more radical challenges from the left. As I shall suggest in part II of this talk, Marx, and, especially, Engels were strongly placed to come to terms theoretically with these problems. As enthusiastic advocates of Darwinism in biology, and of naturalism as a general philosophical approach to humanity, the paradox of the increasingly conservative character of social Darwinism in the last quarter of the nineteenth century presented itself to them in a particular extreme and pressing way. The remainder of my talk draws upon the arguments used by Marx and Engels in defending their own naturalistic and materialistic philosophy of human nature whilst simultaneously rejecting politically conservative forms of social Darwinism.

II

So far I have tried to expose a number of paradoxes and problems which must be faced by both the political left and the defenders of the autonomy of the social sciences if they are to persist in their opposition to biological determinism. I now want to turn to the more positive task of exploring prospective solutions to these problems and paradoxes.

The first part of my argument is an attempt to show, beginning with premises broadly favourable to sociobiology, and deploying arguments (hopefully!) consistent with modern biological theory, that the autonomy of culture is itself a consequence of human biology.

The intent of this part of the argument is to demonstrate, on biological assumptions, the autonomy of human culture in at least two respects. First, the claim is that there is an indeterminacy in the relationship between human genotype and specific behavioural repertoires, such that the latter cannot be explained in terms of the former. Second, it is argued that culture is autonomous in the sense that it operates as a distinct causal order with determinate effects on human biology. This first part of my argument, then, is designed to sustain the positions of both political and social scientific critics of sociobiology, but by means of an argument which ought to win the approval of the sociobiologists themselves.

The second part of my argument begins by further sustaining the thesis of the autonomy of culture from human biology, but goes on to show that this autonomy must be recognized to be an 'autonomy-within-limits', only. It is further argued that, though these limits to the autonomy of culture are themselves historically variable, there nevertheless remain ultimate 'outer' limits to the variability of cultures. These outer limits are, it is argued, both biological and, more broadly, 'natural', and they are non-trivial in their political and in their social scientific implications. The main burden of this part of the argument, then, is to show that the thesis of the autonomy of culture is quite consistent with a weak, but non-trivial biological determinism. Moreover, any explanatory strategy in the human sciences which failed to take this into account would be fundamentally flawed, as would any political strategy of the left.

(a) *Biological Assumptions and the Autonomy of Culture*

I shall begin with an assumption which, stated in very general terms, would command wide assent among both sociobiologists and their leading opponents. This is that, whether or not any specific human behavioural repertoires are subject to genetic determination, it is plausible to assume that human beings possess some *general capacities* and tendencies which *are* subject to genetic determination. At least some of these must be supposed to be conditions of possibility of culture itself. The capacity for sensory discrimination is, I suspect, one such capacity that would be accepted uncontroversially by each side. Such natural capacities, we may suppose, whilst being conditions of possibility of culture in general, will be exercised, or manifested, in diverse ways in different environmental or cultural contexts.

Now, before attempting the much more controversial exercise of specifying, in a more detailed way, some of these natural capacities and tendencies, I will try to guard against three possible types of misinterpretation. First I am not, in specifying these capacities or tendencies, claiming either that they amount to a *complete* theory of human nature, or that these natural characteristics are of special significance *vis-à-vis* the others. They are selected for the purposes of my present argument. That is all. Secondly, I do not intend it to be understood that I regard these natural capacities as part of a theory of human nature in the sense that their possession is *distinctive* of *Homo sapiens*. It is quite consistent with my thesis that they are possessed by other species (indeed, I think they all are, to some degree at least, so shared). Thirdly, and perhaps most important, I do not mean by a 'natural' capacity or tendency, one which could be manifested by a human being in abstraction from some specific cultural form. I take it as established, since the time of Adam Ferguson,[8] that the social state is the natural state for human kind, such that not only the greater part of human activity, but even sustained existence itself is not possible independently of some sort of cultural context.

My initial assumption, then, is that a distinction can be made between two sorts of human capacities (and related tendencies, dispositions, and so on). The first sort (let us call them 'natural capacities') are distinguished by their generality in the human species, across historical periods and diverse cultures. Their *possession* is, then, independent of membership in, or acquisition of, any *specific* culture. They are, of course, *exercised* in specific cultural contexts and forms, and they, like their possessors, can only exist in a stable way in *some* cultural context or other. The point is simply that their *possession* is dependent on no *specific* cultural acquisition. Indeed, where these natural capacities are shared with other animals, they may be both possessed *and* exercised in the absence of any cultural context. The capacities underlying feeding, locomotion and mating would be obvious examples here.

The second sort of human capacity is distinctive in that not only its exercise, but its very possession is dependent upon some specific cultural acquisition. Since such capacities are multiplied by the historical development of the human species I shall call them 'historical capacities'. If we take the capacities underlying feeding-behaviour as an example of such natural capacities, then, of course, in the human case, specific feeding-behaviours, specific *exercises* of these capacities, will indeed be culturally specific. By contrast, the capacity to cook food is a capacity whose specific exercises are subject to enormous cultural variability, but which cannot exist even as a capacity unless certain specific cultural conquests are already established: manual skills have to be acquired, fire, or other sources of heat have to be understood and subjected to minimal deliberate control, a store of knowledge as to the effects of heat on different food-substances has to be acquired, and so on.

Though I have so far done no more than distinguish, in an elementary way, these two sorts of capacity, it is important for the subsequent line of argument to notice that there are definite logical relationships between them. Most significantly for my purposes, there is an asymmetrical relationship, such that for any specific historical capacity, its possession presupposes the prior possession *and exercise* of some set of natural capacities, whilst, conversely, the mere possession of any specific set of natural capacities neither presupposes nor implies the possession of any historical capacity.

[8] A. Ferguson, *An Essay on the History of Civil Society* (Edinburgh: 1767).

A capacity to 'A' may be said to be a natural capacity of human beings if it is generally true of normal adults that in virtue of their structure, constitution and state they are able to perform A, provided A's external conditions of possibility are present. A tendency to 'B' on the other hand, may be said to be a natural tendency of human beings if it is generally true of normal adults that they will do B when subject to the appropriate internal and external stimuli unless there are countervailing pressures. A natural tendency in this sense always presupposes a natural capacity. In my view sensory discrimination, cognitive appraisal, symbolic co-ordination of activity and deliberate intervention into natural processes are all general types of activity the capacity to perform which is a natural capacity for human beings. Although any specific exercise of these capacities may be regarded as a cultural activity, mere *possession* of them may be regarded as a general *condition of possibility* of the relevant cultural activity (or of cultural activity in general) and does not presuppose any specific prior cultural acquisition. As examples of natural tendencies we may take seeking sexual satisfaction in the context of more or less extended pair-relationships, and co-operative acquisition of means of subsistence.

My assumption is that these tendencies and capacities (along, probably, with many others) are natural to human beings, in the sense specified above, and so may be regarded not as cultural acquisitions, but, instead, to have arisen as a result of the operation of natural processes, presumably, in the main, as the outcome of natural selection acting upon the genetic constitution of our ancestor-populations. I shall regard it as relatively uncontroversial that such capacities and tendencies may be regarded as being explicable (in principle, at least) diachronically in terms of natural selection, and synchronically in terms of human anatomy and physiology. It is important to note that my assumption here is restricted to the explanation of the capacities and tendencies, and not to any *specific* behavioural exercise or performance, but it is still an assumption that would find favour with most sociobiologists.

Now, once the capacities for cognitive appraisal, for symbolic co-ordination of activity, for deliberate intervention in natural processes, together with a tendency to seek co-operatively for means of subsistence have become established in an organic population (human, or, more broadly, primate), certain consequences follow. First, the systematic exercise of these capacities in a given natural environment constitutes the acquisition of a culture. This means, among other things, acquisition of specific knowledges, organizational competences and practical skills. These acquisitions are cumulative and are the foundations of new, *historical* capacities and tendencies. A historical capacity as defined above is one possessed by members of only some cultures and which is distinguished from a natural capacity in that its very *possession* presupposes some specific cultural acquisition.

If we now suppose the co-existence of more or less practically isolated sub-populations of our species, existing in more or less diverse environmental conditions for more or less extended periods of time, the cumulative, and therefore directional character of their cultural acquisition may be expected to result in significant and increasing degrees of cultural diversity. If we now adopt, for the sake of argument, the sociobiologists' view that the units upon which natural selection operates are the elements of the individual genotype, then the following important consequences follow. First, that the reproductive success of individuals, and hence the differential distribution of genetic material in the total population will be determined in part, at least, by the cultural acquisitions of the whole interbreeding sub-population. For average members of two distinct sub-populations of hunting-and-gathering people, for example, reproductive potential will be in part determined, no doubt, by sheer availability of means of subsistence, but it will also be determined in part by differential acquisitions of organizational competences, knowledges and manipulative skills as between the two cultures. Second, since both sub-populations may be supposed to embody the natural human tendency to seek means of subsistence co-operatively (a sexual and often also an age-division of labour, forms of co-operation in hunting, etc.) consumption is no longer a matter of a direct interaction of individual and enviroment, but the result of yet another variable cultural acquisition: norms of distribution of co-operatively acquired means of subsistence. As between individuals *within* each sub-population, now, differential reproductive prospects must arise on the basis of the application of these norms of distribution. In cases of extreme hardship these norms may decide who lives and who dies.

On the basis of these considerations, then, we may say that even on the assumption that certain capacities of human beings are natural capacities, and are wholly explicable, both synchronically and diachronically, in biological terms, the consequences of sustained, *exercise* of these natural capacities are:

1. The acquisition of culture (for my purposes, this may be taken as equivalent to the acquisition of historical capacities).
2. The subjection of individual reproductive success, and therefore of the gene-pool of the population, to at least two levels of cultural determination.
3. A partial abrogation of natural selection with respect to the reproductive prospects of each individual member of a culture. In so far as natural selection continues to operate, it does so through

the refracting medium of the (presumably and predominantly) contingent and unforeseen effects of normative choices on genetic survival. [Eugenics, in this interpretation, would be a practice of deliberate intervention in a natural process (human reproduction) on the basis of normative choices made for the sake of *foreseen* effects on genetic survival. Only with eugenics does Darwin's metaphor of 'natural selection' truly return to its source. For the most part, the genetic effects of human social practices are unintended, unforeseen, and unrecognized consequences of them.]

Further consideration of the distinction between natural and historical capacities will allow me to make clearer the precise bearing of these points on the questions at stake between advocates of biological determinism and the autonomy of culture. Once those capacities which are the natural conditions of possibility of culture are exercised in a sustained way, the result, as we have seen, is a diversification of cumulative cultural forms. The cumulative acquisition of culture is itself sufficient to establish in human beings new capacities, historical capacities, which would not otherwise be possessed. The capacities for aesthetic creation and appreciation, for example, presuppose natural capacities such as sensory discrimination and deliberate intervention into natural processes, but these and other natural capacities are jointly *insufficient* to establish aesthetic capacities. To acquire these capacities, human individuals must learn, and so belong to cultures which can teach, a common stock of relevant knowledges, skills, normative rules and symbolic means. I shall consider another example a little later. Now, in so far as specific behavioural repertoires, possible in some cultures, and at some periods in their history, but not at others, have to be regarded as manifestations of *historical* capacities, then the relationship between these repertoires and any natural capacities will be indirect, mediated, and attenuated. In other words, the long-term consequences of the exercise of natural powers is the emergence of behavioural repertoires which are increasingly autonomous *vis-à-vis* the natural capacities, and, hence, genetic constitution which were their original condition of possibility.

Several important consequences for the relationship between human culture and human biology can now be shown. First, the biological individual, the 'privileged' site for selective pressures according to contemporary social Darwinism, must be regarded as subject to selective pressures of two radically heterogeneous types. The chances for reproductive success of the individual are jointly determined by the natural and by the social, or cultural environment. Some proponents of the autonomy of culture would here argue that once cultural forms have

125

become established, all of the interactions between individuals and nature are mediated by it, so that the natural/cultural environment distinction falls. Instead of answering this argument directly, I shall continue to beg the question, apparently in favour of biological determinism, since I hope to show that, in doing so, I can, in fact, strengthen the argument for the autonomy of culture.

I shall consider first the effects of the existence of culture on the continued action of natural selection. To the extent that the reproductive success of the individual members of a human culture is a function of the overall cultural achievement of the sub-population to which he/she belongs, then to that extent, the primary site of natural selective pressures is displaced from individual to group, or cultural competition. (It should be noted that, in this very general version, the idea of group-selection is not subject to the standard objections to group-selection explanations of the specific trait of 'altruism'.) It is a further consequence of this displacement to group competition that, in so far as natural selection continues to affect the human gene-pool at all, its tendency will be to produce an intensive and extensive augmentation of those very natural capacities which facilitate cultural achievement. In short, the *effect* of any continued operation of natural selection is to produce characteristics which progressively *reduce* the causal importance of natural selection itself.

Turning, now, to the implications the emergence of social, or 'cultural' selection, it can be shown that these sustain the thesis of the 'autonomy of culture' in a further respect. First, the flexibility and variability of behavioural repertoires) what a prominent sociobiologist, Richard Dawkins has recently referred to as 'flexible reprogrammability'[9]) *vis-à-vis* underlying natural capacities, probably augmented by continuing residual natural selection, means that those behavioural characteristics upon which *cultural selection* operates will be increasingly distantly related to individual genotypes. This makes it highly implausible to suppose that any specific behavioural repertoire could ever become genetically 'fixed' through the operation of cultural selection. This could happen only if such behavioural repertoires were phenotypical expressions of genotype (or, at least, strongly correlated with them) and if culturally selective pressures were sustained over very long periods of time. *Ex hypothesi* the satisfaction of the first condition is ruled out, whilst the second is rendered implausible by the relative rapidity of cultural change as compared with biological. The social structures, such as kinship systems, which distribute genetic life-chances are just not stable for sufficiently long periods of time. Even the very 'optimistic' thousand-year rule proferred by Lumsden

[9] R. Dawkins, *The Selfish Gene* (Oxford: Oxford University Press, 1976).

and Wilson[10] for significant genetic change to occur seems to place implausible requirements on the stability of the relevant cultural forms.

In so far, then, as 'cultural selection' may be supposed to operate as an autonomous causal order, with effects on the human gene-pool, these effects will not be to biologically fix specific behavioural characteristics. If, however, those natural capacities (cognitive appraisal, symbolic co-ordination of activity, and so on) which are conditions of possibility of culture, or which facilitate the acquisition of culture are possessed to different degrees in different individuals, or in different human sub-populations we may suppose that the long-term effects of cultural selection will be to augment those biological characteristics which are the basis of such natural capacities. Dawkins' 'flexible reprogrammmability', for example, would, on this view, be a natural capacity which could be expected to be augmented by the long-term effects of cultural selection. This, in turn, means further pressure towards indeterminacy in the relationship between individual genotype and specific behaviour repertoires.

Three important conclusions with a bearing on the biological determinism/cultural autonomy can now be drawn:

1. Starting out with assumptions favourable to sociobiology and using arguments which are (I hope!) consistent with contemporary biological theory, I have generated conclusions favourable to the thesis of the autonomy of cultural practices *vis-à-vis* human genetic constitution, an autonomy rooted in human biology itself.
2. The case advanced by Sahlins and other advocates of the autonomy of culture from biological determinants is sustained and strengthened, but at the same time shown to be consistent with, and even partially explained in terms of, a weak biological determinism of the kind advocated by Rosenberg and other proponents of sociobiology.
3. The argument, whilst maintaining the pertinence of a biological approach to understanding and explaining human capacities and activities, nevertheless undermines the rationale of at least two specific types of use of biological ideas to which the political left has objected. First, the literature deriving from animal ethology. The main argumentative strategy used in this literature is to 'naturalize' and so 'eternalize' certain human behavioural repertoires on the basis of analogies between them and the behaviour repertoires of other animals (aggression, territoriality, etc.). Now, the biological arguments presented here, which show these repertoires to be, in general, manifestations of historical

[10] C. J. Lumsden and E. O. Wilson, *Genes, Mind and Culture* (Cambridge, Mass.: Harvard University Press, 1981).

rather than natural capacities, in the human case, make it highly
implausible to suppose that classifications of behaviour made on
the basis of animal/human analogies denote natural kinds. Similar
considerations apply to the controversial attempts to interpret
behavioural repertoires, such as successful performance of IQ
tests, as wholly or mainly expressions of genotype. Again, the
important point here is not that this can be shown, but that it can
be shown by an argument which begins with assumptions
favourable to a biological interpretation of human behaviour.

(b) *Biological Nature and the Limits to the Autonomy of Culture*

So much can be derived from a consideration of the implications of the
sustained human exercise of capacities, on the supposition that they are
'natural', and acquired in accordance with the principles of modern
biological theory. We are now in a position to embark on the next stage
of the argument which will begin by further sustaining the 'autonomy of
culture' thesis, but end by showing that it is subject to continuing
limitations which are of both social scientific and political significance.
Though the general drift of my argument so far owes a good deal to the
work of Marx and Engels, this part of it is more specifically based on a
very condensed argument used by both of them against social
Darwinism. The argument concerns the effects not of culture as such,
but of one historical capacity in particular, that of production. The
natural capacities for cognitive appraisal, symbolic co-ordination of
action, and deliberate intervention in natural processes are separately
necessary for production, but they are not jointly sufficient. Definite
organizational competences, technical skills and stocks of knowledge
are indispensable to the historical emergence of the historical capacity
to produce (a conceptual truth which is illustrated by the relative
lateness of the appearance of productive, as distinct from hunting-and-
gathering, cultures in human history). The exercise of productive
powers, productive activity, can be characterized as an organized
intervention into natural processes the outcome of which is the
provision of means of subsistence which would not otherwise be
available—i.e. which would not be provided by nature unaided by
human social practices. The first stock breeders and agriculturalists
are, in this sense, the first producers.

For Marx and Engels the historical emergence of production is a
decisive moment. Once human beings are able to produce means of
subsistence which nature would not otherwise provide they immediately mitigate the consequences of the Malthusian struggle for existence.
As is well known, Malthus's law of population postulated a necesary
struggle for existence deriving from a mathematical disparity bctween

the reproductive powers of a species and the rate at which means of subsistence could be expected to expand. Since the former necessarily outstripped the latter, availability of means of subsistence must exert a persistent mediate or immediate pressure on population: of all the offspring produced, only some will survive in the struggle for life. Applied to the human species, Malthus's law was taken to be a powerful argument to the effect that well-meaning attempts to improve the lot of the poor were bound to be self-defeating. The struggle for existence, with its associated misery and vice would simply reassert itself at new, higher population levels.

Now, as Marx and Engels argued, the historical emergence of the power of production modifies the effects of the law so far as the human species is concerned. The pressure on population exerted by shortage of means of subsistence can be offset in a way which is subject to no obvious outer limit by the cumulative expansion of human productive powers. Human offspring have their survival chances greatly enhanced once they inhabit cultures which have acquired the power to produce what nature would not otherwise have provided. The struggle for existence is gradually transformed, in the human case, into a struggle for wealth, social power, and other cultural acquisitions. As for the other side of the Malthusian balance, it was left to the German Marxist, August Bebel, in his *Women and Socialism*,[11] to show that the rate at which human beings exercise their reproductive powers, too, is a quantity regulated not by biology, but by culture, and is significantly affected, among other things, by the degree of subordination or emancipation of women.

In his later years Engels was faced by the apparent paradox that Darwinian theory, which he had welcomed enthusiastically from the start, was now being increasingly used to support conservative political causes. Engels's response was to deploy these already available arguments against Malthus to undermine social Darwinism. The point of application of the arguments is the supposed reliance of Darwin's concept of natural selection on the Malthusian idea of a necessary struggle for existence. Whereas Malthus had drawn no conclusions for the biological *quality* of populations from his law, Darwin saw that such consequences would follow. Amongst the innumerable inherited differences possessed by members of a population, some would confer advantages in the struggle for existence and so would result in differential survival chances and opportunities for reproduction. Directly, then, production consolidates and augments the abrogation or mitigation of natural selection on human populations which has already been established with the acquisition of culture itself. The

[11] A. Bebel, *Die Frau und der Socialismus* (Dietz, 1980).

phasing out of the struggle for existence which production ushers in is at the same time the phasing out of 'selection' of both types—social and natural. This is all Engels needs. It is enough to show the error involved in the social Darwinists' representation of, for example, capitalist competition as the direct expression of a biological law.

Unfortunately, the argument is flawed, in that Engels, like Darwin himself, was mistaken in supposing that the Darwinian and Malthusian struggles for existence are the same. In fact they are quite different, although it may be that enough of an analogy persists for Engels's argument to be successfully reconstructed. What is of interest for my themes, however, are Marx's and Engels's arguments against the applicability of the specifically Malthusian struggle to the human case beyond the emergence of production. Much of my argument so far, and, indeed, much of our contemporary debate, poses the question of the pertinence of biology to the understanding of the human species as if this were the same as the question of the pertinence of genetics. In fact, Malthus's law can be seen as a putative law of human ecology. It sets out to indicate the parameters which circumscribe variations in the size of populations under given environmental circumstances: in abstraction from any supposed *qualitive* implications of the law, its purely quantitative ones are of biological significance. The idea of the struggle for existence is a putative explanation of the tendency of natural populations to remain within limits set by their environmental conditions of life.

In the human case, the argument of Marx and Engels suggests that the human productive power to modify those environmental conditions offsets the natural mechanism which equilibrates population densities with environmental resources.

But it is at this point that the question has to be confronted: to what extent is this apparent autonomy which human beings, through their acquisition of cultural and historical powers, have established *vis-à-vis* internal and external nature, thinkable as an *absolute* autonomy. In what sense, if at all, does it continue to be an 'autonomy-within-limits'? First, it is significant that Engels does not speak simply of an end to the struggle for existence with the emergence of production. *Struggle* persists, but in new forms, which are changed with each successive historical change. These new forms of struggle are, it seems reasonable to suppose, thought of by Engels as 'transformed forms' of the struggle for existence, or as the struggle for existence mediated and refracted in culture. This is one way of giving sense to the Marxian idea that individuals enter into production relations which are independent of their will. Though production relations are certainly social relations, their relative inflexibility can be seen to derive in part from their character as forms of mediation between nature and culture. If this is so, then it suggests that specific extents and types of autonomy of culture *vis-à-vis* the constraints of external nature are localized historical conquests of particular cultures: given forms of knowledge, organizational capacities and practical skills determine a specific type and level of autonomy from a continually present modifiable-only-within-limits natural environment. On this view, human cultural autonomy certainly is an autonomy-within-limits, though the limits here are themselves historically variable.

This, in turn, leads to a new question—or perhaps it is just a new way of posing the original one. Given that the limits within which culture is autonomous are historically modifiable, is there any outer limit to the extent of this modification? There are interpretations of the Marxian idea of communism as a 'realm' of freedom', by contrast with its human pre-history as a 'realm of necessity', which suggest a negative answer to this question. The autonomy of human culture from its natural context is potentially absolute: a complete, multi-faceted, 'humanization of nature'. That this cannot be the case is demonstrable on the basis of the concepts and distinctions so far advocated. Both natural and historical capacities are defined as human abilities to engage in certain activities in the presence *of their external conditions of possibility*. For human beings, these external conditions are both natural and social. The capacity for production, for example, may be lost due to a cultural degeneration, or a collapse of the social order. More centrally for my present argument, this capacity may be lost as a result of the absence, or prior destruction, of its natural conditions of possibility. Apart from the physical and mental powers of human beings, these natural conditions of possibility in the case of production will include both the means of production and the raw materials involved in the process. Of course both these elements will usually be natural objects or materials which are already 'worked' by human activity, but 'worked' nature always has as its ultimate condition of possibility, unworked nature.

Now, since the cumulative exercise of human productive powers tends to extend the scope and magnitude of our interventions into natural processes, without foreseeable limits, the future continuation of this cumulative power poses this possibility: the possibility that among the (presumably unintended) consequences of this continued advance will be interventions into natural processes which undermine the maintenance or reproduction of those very natural mechanisms upon which human productive activity, and even human life itself, is premised. In short, the pursuit of the autonomy of culture, in at least one of its aspects, carries with it a risk, proportionate to its success, of an environmental catastrophe. This risk, perhaps the most dramatic possible exemplification (apart, perhaps, from nuclear warfare, whose possibility can be explained in similar terms) of the non-triviality of biological constraints on human culture, is itself a corollary of the specific autonomy acquired by human populations from the ecological principle governing the populations of other species. This argument can itself be understood as but one detailed specification of the relationship between the human species and its natural conditions of existence which was expressed more succinctly and more elegantly by Marx in his *Economic and Philosophical Manuscripts* of 1844: 'Nature is man's *inorganic body*—nature, that is in so far as it is not itself human body. Man *lives* on nature—means that nature is his *body*, with which he must remain in continuous interchange if he is not to die. That man's physical and spiritual life is linked to nature means simply that nature is linked to itself, for man is a part of nature'.[12]

I hope I have shown that a weak biological determinism, one which does not seek to explain specific cultural contents, but restricts itself to an attempt to specify underlying natural capacities and tendencies which operate as limits on the variation of culture is, for all that, not trivial in its consequences for our view of human history and its prospects. In this respect, at least, Sahlins is wrong when he says limits are mere 'negative determinations', of no great interest to social scientists. I hope I have also shown that a weak biological determinism of this sort is by no means incompatible with cultural diversity and major historical change. Indeed, it goes some way to explain the underlying conditions of possibility for both, though it can of its own resources actually explain neither. Further, I have used weak biological determinism to show how the rationale of the most influential conservative appropriations of biological ideas in the human sciences may be undermined.

Finally, since I think it can also be shown that capitalism is an economic system perfectly designed as an instrument for bringing about ecological catastrophe as its long-term effect, I think I have provided strong arguments for the political left, not to mention anyone else who favours the survival of the human species and all those other species we are liable to take with us, to simultaneously embrace biological determinism and work for the end of capitalism.

---

[12] K. Marx 'Economic and Philosophic Manuscripts of 1844', in K. Marx and F. Engels, *Collected Works*, 3 (London; Lawrence and Wishart, 1975), 276.

Select Bibliography

D. Barash, *Sociobiology: The Whisperings Within* (London: Fontana, 1979).

T. Benton, 'Natural Science and Cultural Struggles', in *Issues in Marxist Philosophy* II, Ruben and Mepham (eds) (Hassocks: Harvester, 1979); 'Social Darwinism and Socialist Darwinism in Germany 1860 to 1900', *Rivista di Filosofia* **22–23** (giugno 1982), 79–121.

R. Dawkins, *The Selfish Gene* (Oxford: Oxford University Press 1976).

S. J. Gould, *Ever Since Darwin* (New York: W. W. Norton, 1977).

D. Lockwood, 'Race, Conflict and Plural Society', in *Race and Racialism*, S. Zubaida (London, Tavistock, 1970).

D. Morris, *The Human Zoo* (London: Jonathan Cape, 1969).

A. Rosenberg, *Sociobiology and the Preemption of Social Science* (Oxford: Blackwell, 1981).

M. D. Sahlins, *The Use and Abuse of Biology* (London: Tavistock, 1977).

J. Maynard-Smith, *The Theory of Evolution* (Harmondsworth: Penguin, 1975).

E. O. Wilson, *Sociobiology, The New Synthesis* (Cambridge, Mass.: Harvard University Press, 1975); *On Human Nature* (Cambridge, Mass.: Harvard University Press, 1978).

Moral Objectivity

JONATHAN LEAR

Morality exercises a deep and questionable influence on the way we live our lives. The influence is deep both because moral injunctions are embedded in our psyches long before we can reflect on their status and because even after we become reflective agents, the question of how we should live our lives among others is intimately bound up with the more general question of how we should live our lives: our stance toward morality and our conception of our lives as having significance are of a piece. The influence is questionable because morality pretends to a level of objectivity that it may not possess. Moral injunctions are meant to be binding on us in some way that is independent of the desires or preferences we may happen to have. When one asserts that a certain action is morally worthy or shameful one is, *prime facie*, doing more than merely expressing approval or disapproval or trying to get others to act as instruments of one's own will. If moral assertions were shown, at bottom, to be merely such exhortations, then they would be shown to wear a disguise. Morality would be revealed as pretending to an objectivity it does not have, and such a revelation could not but have a profound impact on our lives. It is doubtful that such a revelation could be kept locked up inside our studies.[1]

The debate over the objectivity or non-objectivity of ethics takes place in the shadow of Kant. He has bequeathed to us both a powerful conception of morality and the framework for discussing questions of objectivity. The appeal of Kantian ethics is that it directly links morality to a dignified conception of man as a rationally free agent. Kant severed the tie between morality and the pursuit of happiness because, he argued, morality cannot be binding on an agent in virtue of desires he just happens to have. The agent might have lacked those desires and, Kant argued, it was intolerable that an agent should be bound to morality by so contingent a thread. Morality should bind an agent solely in so far as he is rational; thus morality, for Kant, should be constituted by the formal laws of rationality alone. In regarding himself as a purely rational agent, for the purposes of making a moral judgment, a man treated himself as free of the causal sway of particular desires, passions, interests that might otherwise engage him. In morality, as Kant conceived it, man could realize his highest freedom.

[1] See Bernard Williams, *Shame and Necessity* (London: Faber and Faber, forthcoming); and my "Ethics, Mathematics and Relativism", *Mind* 92 (1983).

Such a conception has an austere, awesome appeal. And Kant's negative critique seriously challenges its intended target; namely, those eighteenth-century moral theories which based morality on the pursuit of happiness. But as a critique of Aristotelian ethics, in which ethics is treated as a practical guide that enables a man to achieve *eudaimonia*, it misses the mark. *Eudaimonia*, which has often been translated as 'happiness' but which is perhaps better translated as something like 'human flourishing' is not based on the satisfaction of desires that an agent may or may not possess.[2] According to Aristotle, man has an essence: there is something definite and worthwhile that it is to be a human being. *Eudaimonia* consists in the living of this potentially noble life to the fullest possible extent. Let us, for the sake of argument, translate '*eudaimonia*' as 'happiness'. Then when Aristotle asks

> Why should we not call happy the man who exercises his abilities according to the highest standards of virtue and excellence in a context which affords him sufficient resources and not merely for a brief moment but throughout his life?[3]

the answer cannot be: 'Because a man's happiness depends upon the satisfaction of his desires which may or may not bear any relation to his living a virtuous life'. The pursuit of happiness, for Aristotle, must be clearly distinguished from the pursuit of pleasure, though many mistakenly suppose that in pursuing pleasure they pursue happiness. In devoting themselves to pleasure, they act slavishly toward their desires and, in effect choose the life of an animal.[4] Kant's critique does not undermine a morality based on *eudaimonia*, not because *eudaimonia* must be conceived of independently of all desires, nor because the desires involved in *eudaimonia* are non-contingently shared by all humans, but because they are non-contingently shared by those who are living a life of *eudaimonia*.

The most important defect of Kantian ethics, Hegel argued, is that it lacks content.[5] From a purely formal principle of rationality one cannot derive any substantial conclusions about how to act. Yet there is one important point on which Kant and Hegel agreed: that Kantian ethics

[2] For a discussion of '*eudaimonia*' as 'human flourishing', see John Cooper, *Reason and Human Good in Aristotle* (Cambridge, Mass.: Harvard University Press, 1975).
[3] *Nicomachean Ethics* I.10, 1101a14–16.
[4] *Ibid.* I.5, 1095b14–22; I.9, 1099b32ff.
[5] See e.g. G. W. F. Hegel, *Phenomenology of Spirit*, A. V. Miller (trans.) (New York: Oxford University Press, 1977), §§ 599–671; *Philosophy of Right*, T. M. Knox (trans.) (New York: Oxford University Press, 1980), §§ 105–140 (*N.B.* the remarks to § 135 and § 139); *History of Philosophy*, III, E. S. Haldane and F. H. Simson (trans.) (New York: Humanities Press, 1974), 457–464.

represented a significant advance in moral thinking. In conceiving himself as a purely rational agent, man could legislate the moral law to himself. For Kant, morality was at last freed from the slavish pursuit of happiness or the unreflective obedience to divine dictates. For Hegel, man at last realized his subjectivity, that the moral law must be self-legislated, and this was a necessary stage in the development of an adequate ethical consciousness. The virtuous citizen of the Athenian polis, Hegel thought, unreflectively identified with the polis and obeyed its laws. The radical subjectivity of Kantian ethics separated the moral agent from his social context—at the price, Hegel thought, of emptiness—but it paved the way for a higher reconciliation between the reflective moral agent and the objective social world.

The charge of emptiness continues to be made against Kantian ethics, and it is a charge that ought to be investigated seriously. For there remains widespread agreement that Kantian ethics describes what the objective stance in morality is:[6] in viewing the world objectively I reflectively detach myself from my present concerns, interests and situation and conceive of myself simply as one agent among others. But, Bernard Williams has recently argued, if one actually succeeds in viewing the interests and concerns of all agents, including oneself, from a genuinely detached perspective, there seems to be no motivation left for acting in any particular way at all.[7] The detached standpoint carries with it no positive attitude to any agent's interests and desires. Ironically, this is an analogue in the realm of practical reason to an objection Kant himself made in the realm of pure reason. In the Paralogisms Kant argued, roughly, that if one abstracts from the ego all its conditions and determinations except for the 'I think' that must be capable of accompanying all my thoughts, then one will not be able to derive any substantial conclusions about this I which thinks.[8] Williams' point is that from the detached perspective of a mere 'I will' there are no substantial conclusions to be derived about the I

[6] See e.g. John Rawls, *A Theory of Justice* (Cambridge, Mass.: Harvard University Press, 1971); 'Kantian Constructivism in Moral Theory', *Journal of Philosophy* **77**, (1980); Thomas Nagel, *The Possibility of Altruism*, op. cit.; 'The Limits of Objectivity', in *The Tanner Lectures on Human Values*, I, S. M. McMurrin (ed.) (Salt Lake City: University of Utah Press, 1980); 'Subjective and Objective', in *Moral Questions* (Cambridge: Cambridge University Press, 1979); Bernard Williams, 'Persons, Character and Morality', 'Internal and External Reasons' in *Moral Luck*, op. cit.; 'The Presuppositions of Morality', Thyssen Conference on Transcendental Arguments, Cambridge (September 1981).

[7] Cf. Bernard Williams, op. cit. Conference on Transcendental Arguments, Cambridge (September 1981).

[8] Immanuel Kant, *Critique of Pure Reason*, N. K. Smith (trans.) (New York: St Martin's Press, 1965), A341–405, B399–432.

which wills, including of course what it should will. In response neo-Kantians have argued that the aim of the detached perspective is not to generate motivations to act but only to endorse motivations which already exist from a standpoint outside of these motivations.[9] But it remains enigmatic how the detached point of view is supposed to accomplish this, and one suspects that either it will be impotent to endorse any motivations or that it will endorse some by being covertly guilty of heteronomy: of smuggling into the 'detached' perspective the very motivations it ends up endorsing.

To gain a clearer focus let us, following Williams, distinguish internal reasons for action from external reasons.[10] There are two sorts of interpretation which can be given to sentences like 'A has reason to ϕ' or 'There is a reason for A to ϕ'. As an *internal reason*, A has some motive which will be served by his ϕ-ing, and if this is not so, the sentence is false. As an *external reason*, the sentence is not falsified by the absence of an appropriate motive. Now it would seem that there is no point in adopting the detached perspective if there are no external reasons for action.

In *The Possibility of Altruism*, Thomas Nagel argued that ultimately the only acceptable reasons for action are ones that can be formulated completely impersonally—with no reference to one's particular motives, interests or desires.[11] Even if one acts from subjective principles and motivations, Nagel argued that one is guilty of a type of irrationality if one cannot back up one's actions with reasons which are completely impersonal. 'To regard oneself as merely a person among others, one must be able to regard oneself in every respect impersonally.'[12] It follows, Nagel argued, that one's principles of practical reason must be universal, for if one operates solely with a subjective set of principles that cannot be applied from the impersonal standpoint, one is guilty of a type of dissociation: one has failed to see that one is merely one person among others.[13]

Nagel's argument does not, I think, succeed for it presents what is in fact a tautology as a substantial insight of practical reason.[14] Of course,

[9] Cf. Thomas Nagel's response to William's 'The Presupposition of Morality', Thyssen Conference on Transcendental Arguments, Cambridge (September 1981).

[10] See Bernard Williams, 'Internal and External Reasons', *Moral Luck* (Cambridge and New York: Cambridge University Press, 1982).

[11] See Thomas Nagel, *The Possibility of Altruism* (Oxford: Clarendon Press, 1970). These are what Nagel calls 'objective reasons'; cf. Ch. X.

[12] Ibid. 162.

[13] Ibid. See especially Ch. IX, §§ 5–7.

[14] *N.B.* that Hegel accused Kant of trying to derive substantial moral conclusions from formal tautologies. See note 5 above.

if one is 'to regard oneself as merely a person among others, one must be able to regard oneself in every respect impersonally', but the question arises: why regard oneself as *merely* one person among others? 'Merely' is doing too much work, for Nagel concludes that if any of one's practical reasons for action cannot be justified from the impersonal standpoint then one suffers a type of dissociation: one fails to recognize oneself as one among others. But this does not follow; one can recognize oneself as one person among others without thinking that one is merely that. Indeed, it seems to involve dissociation to regard oneself as merely that, and thus the man who seeks to justify all his reasons from a detached viewpoint seems to be the one who is suffering from dissociation.[15]

The argument against there being any external reasons portrays itself as neo-Human.[16] No external-reasons statement can by itself explain an agent's action, for the external-reasons statement can, by hypothesis, be true of an agent totally independently of his beliefs and motivations. Now it may be that an agent's believing that an external-reasons statement is true of him will help to explain his action, but of such an agent an internal-reasons statement is also true, namely, that he is motivated to act when he believes an external-reasons statement is true of him. So to understand the content of an external-reasons statement we must understand what it is for an agent to come to believe one. But how, it is asked, can an agent who does not already believe the external-reasons statement and who does not already have the appropriate internal reason come to believe the external-reasons statement? The external-reasons statement 'A has reason to ϕ' entails the claim that

(1) If the agent rationally deliberated then, whatever motivation he originally had, he would come to be motivated to ϕ

and it is objected, on Humean grounds, that all such claims are false. For, by hypothesis, there is no motivation for the agent to deliberate from to gain the new motivation.

One may object that this argument depends on a Humean anatomy of the mind, which unacceptably separates cognitive and motivational faculties, but such an objection does not get to the heart of the matter. For the argument is directed *ad hominem* against a Kantian external-reasons theorist, who believes that from rationality alone one can be motivated to act. The internal-reasons theorist need only maintain that this is not so (he may also believe that reasons and

---

[15] For a good example of this dissociation see Nagel's discussion of the practical reasoning involved when someone steps on my toe, ibid. 112–113.
[16] Williams, 'Internal and External Reasons', op. cit.

motivations are indistillably mixed). One might also try to build into the notion of rational deliberation certain ideal conditions such that once an agent is placed in those conditions he will be motivated to ϕ. Such a strategy has its attractions, but it is open to the internal-reasons theorist and, more generally, to the moral sceptic, to deny that rational deliberation requires any such ideal conditions.

What I think does turn out to be a problem for the internal reasons theorist is that his argument is *ad hominem*. Any *ad hominem* argument may legitimately adopt assumptions of the position it is trying to undermine; but if the argument purports not merely to undermine an opposing position but also to establish certain positive conclusions, then one must look carefully at the shared assumptions. The internal reasons theorist, has I think, ingeniously undermined the existing arguments that moral imperatives can be derived from rationality alone. However, if the argument is also taken to establish the positive conclusion that the only reasons for action are internal reasons, then it turns out that the internal reasons theorist is himself committed to important Kantian assumptions about practical reason. First, he assumes that reasons are divided exhaustively into those that are derivable from an agent's subjective motivations (plus any additional premises which serve to correct for false belief or add non-evaluative information) and those that are derivable from rationality alone. There is no basis for thinking that a subjunctive conditional like (1) follows from the existence of an external reason unless one assumes that if there were any reasons not based on an agent's internal motivation, they would have to be grounded in rationality. No room is left for any other type of reason; yet, I shall argue, there ought to be room.

Second, the internal-reasons theorist must to some extent treat an agent as a detached consciousness removed from the full particularity of his life. On reflection, it should not be surprising that the internal-reasons theorist should face such a problem. For he has chosen to undermine Kantian ethics via a neo-Humean acccount of practical deliberation. But Hume himself had notorious difficulty in giving any positive account of the self. Not only couldn't he find any self as an object of introspection, but more importantly for our present purposes he could give no satisfying account of a self which endures over time. However many deep philosophical problems are raised by Hume's account of the self, it remains that any account of practical reasons which does not capture the fact that we are beings who endure over time is likely to fail to portray accurately the lives we find ourselves living.

Consider, as a first example, Herman, an insurance salesman who at this moment is sitting in his car which is parked on the railroad tracks. Herman took various premiums which he received and invested them in a get-rich-quick scheme. His plan was to pay in the premiums as soon as his investment paid off; however his investment failed and in the meantime one of his clients has died. Herman is simply unwilling to face up to the shame, embarrassment and punishment that is about to fall on him. In fact, were Herman forced to live through the shame, he would at some later time come to find life worth living. Even he recognizes this, for he knows that he is not one to dwell on the past; he is too busy planning his next scheme. But this recognition does not weigh with him at all, for what he finds intolerable is present or imminent shame. There is neither an internal nor an external reason for Herman to get off the tracks. There is no internal reason because Herman lacks any motivation for going on living—he is not someone particularly tied to life—and he is strongly motivated to avoid facing up to the consequences of his actions. There is no external reason, for the subjunctive conditional

(1') If Herman rationally deliberated then, whatever his original motivations, he would come to be motivated to get off the tracks

is not true. Herman's problem is not that he is deceived about his motives, nor that he is unable to deliberate rationally; his problem is that he is motivated to avoid shame at all costs and in this case the cost seems to be his life. Yet if we think about the life Herman would lead if, somehow or other, he got through the period of shame and punishment, it seems that there is some reason for Herman to get off the tracks (whatever weight he or we assign to it).[17]

The internal-reasons theorist cannot do justice to Herman's life because his life stretches over time and, until it is over, partially consists in possibilities which may or may not be realized. However, the internal-reasons theorist has to maintain that the only reasons that can exist for Herman at a given time are reasons he would come to recognize *at that very time* given only that he had true beliefs, accurate insight into his motivation and could rationally deliberate. This is to treat Herman as a spatio-temporal slice. To say that Herman has no reason to get off the tracks is to detach him from his full life—the life he has led, is leading and might lead—and to consider him solely in terms of his consciousness at a given moment. Of course that moment is a special one; it is the present, and we regularly have to make decisions based upon current motivation. Indeed, the virtue of the internal reasons account is that it does explain how an agent's choices are based upon his current motivation. I do not wish to play down the importance of current motivation for practical reason: it is precisely because Herman lacks any motivation to go on living that, if left to his own devices, he will remain on the tracks—whether or not he engages in rational

[17] Cf. Nagel's prudential reasons which are supposed to be able to explain prudential *conduct* irrespective of whether they are also internal reasons.

deliberation as he listens for the far-off whistle. I only wish to make the weaker claim that it is implausible that all reasons for Herman to be on or off the tracks should be derivable either from pure rational deliberation or from deliberation on his current motivation.

Though Herman is a dramatic case, he represents a phenomenon which is, I think, common in life: that a single human life can contain discontinuities of motivation. Variations on the rationally deliberated suicide are easily proliferated (I leave the heartbroken lover and the cancer victim who refuses chemotherapy as exercises for the reader) and I shall confine myself to one other type of example.

Consider Eli, a drunk who has a strong desire for a drink and no conflicting desires that he refrain. Were he sober, Eli would be motivated not to have another drink but, having become drunk, he cheerfully throws himself entirely into the maintenance of his current state. The problem which Eli presents is how to analyse the subjunctive conditional

(1*) If Eli rationally deliberated then, whatever motivation he originally had, he would come to be motivated not to have another drink.

If, on the one hand, we assume that Eli, while drunk, is incapable of rational deliberation, then the conditional (1*) will come out true. For when sober Eli is motivated not to drink, irrespective of his motives when drunk. Thus there will be an external reason not to have another drink. The only way to avoid this conclusion, while nevertheless agreeing that drunken Eli is incapable of rational deliberation, is to posit the existence of a motivation not to drink that is hidden to him while drunk or overruled by other motivations. Were such a motivation present in him, it might be argued, his rational deliberation would not be irrespective of his original motivations. Now such a motivation may be hidden in the bosom of many drunks, but it is artificial to insist that it *must* be present in Eli. What makes Eli a charming drunk is, among other things, the wholehearted way in which he enjoys his drunkenness and the apparent transparency of his motives to himself and to us. Eli is simply someone whose motivations differ when he is drunk from when he is sober. So to maintain that (1*) is false, one must conceive of Eli *both* as drunk *and* as somehow able to calculate rationally means to ends. He tabulates the available means to the given end of having a drink and, of course, does not acquire a motivation not to have another drink. But is this not to treat Eli as a mere rational will, an abstract consciousness? For the subjunctive conditional to come out false, it cannot be *Eli*, in his full particularity, who deliberates, but a mere rational consciousness that is able to calculate Eli's actual means and ends.

Finally, both the internal reasons theorist and the Kantian treat the individual as the absolute focus of practical reason. Because it is assumed that what requires explanation is an *individual's* actions we are forced to concentrate on the individual's will; from this vantage point it looks incredible that there might be anything else to appeal to. This is not the only available vantage point, however; another can be extracted from Aristotle's political and ethical writings.[18] Aristotle took it as evident that man is a political animal:[19] he can fully realize his nature only within a political society that promotes human flourishing. Indeed, human flourishing consists, in part, in an active life within political society. It is characteristic of man that he has a sense of justice, a moral sense; he is the only animal with speech and this enables him to develop a more general social capacity.[20] Political society is the developed form in which these capacities can be fully exercised. Society, for Aristotle, is much more than an arena in which individuals can obtain certain goods.

Aristotle compared the man living outside of political society to 'an isolated piece at draughts'.[21] This is a remarkable comparison, for an isolated piece at draughts is not, strictly speaking, a piece at draughts at all. A draughts piece gains its very identity, and thus in a sense its existence, by its relation to the game of which it is part. No draughts piece can, so to speak, live outside the game of draughts. Aristotle is clearly willing to accept that analogous relations exist between men and political society. He sees society as a functioning organism and argues on general principles that it is metaphysically prior to, more substantial than, the individual.[22] Just as the parts of a functioning organism gain their identity and role in relation to the whole functioning organism—being a severed hand or the hand of a dead man is not a way of being a hand, it is a way of not being a hand—so a man's function is defined by his relation to society. This is made evident, Aristotle thought, by the fact that an individual separated from society could not be self-sufficient (*autarkes*).[23] Modern critics like to make fun of Aristotle's high esteem for self-sufficiency—as though if only an

---

[18] A forceful critic of Kantian ethics and advocate of Aristotelian ethics is Alasdair MacIntyre, see *After Virtue* (London: Duckworth, 1981) from which I have drawn much inspiration. However, I disagree with MacIntyre's interpretation of how Aristotelian ethics might be applied in the twentieth century, as will become clear at the end of this essay.

[19] *Politics* I.2, 1253a2; and *Nicomachean Ethics* I.7, 1097b11.

[20] *Politics* I.2, 1253a1–39.

[21] Ibid. 1253a7. Cf. Hegel's account of this passage in his *History of Philosophy*, III, op. cit. 207–210.

[22] Ibid. 1253a18–29.

[23] Ibid. 1253a26.

individual could shed the regrettable necessity of depending on others he would be truly happy—so it is worth noting that he conceived it as a political virtue.[24] Self-sufficiency is expressed in one's relations with one's family, friends and fellow citizens. It is taken to be 'that which makes life desirable and lacking in nothing' and it is thus identified with *eudaimonia*.[25] The self-sufficient life, the flourishing life, can only be lived within political society, and it should be contrasted with the solitary life which, Aristotle thought, could not flourish.[26]

Thus an individual who thinks of himself as the complete locus of practical reason has, on Aristotle's account, a misleading picture of reality. It is as though one's hand could ask why it should bother lifting food to a mouth. Political science enables man to get a clearer understanding of his relation to society and its aim is to help men form societies in which they can flourish.[27] Having seen that there is room for a type of reason which need be neither internal nor external, one can, with this conception of political science, make sense of the notion of an *objective* reason for action. An agent has an *objective reason* to ϕ if either ϕ directly promotes human flourishing or ϕ contributes to the society's ability to promote human flourishing. These reasons need not be derivable from rationality alone. In ideal conditions objective and internal reasons will either coincide or be harmonious. For, of course, an objective reason may also be an internal reason and it is an important fact that this will often be so: men naturally tend to desire to flourish and thus will be motivated to act in certain ways if they come to believe that so acting will promote it. It is upon the widespread presence of such motivation that human flourishing, ethical life within a society, and thus the existence of man as the political animal Aristotle understood him to be, depend. But it will certainly not always be the case that internal and objective reasons coincide: a person may be motivated by a mistaken conception of flourishing—for example, the unremitting acquisition of material goods—or, more radically, he may simply not be interested in flourishing. People get depressed, they become drunk, they become suicidal. Yet it is precisely by understanding that they lack internal reasons, though there are objective reasons, that we gain insight into what their position is. If the drunk or depressive lacks an internal reason to flourish, then reasoned discourse with him will not, as reasoned discourse, motivate him to flourish (it may motivate him as an expression of our caring for him). Thus he will also lack an external reason to flourish, but recognizing that he does have objective reasons we can do justice to the fact that his motivations

[24] *Nicomachean Ethics* I.7, 1097b7–22; cf. V.6, 1134a27.
[25] Ibid. 1097b15.
[26] Ibid. I.8, 1099b3–6.
[27] Ibid. I.2, 1094a18–28, b7–9; I.4, 1095a16; I.7, 1097a22–34.

are not merely one set among others, all being equally good or bad, but are genuinely deficient.

This gap between internal and objective reasons provides at least one way of justifying a paternalistic attitude toward such a person. While it is not clear how we should interpret the subjunctive conditional (1*), it is clear that Eli is incapable, in his drunken state, of rational deliberation. If we are to help him then we must treat him as something other than as a rational agent. Now of course the question of our behaving paternalistically towards him will not even arise if we do not have internal reasons to help him. But our subjective motivation will not in itself justify paternalistic action. If on reflection we found that there was no justification for our motivation, that realization might be instrumental in deciding to refrain from interfering in another person's life. Whilst there may be other ways to justify behaving paternalistically toward someone, one way is by showing that we are acting on reasons which he has. It is precisely because we can see that there is objective reason to help the drunk that our internal reasons for helping him survive reflective testing. This argument can of course be misused and horrible things have been done to people in the name of their own good. That in itself does not impugn the argument, it means that one should take a paternalistic stance only with extreme caution and circumspection.

There is a cluster of challenges to this Aristotelian approach which might loosely be grouped under the heading 'the problem of other cultures'. The general refrain is, perhaps, too familiar: other cultures embody or have embodied different conceptions of human flourishing, different moral outlooks, different conceptions of the good. Does this not impugn the objectivity of morality? From what vantage point can one criticize the moral values of another culture? Are not moral values relative to the culture one lives in? Underlying these questions are two significant trains of thought. The first, *the Wittgensteinian challenge*, concerns the relative autonomy and immunity from external criticism of a society's practices and beliefs.[28] The second, *the problem of*

[28] I do not mean by this title to imply that Wittgenstein himself is the author of this challenge as will become clear in what follows; cf. Peter Winch, *The Idea of a Social Science* (London: Routledge and Kegan Paul, 1958) and 'Understanding a Primitive Society' in *Rationality*, B. Wilson (ed.) (Oxford: Blackwell, 1970). See also Bernard Williams, 'Wittgenstein and Idealism', in *Moral Luck* op. cit.; Charles Taylor, 'Understanding and the *Geisteswissenschaften*' in *Wittgenstein: To Follow a Rule*, C. Holtzman and S. Leich (eds), (London: Routledge and Kegan Paul, 1981). But cf. Norman Malcolm, 'Wittgenstein and Idealism' and Derek Bolton, 'Life-form and Idealism' both in *Idealism Past and Present*, G. Vesey (ed.) (Cambridge: Cambridge University Press, 1982).

ideology, presents the possibility that we are (self-) deceived about some specific moral and social beliefs. Anthropology has made us aware of the functional role moral beliefs play in maintaining the stability and viability of a culture; philosophy, psychology and sociology have made us aware of the phenomenon of false consciousness. Perhaps Aristotle was a victim of false consciousness in his defence of the natural inferiority of slaves; perhaps we are similarly deceived about some contemporary moral cliché?

The Wittgensteinian challenge is, roughly, an amalgam of two theses which have dominated much theorizing about social explanation. The first is that to understand the beliefs and practices of any society one must, to some extent, go native. The heart of a society is revealed in the various practices, customs and rituals that constitute a 'form of life'. These practices can be thought of as rule-governed behaviour, but there is no way of undestanding the rules except from inside the rule-governed practices themselves. One is trying to understand the actions of a group of agents and to succeed in this one must absorb oneself in the native beliefs and practices: one must come, at least to some extent, to see the world as they do. Otherwise one will merely be imposing a set of alien categories on a culture one has failed to understand. But once one is 'inside' the culture one will see that the beliefs and practices have their own 'rationality'.

The second thesis is that all patterns of justification come to an end, and in the end they are grounded in the practices of a group. An explanation or a justification is supposed to reveal why the agents acted in one way rather than another. But, as Wittgenstein repeatedly pointed out, any such chain of explanations or justifications must come to an end somewhere;[29] so, ultimately, all one can say is that they are the sort of group who tend to act for these reasons. This is not intended as an explanation of their actions—i.e. as an account of why they acted one way rather than another—for all explanations have already been given. It is meant to provide non-explanatory insight into how they go on. The upshot of this line of reasoning is the autonomy of a culture's beliefs and practices. From outside the culture there is no legitimate vantage point from which to criticize them. From inside the culture the beliefs and practices will 'make sense'.

Ironically, such a line of thought tends to undermine *our own* beliefs and practices rather than reinforce them. Our moral beliefs do not initially present themselves merely as the way we happen to go on here

[29] See e.g. Ludgwig Wittgenstein, *Philosophical Investigations*, I, G. E. M. Anscombe (trans.) (Oxford: Blackwell, 1978) §§ 109, 126, 211, 213, 261, 325–326, 467–468, 469, 516, 599; *Zettel*, G. E. M. Anscombe and G. H. von Wright (eds and trans.) (Oxford: Blackwell, 1967), §§ 216, 313–315, 608–611.

in Western civilization at the end of the twentieth century. If we are led to believe that they are, at bottom, one way which one tribe happens to go on, then a single question becomes unavoidable and unanswerable: why not go on some other way? Philosophy, Wittgenstein emphasized, should be non-revisionary; it should leave our beliefs and practices as they are.[30] Wittgensteinian philosophers of social science have applied this in terms of respecting the rationality and autonomy of each culture, but such an application is inherently unstable. For if we have to respect the rationality and autonomy of every culture it turns out that there is one culture whose rationality and autonomy we cannot respect: our own. Our moral beliefs present themselves as basic truths about how humans beings should act, but we are now supposed to respect incompatible moral beliefs just so long as they are actually embodied in a culture. By the standards of rationality available in our tribe these two stances are incompatible: being forced to accept that alternative incompatible moral outlooks are equally justifiable (or equally unjustifiable) cannot help but undermine the confidence of reflective moral agents.

Why should anyone believe that philosophical reflection ought to leave our beliefs and practices intact? How, in particular, can the insight that there are certain things we think and do for which there is no explanation or justification be expected not to impel us towards revisions? The answer, in Wittgenstein's case, is that there are no coherent alternatives. Let us say that a person is *minded in a certain way* if he has the perceptions of salience, routes of interest, feelings of naturalness in following a rule, that constitute being part of a form of life.[31] Then Wittgenstein tries to awaken us to the insight that even a basic arithmetical truth like '2+2=4' is not totally independent of our being minded as we are: there is no Platonic fact which guarantees its truth. And our being so minded itself has no explanation or justification. Explanations and justifications take place within the context of our form of life: it is, for Wittgenstein, only because we are so minded that we find certain accounts explanatory or justificatory. Yet this insight does not enable us to contemplate an alternative arithmetic—say one in which 2+2=3—for in this breadth of context there is no coherent possibility of being other minded. The possibility of our being minded in any way at all is the possibility of our being minded as we are. We explore what it is to be minded as we are by moving around our mindedness self-consciously and determining what

[30] See e.g. *Philosophical Investigations*, I, 124, 133; and cf. my 'Leaving the World Alone', *Journal of Philosophy* **79** (1982) where I discuss Wittgenstein's non-revisionism in detail.

[31] See my 'Leaving the World Alone', op. cit.

makes more and less sense; when we try to move, so to speak, outside of our mindedness we lapse into nonsense.

It is *only* because Wittgenstein is working within such a broad context that he is able to maintain both that philosophy provides insight into the unjustifiability of our thoughts and actions and that it should be non-revisionary. The insight into 'how we go on' is not meant to apply only to one tribe among others, but to encompass all rational creatures. One might thus be tempted to claim that Wittgenstein's use of 'we' is dispensable, that he is in fact investigating the conditions of rationality. Though such a claim has a germ of truth, it is misleading. According to the later Wittgenstein, rationality is not, as Kant thought, a fixed structure revealed by transcendental argument, nor does it Platonically exist totally independently of us: it is somehow constituted by our thoughts, actions, feelings of naturalness, perceptions of salience, etc. One might similarly be tempted to remove the 'I' from the Kantian 'I think' and claim that Kant is just investigating the conditions of thought. But this flattens the Kantian insight that thought is thought by a thinker: there must be a subject who is having the thoughts. In this sense, the Wittgensteinian 'we' is a pluralization of the Kantian 'I'. except that it is not merely a case of 'we think' but 'we think, feel, see, react . . .'.

By taking the Wittgensteinian 'we' to pick out one tribe among others, philosophers of social science have developed an implausible account of social explanation. For if one draws a 'form of life' narrowly to pick out a single culture, then the rationale for thinking philosophy to be non-revisionary disappears. One might consider here how a philosopher like Socrates differs from Wittgenstein. Socrates was in his dialogues continually trying to get his interlocutor to see that he was engaged in social practices, had beliefs about customs, for which ultimately he had no explanation or justification.[32] But this reflective exercise was not meant to leave everything as it was. The reflective awareness that certain social mores lacked justification was an agent for social change. The Athenian polis, Hegel argued,[33] correctly perceived that Socrates threatened its stability by inducing this reflective awareness. Wittgenstein's dialogues, by contrast, encourage a very different type of reflective awareness. We are not simply 'sunk in a form of life' unreflectively inferring Q from P and *If P, Q*: we are seemingly able to gain some reflective awareness of how we go on. Yet while this reflection seems to reveal, superficially at least, an ultimate contingency in the things we do, it also reveals that there is no alternative. It seems to me no accident that Socrates went to jail, and Wittgenstein went to the movies.

[32] See e.g. Plato, *Euthyphro*.
[33] Hegel, *History of Philosophy*, I, op. cit. 425–488.

If there are genuine alternatives to the things we think and do, and if some of these beliefs and practices lack explanation or justification, then reflecting on this can be an impulse to social change. By ignoring this, post-Wittgensteinian social science represents a retreat from insights that emerged in Hegel's social and political philosophy. Both Hegel and Wittgenstein emphasized that the beliefs of a group are concretely embedded in their practices, and that it is only in terms of the practices that the beliefs can be fully understood. But Hegel allows, in a way that Wittgensteinians do not, for agents in society to become reflectively aware of how their beliefs are embedded in practices and to subject them to criticism. It is beside the point to insist on the 'rationality' of the beliefs and practices of a tribe. Given a tribe engaged in a primitive form of capitalist production, it may be 'rational' for the bourgeois members to believe that they are responsible moral agents acting for the good of the whole tribe. However, if other members of the tribe should come to realize that this moral claim is being used to sanction domination, then this realization may well have an undermining effect. The 'rationality' of a tribe's beliefs and practices is taken by Wittgensteinians to be sacrosanct in part because they ignore the possibility that the tribe may contain natives who are engaged in a reflective examination of their own beliefs and practices.

The Wittgensteinian challenge does not undermine our sense of moral objectivity because it does not rob us of the right to criticize the moral practices of another culture. Consider, for example, the infamous Ik, a group of mobile savages who have lived for a prolonged period in conditions of extreme deprivation.[34] They have, according to Colin Turnbull, developed a mode of social life that, except for a few atavistic traces, is devoid of a moral sense. They regularly lie and cheat, they treat their neighbours, even their own families, terribly and regard acts of benevolence as absurd and ridiculous. According to Wittgensteinian social science, there is no legitimate place from which to criticize the Ik: from outside of their practices we will just be imposing an alien set of categories, from inside we will be too busy scrounging, robbing and cheating, to reflect on the moral worth of our actions. The fallacy lies in the assumption that the imposition of an alien set of categories must be illegitimate. If Ik society has no room for reflective moral awareness, then any set of concepts used self-consciously to evaluate moral worth will be alien. This does not imply that Ik behaviour is completely outside the bounds of moral evaluation as, say, the behaviour of a community of ants might be. We can take on the role of reflective moral agents which Ik society lacks. Such a stance of course

[34] See Colin Turnbull, *The Mountain People* (New York: Simon and Schuster, 1972).

requires a sensitivity to their culture, to the 'rationality' of their modes of social behaviour and a sympathetic understanding of the lives they (may have to) lead. Taking such a stance is fraught with the dangers of misinterpretation, projection, self-deception and cultural imperialism, but it is not theoretically impossible as it would be, for example, to take on the role of the reflective moral consciousness of a community of red ants. Had external conditions been more benevolent, a reflective moral awareness might have grown up within Ik society. Indeed, there is evidence that in the past the Ik had a richer moral life than they do now, since the few bonds that hold that society together appear to be atavisms. In any case, we take on this role for our sake, not the Ik's. Trying to absorb and develop the moral consciousness of another culture—or of our culture at a different historical period—is one way of becoming reflectively more aware and critical of our own moral consciousness.

Of course, any such critical endeavour is threatened by the problem of false consciousness. We may for various reasons having to do with social organization, class or role be deceived about what human flourishing is or about the part we play in promoting it. This, of course, is the *problem of ideology*. Much of the work of Jurgen Habermas and other critical theorists of the Frankfurt school has been devoted to the problem of how one discovers that a form of consciousness is false.[35] Critical theory is, however, vitiated by a deep intellectual ambivalence, revealed in the disparate interpretations which have been placed on its cardinal principle: that the agents themselves must in principle be able to come to realize that they are suffering false consciousness. On the one hand, this principle insists that what human flourishing is cannot be completely unavailable to human consciousness. On the other hand, the principle makes the notion of flourishing remarkably unavailable. For, according to critical theory, the agents of each society ought to be the arbiters of their real interests and of what it is for them to flourish. But this leaves open the possibility that two societies could emerge with deeply incompatible outlooks, each of which was validated by what each group took to be acceptable critical methods. Though critical theory has developed from Hegelian and Marxist social theory, there is

[35] See especially Jurgen Habermas, *Knowledge and Human Interests*, J. Shapiro (trans.) (London: Heinemann, 1972); 'Wahrheitstheorien', in *Wirklichkeit und Reflexion: Walter Schulz zum 60 Geburtstag*, (Pfullingen: Neske, 1973); *Theorie der Gesellschaft oder Sozialtechnologie—Was leistet die Systemforschung?* (with N. Luhman) (Frankfurt: Suhrkamp, 1971); *Theory and Practice* J. Viertel (trans.) (London: Heinemann, 1974); *Legitimation Crisis*, T. McCarthy (trans.) (London: Heinemann, 1976). Cf. Theodor W. Adorno, *Negative Dialectic*, E. B. Ashton (trans.) (New York: Seabury Press, 1973).

a crucial feature of Hegelian and Marxist thought which critical theorists have tried to abandon: a definite conception of flourishing against which a form of consciousness can be measured. What human flourishing is, Habermas has argued, is what the agents of a community agree it to be in conditions that are free of distortion and coercion.[36] There is no notion of flourishing that exists independently of a community's consensus.

I do not think that the theoretical underpinning of the consensus theory is very firm. I shall argue, first, that critical theory presupposes a substantial conception of human flourishing: second, that in its explicit attempt to avoid any such presupposition it is forced to adopt various unattractive Kantian features of practical reason. The consensus is a socialized descendant of the Kantian demand that moral agents be self-legislating. But, like Kantian morality, the consensus theory does not take seriously who the agents are who are doing the legislating.

If social value is to emerge from a consensus of the agents in a society, one must begin with the individual agent, with his particular needs, desires and interests, who must non-coercively be brought into the consensus if there is to be one. Thus there is a powerful presupposition of the priority of the individual in the construction of the good society. In particular, one ought never to have to appeal to society's interest to explain an individual's interests. Society's interest can be nothing more than the consensus that would emerge under certain conditions. Since the individual would, under those conditions, presumably be part of the consensus, appeal to the society's interest should be both otiose and metaphysically misleading.

So an individual's real interests must be generated from within the individual himself: on this point the critical theorist and the internal-reasons theorist agree. Consider again our drunk who has a strong desire for a drink and no desire to refrain. Can the critical theorist make any case that it is in the drunk's real interest to refrain from drinking? It would be relatively easy if the drunk shared our conception of the good life or had some false belief, say, that drinking was the key to immortality—though not as easy as critical theorists assume. They tend to identify an agent's real interests with that which contributes to his realizing his own conception of flourishing.[37] Then if any of his immediate interests, say having a drink, conflicts with his real interests they are said to be merely apparent or phenomenal interests. It

[36] This is Habermas's so-called consensus theory of truth. See 'Wahrheitstheorien', op. cit.

[37] See Raymond Geuss's excellent exposition of critical theory's account of real interests in *The Idea of a Critical Theory* (Cambridge: Cambridge University Press, 1981), 45–54. In the next few paragraphs I discuss Geuss's argument in detail.

is certainly possible that an agent's long- and short-term interests may conflict, but why should we assign importance to an agent's avoiding conflict? And from what perspective does one give precedence to the long-term interests by calling them 'real' and slight the short-term interests with the pejorative 'phenomenal'? One cannot legitimately appeal to the fact that an inconsistent set leads to frustration and unhappinesss, and that frustration and unhappiness violate the agent's own conception of the good life. For this is simply to repeat that there may be conflicts and to give precedence to the long-term interests. The agent may be willing to put up with a certain amount of stress and frustration in order to realize as far as possible incompatible desires. One cannot appeal to the fact that the agent will thereby lead a disharmonious life; first, he may not be interested in harmony and, second, even if he is it may be only one of his interests, others of which conflict with it. The danger of course is that *we* are imposing value on leading a harmonious life or on satisfying long-term goals—which, from a proper critical perspective, is taboo. So if a critical theorist is legitimately to attach importance to an agent's long-term goals, calling them his 'real' interests, it must be in virtue of choices the agent himself would make. If informing an agent that his continued drinking frustrated his larger goals were to motivate him to cease, then the critical theorist would have grounds for claiming that it was in the agent's real interest to cease. From the meagre ingredients of an agent's conflicting desires, false beliefs and hypothetical choices, a watery theory of real interests can be made.

But our drunk does not fit easily into this picture. His conception of the good life does not extend far—perhaps to being able to drink *ad libitum*—and his desire, if it is based at all, is based on the true belief that it brings him pleasure. Either the critical theorist must admit that the drunk has no real interest in refraining or he must argue that under theoretically acceptable conditions the drunk would decide that it was in his interest to refrain. The first option is, I think, an admission of failure. One has only to remember the examples of human degradation one has seen to be intuitively convinced that any theory which asserts that such degraded humans have no real interest in improving their lot is simply not a theory of real interests.

So if he is to generate real interests for our drunk, the critical theorist must concentrate on choices the drunk would make under certain theoretically acceptable conditions. But what conditions are theoretically acceptable? One suggestion is that we consider the choices an agent would make if he had 'perfect knowledge':

(2) An action ϕ is in an agent's *real interest* if and only if he would choose to perform ϕ if he had perfect knowledge.

There are two reasons for thinking that this condition will not generate any substantial conclusions. First, the perfect knowledge with which we hypothetically endow the agent cannot consist of any theory—say Aristotelian ethics, Marxism or psychoanalysis—which contains a substantial notion of human flourishing. What human flourishing is is supposed to emerge in the consensus, and it would be begging the question artificially to inseminate the agents with a conception of flourishing which they would then, rather unmiraculously, agree to. The 'knowledge' must be pretty sterile—the Krebs cycle, molecular structure of DNA—and thus will be unhelpful in making any decisions other than in the straightforward and boring cases where the drunk is acting on a clearly false belief: e.g. that drinking is an aid to longevity and mental acuity. So this condition, inasmuch as we can make sense of it, seems empty.

Second, the condition (2) is, I think, ultimately incoherent. Giving the truth conditions of subjunctive conditionals is a tricky business. One takes a subjunctive like

> If Harry had known that the horse had been drugged he would not have bet on it,

to be true if given a situation very much like the one that actually obtains, differing in that Harry knows that the horse has been drugged and whatever *minimal* changes are necessary for Harry to have that knowledge, Harry does not bet.[38] It does not affect the truth of the conditional to consider the case in which Harry, having learned that the horse is drugged, is immediately hypnotized by a Martian and commanded zombie-like to place the bet anyway. The truth of the subjunctive is not affected by such far-out possibilities, for we are concerned with what Harry might do in slightly different circumstances. Now the problem with a conditional like (2) is that we want to know what an agent would do under a given set of conditions, but these conditions are themselves so dramatically unlike anything that actually obtains that the most likely situation in which they obtain is too unlikely to give us any enlightenment. We want to know what an agent would do in a situation very much like the actual one, differing only in that the agent has perfect knowledge. We have no way to handle such a conditional: for there is *no* situation which is very much like the actual one, differing only in that the agent has perfect knowledge. The conditional asks us both to consider what *the agent* would choose and to abandon any sense that it is the agent who is doing the choosing. 'Endowing him with perfect knowledge' is not something we can do to an agent without destroying his integrity as an agent. It turns 'him' into

[38] David Lewis, *Counterfactuals*, (Oxford: Blackwell, 1973).

a mere Kantian rational consciousness. Our understanding of subjunctive conditionals is too finely tuned to withstand such a violent procedure.

A second suggestion is that we generate real interests by considering what the agent would do under 'optimal conditions':

(3) An action ϕ is in an agent's *real interest* if and only if, under optimal conditions, the agent would choose to ϕ.

The problem with this condition is that the notion of optimal conditions presupposes a substantial conception of human flourishing. What human flourishing is is not being constituted by a consensus, it is being presupposed in the optimal conditions that make a consensus possible. If the drunk were to undergo a cure, he would in this sober and educated state choose to refrain from excessive drinking. If we were to sink into his state of torpor, however, we would choose to have another drink. What makes one set of conditions rather than the other optimal? They cannot be discriminated by the choices the agents would make in those conditions, for they are symmetrical in that respect. One might try to avoid presupposing a substantial conception of flourishing by allowing the agent to decide for himself what he takes to be optimal conditions. But the drunk would choose unlimited availability of alcohol, and under such conditions he would choose to have another drink. Is that in his real interest? The optimal-conditions approach faces the following dilemma. If the *raison d'être* for invoking optimal conditions is that it is believed that an agent's current choices are distorted by the condition in which he lives, then presumably his current choice of optimal conditions may also be distorted. If, on the other hand, *we* specify the optimal conditions—subject perhaps to the proviso that the agent endorse these conditions as optimal once he has realized them then we have presupposed what constitutes flourishing.

This dilemma becomes acute when we consider alternative value-systems that have developed in other societies. The Ik seem to value lying and cheating, they admire nasty tricks and are genuinely amused by displays of altruistic behaviour. There is no doubt that their value-system has emerged in response to the depraved conditions in which they have had to live, and by focusing on optimal conditions we try to compensate for that. Yet two questions need to be asked. First, are the 'optimal conditions' meant to be conditions the Ik might actually realize in their lives, given a few fortunate turns of circumstance, or are the optimal conditions well beyond anything they might actually experience? Second, who specifies the optimal conditions, us or them? Suppose we allow them to specify the optimal conditions and by 'optimal conditions' we mean circumstances they might actually realize. (For example, they could specify repeated good harvests, successful breeding of livestock and beneficial trading with neighbours; they could not choose a penthouse suite at the Nairobi Hilton.) The virtue of this reading of optimal conditions is that we can make sense of the subjunctive conditionals. But the available empirical evidence suggests that under these 'optimal conditions', they would choose a life of improved cheating and stealing. Their value-system may have emerged in deprived conditions, but the anthropologist who studied them says that it has stabilized and remains intact through periods of good fortune. So if we restrict ourselves to choices they would make in conditions which they might, just possibly, realize, the evidence suggests that they would make rather nasty choices.

If, however, we try to stretch the notion of 'optimal conditions' we rapidly lose the sense that it is the Ik who would be doing the choosing or that the choices will be in the Ik's real interest. Consider, for example, the following claims:

> We have reason to believe that the Ik realize that their situation is dismal and that they would prefer not to live as they do. That their circumstances are horrible is not just a judgment we as outsiders make. If the Ik would prefer not to live in their present state of extreme malnutrition, presumably they would also prefer not to have to form their desires and interests in such circumstances. Now if the Ik are assumed to have perfect knowledge part of what they will know is what the 'optimal conditions' for forming desires and interests are. These condition are conditions of non-deprivation, non-coercion and minimally correct information. With perfect knowledge the Ik would know what interests they would form if they were to live in 'optimal conditions', and we may safely assume that they would prefer to live in optimal conditions.[39]

> . . . if the Ik recognize—as we assume they do—that there is another set of interests they would prefer to have, namely the ones they realize they would acquire in the circumstances in which they prefer to live, then those are their real interests (and not the sophisticated but bestial ones we see them actually pursue).[40]

There is no evidence for the presumption that the Ik would rather form their desires and interests in other circumstances. The evidence only

[39] Geuss, op. cit. 52. It should be noted that Geuss confines himself pretty strictly to expositing critical theory, so the criticisms in this essay should be thought of as directed against certain ideas in critical theory, not against Geuss' position.

[40] Ibid. 53. *N.B.* that the argument contained in these quotations is crucial to the subsequent identification of the perfect knowledge and optimal conditions approaches (p. 53). So if the argument here fails, so does the identification.

suggests that they would prefer to exercise their desires and interests in other circumstances—circumstances in which they would be more readily realized. Further, if we assume that the Ik, with perfect knowledge, would know what the 'optimal conditions' for forming desires and interests are, then we are building into the initial conditions a substantial conception of human flourishing. We should not, therefore, think that what constitutes flourishing is merely what emerges from the consensus. Finally, there is no evidence either that the Ik would prefer to live in these 'optimal conditions' or that they would prefer to have the desires they would acquire in these circumstances. If the 'optimal conditions' differed more than minimally from the Ik's actual conditions, there is no reason to think that the Ik, from their current perspective, would find them preferable or even attractive. Again, a fragile subjunctive conditional:

> The Ik's real interests are revealed by the choices they would make under optimal conditions

cannot withstand the pressure of these so-called 'optimal conditions'. This is because the Ik cannot sustain the change to 'optimal conditions' they are too far removed from anything the Ik might be likely to encounter in their lives.[41] By including perfect knowledge among the optimal conditions, one transforms the Ik into a mere set of rational consciousnesses and one thereby loses the sense that it would be the Ik who were making the choices. For this reason, the optimal conditions approach appears to generate a deeply unreal set of interests for the Ik. It is not plausible to assume that the choices a set of informed rational consciousnesses would make under certain conditions reveal the real interests of a group who could never expect to live in even remotely similar circumstances. The cardinal tenet of critical theory, that it should be available to the agents themselves, seems to be destroyed by the optimal-conditions approach.

Perhaps problems such as these prompted Habermas to argue that the very possibility of a speech community requires that all its members 'anticipate the ideal speech situation'.[42] The ideal speech situation is one in which absolutely free and equal agents engage in uncoerced and unlimited discussion. It would be up to the people in the ideal speech situation to recognize that they were in it and then to determine,

---

[41] In this regard, note Adelaide's lament about Nathan Detroit: 'For fourteen years I've tried to change Nathan. I've always thought how wonderful he would be if only he was different' (*Guys and Dolls*, book by Jo Swerling and Abe Burrows, music and lyrics by Frank Loesser).

[42] See *Theorie der Gesellschaft oder Sozialtechnologie—Was liestet die Systemforschung?*, op. cit.; 'Wahrheitstheorien', op. cit.

precisely, what it is. The choices made in the ideal speech situation world reveal real interests, beliefs agreed to would be *ipso facto* true beliefs. The ideal speech situation may be unlike anything the Ik (or we) could ever expect to live in but, if Habermas's argument were successful, it would bind the Ik (and us) to the optimal conditions in which their real interests are revealed. For though the optimal conditions may be far removed from the Ik's lives, they would not be totally removed. According to the argument, every Ik action and in particular every Ik speech act 'anticipates' those optimal conditions; that is, by their acts they commit themselves to acceptability in the ideal speech situation as a criterion of truth and moral worthiness. It has been objected that Habermas's transcendental argument is unconvincing, that he has not shown that all speakers always and everywhere anticipate the ideal speech situation.[43] Certainly the general failure since Kant to devise valid transcendental arguments for interesting conclusions ought to make one dubious of Habermas's Kantian strategy. But I think that even more damning criticisms can be made which are analogues of criticisms Hegel directed against Kantian ethics. First, the 'freedom' invoked in the ideal speech situation is blank and empty. It conjures up no particular set of circumstances we might actually realize in our lives. Second, by placing the ideal speech situation outside our lives as that which is *anticipated* by our acts, critical theory reveals itself as another form of unhappy consciousness. Critical theory, like Kantian ethics, must postulate a reconciliation outside of the world—in the ideal speech situation, the critical theorist's heaven—because the actual agents who exist in this world are portrayed as so far removed from their real interests.[44]

Significant problems with the theory are thus shunted off to another, dimly perceived world where, we are assured, they will be resolved. If, however, we lose faith in the other-worldly ideal speech situation, then the problems come back to haunt critical theory. What is it about the

---

[43] Cf. Geuss op. cit. 64–67.

[44] Consider, e.g.: 'We can't be fully free without having perfect knowledge, nor acquire perfect knowledge unless we live in conditions of complete freedom. Our "real interests" are those we would form in such conditions of perfect knowledge and freedom. Although we can be in a position fully to recognize our "real interests" only if our society satisfies the utopian condition of perfect freedom, still, although we do not live in that utopia, we may be free enought to recognize how we might act to abolish some of the coercion from which we suffer and move closer to "optimal conditions" of freedom and knowledge. The task of a critical theory is to show us which way to move' (Geuss, op. cit. 54). But why assume that there is some utopian state that we are moving towards? Is this not merely an empty, removed condition which makes it possible, by comparison, to characterize our current state as deficient?

ideal speech situation that makes it *ideal*? How do we know that agents in the ideal speech situation would not decide that complete freedom for all costs too much—in resources, social organization, etc.—to make it worthwhile? Maybe the ideal speech situation is inherently unstable? Critical theory assumes a universal motivation for freedom because it assigns no negative value to the state of greater freedom. (Is this an Enlightenment heritage?) Yet it cannot seriously consider what negative value greater freedom might have, because freedom is left as a completely blank conception: it is simply a cipher assumed to be absolutely valuable in whatever quantities it is available. Once one sees that there is no substantial conception of freedom and no argument that more for all is always better than less, then one must ask why, say, Machiavelli's *The Prince* should not be regarded as a critical theory.[45] *The Prince*, after all, tries to awaken a few people, princes, to what their real interests are and this consists, in part, in the domination of others. It is not legitimate simply to answer that a social organization envisioned in *The Prince* would never be agreed on in conditions of absolute freedom for, first, we have *no idea* what would be agreed on in such conditions and, second, we lack any argument that engaging in completely uncoerced dialogue would be in the Prince's real interest. We do, by contrast, have a powerful argument offered by Machiavelli that it would be foolish for the Prince to enter such a debate or let any of his subjects do so.

Beliefs are said by critical theorists to be *reflectively unacceptable* if they could only be acquired in conditions of coercion.[46] Thus beliefs are reflectively acceptable if, however they actually were acquired, they could be endorsed in conditions of freedom. Since freedom is such a blank condition, however, we are cut off from knowing which beliefs are reflectively acceptable. Reflection was supposed to be an act we could engage in: we were to step back from some of our beliefs, inspect them from some sort of a 'detached' perspective, and see how well they fit with other beliefs. If they fitted well, if we could endorse the beliefs from this 'detached' perspective, then they were taken to be reflectively acceptable. But if reflective acceptability is identified with acceptability under conditions of freedom it becomes unclear what contribution, positive or negative, the activity we have taken to be reflection makes. Maybe the very activity we have taken to be reflection would not be endorsed under conditions of freedom. The central contradiction, in the Hegelian sense, of critical theory is that it makes possible the very scepticism about ideological distortion that it is trying to overcome. In

---

[45] Here I am indebted to the students at UCLA who attended my seminar on transcendental idealism in the winter term, 1982; especially to Andrew Hsu.

[46] Geuss, op. cit. 62–64.

general, scepticism about one's accurate perception of one's own situation requires the possibility of a removed perspective from which reality can be properly appreciated.[47] For me to entertain the possibility that I am now asleep, dreaming, I need to imagine the possibility of waking up later and discovering that I had been dreaming. To entertain the possibility that I might never wake up, I need to entertain at least the possibility of an evil physiologist, demon or God, who could see me in my true state. Without even the possibility of a true perspective on the world, I lose grip on the notion that the world might really be other than as it appears to me. Thus by making freedom otherworldly, critical theorists *make possible* scepticism concerning our current beliefs about freedom and flourishing. For they postulate the removed standard necessary for scepticism to get started.

One response to this has been to retreat into a pessimistic historicism: to maintain that all there is to 'human flourishing' is a specific society's conception of it at a particular historical period. It is hopeless to try to transcend the social context or historical period in which one lives, to try to say what human flourishing is *per se*. One is better off giving up the 'transcendental baggage' and resigning oneself to the fact that all one's speculation about flourishing will in the end, be a cultural artefact, fossilized in a partial historical and social stratum.[48]

Pessimism is not the only possible response. Pessimism makes sense against a background of there being something desirable which we realize, in all honesty, we cannot obtain. Since we cannot establish *a priori* the transcendental conditions of human flourishing and freedom, we must resign ourselves to our fragile historical product, recognizing that that is all it is. The pessimist's consolation is his self-image of honesty and his belief that he has the truth at last. One way to dissolve pessimism is to show that the allegedly desirable state, which the pessimist argues we cannot obtain, is not so desirable after all. The pessimist is then left with nothing to be pessimistic about. I would like to suggest that post-Kantian social theory has conflated two distinct concerns that Kant himself did not clearly keep separate: transcendental arguments and transcendental conditions for a certain form of empirical experience.[49] Optimists try to embrace both, pessimists

[47] See Thompson Clarke, "The Legacy of Scepticism", *Journal of Philosophy* **69** (1972).

[48] Cf. Geuss op. cit., and Adorno, *Negative Dialectic*, op. cit.

[49] See Ralph Walker, *Kant* (London: Routledge and Kegan Paul, 1978) for an exposition that separates the two. See also my 'Leaving the World Alone', op. cit.; Bernard Williams, 'Wittgenstein and Idealism', op. cit.; Barry Stroud, 'The Significance of Scepticism', in *Transcedental Arguments and Science*, P. Bieri, R.-P. Horstmann and L. Kruger (eds.) (Dordrecht and Boston: D. Reidel, 1979).

jettison both; the correct response, I think, is to forget about transcendental arguments but try to formulate a satisfactory account of the transcendental conditions of human flourishing. There is no valid transcendental argument that the possibility of language depends on or anticipates some substantial conception of human flourishing. But the unavailability of such an argument lends support to pessimistic historicism only if one believes that a transcendental argument is needed to gain any conception of flourishing that is not a prisoner to our times. The antidote is to recognize how rare transcendental arguments are in any area of thought. There is no transcendental guarantee that we are not now all asleep; does that mean that our belief that we are awake is no more than a cultural product of a specific historical period? We live in a world that is relatively bereft of proofs that our way of looking at the world is correct. This does not mean that there is no truth about the world, it only means that the truth must be established by less than *a priori* means.

Though an *a priori* proof is unavailable, I would nevertheless like to suggest that man has a non-empirical interest in flourishing—he is partially constituted by that interest—and that political society provides the only context in which it makes sense to talk about human flourishing. In Aristotelian terms, man is a political animal; in Kantian terms, political society provides the transcendental conditions of human flourishing. Kant gave some content to the transcendental ideality of the phenomenal world by contrasting it, however allusively, to the world as it is in itself. I would like to give some content to the notion of man's non-empirical interests by contrasting the life of man in society with that of a *Homo sapiens* existing outside of all society. We can imagine a member of the biological species *Homo sapiens* existing in the wilderness, never having experienced any human society, but we have no conception of what it is like to be such a being for he is 'like an isolated piece of draughts': man does not come into existence until there are societies in which he can live. This concern for the transcendental conditions of human flourishing differs dramatically from the transcendental idealism advocated in Kant's ethical theory. Kant placed our freedom outside the world, in a noumenal world of pure intelligences, removed from the causal flux: whereas human freedom and flourishing ought, as Aristotle and Hegel stressed, to be placed firmly in the world of human societies.

As I said at the beginning, it is widely believed that the detached impersonal perspective is fundamental to and partially constitutive of the moral standpoint. It is this belief that, I think, ought to be abandoned. Here one must distinguish *seeing oneself from a detached impersonal perspective* from *seeing oneself as one person among others*. There is no detached impersonal perspective from which one can view the world morally. Anti-Kantians are correct to stress that no substantial moral conclusions can be derived from such a detached perspective. This is only to be expected if morality is located within the world, rather than outside it. To see oneself as one person among others is not a matter of seeing oneself from a detached perspective, it is a matter of seeing oneself as one is. One is a person among others and failure to perceive this reveals insensitivity and lack of self-awareness. Self-awareness requires not a detached perspective, but a clear appreciation of an undetached perspective.

If we do abandon the detached perspective and focus our concern on the conditions of human flourishing, it is not obvious that we will emerge with a recognizably *moral* outlook. Indulging in the so-called co-operative virtues, such as justice, was, according to Callicles, an unmitigated hindrance to flourishing. And one cannot reject out of hand the possibility that man, when flourishing, is a rather unco-operative fellow. Callicles might accept that man is a political animal—that he can only flourish within the context of a society that promotes his flourishing—but he would deny that human flourishing in any way consists in contributing to the well-being of society.

There is no *a priori* proof that Callicles' conception of flourishing is mistaken. However, that need not imply that one cannot answer the Calliclean challenge: whether or not one can depends on what one takes the role and function of scepticism to be. Sceptical challenges, in broad outline, seek to undermine the reflective justifications one gives for a set of beliefs or practices. If one takes the reflective justification for a practice, say acting justly, to be a proof which eliminates all alternative possibilities for acting in one's interest other than acting justly, then the mere construction of an alternative possibility will be sufficient to undermine the reflective justification. The sceptic has to do relatively little to undermine the moralist, precisely because the moralist has set himself such a huge task. Such Platonic proofs fail because they are overly ambitious. The key to a moral outlook that is resilient to Calliclean scepticism is to sacrifice ambition. If one abandons the search for such a strong proof, then one will not necessarily be reflectively undermined by the mere construction of an alternative possibility. If one can formulate a reflective justification for certain social and moral practices that is at once weaker than the Platonic proof but nevertheless satisfying one will simultaneously have forced the sceptic to do more if he is to be undermining.

The appropriate strategy is, therefore, to prove *a posteriori* that a significant form of human flourishing consists, in part, in promoting flourishing generally. One does this by pointing *to actual cases* of human flourishing, where the flourishers are actively engaged in promoting the flourishing of others or the society of which they are part.[50] Men often do desire to promote human well-being, they find significance and fulfilment in acting so as to better man's lot, and they often feel frustration when they live in a society or historical period in which they are prevented from so acting. That there are forms of flourishing that partially consist in promoting flourishing is the truth that underlies the common belief that moral behaviour is in one's enlightened self-interest. People also believe that there must be more to moral motivation than enlightened self-interest. The truth that underlies this belief is that in flourishing, one is motivated to promote flourishing generally not because it promotes one's own flourishing but simply because it promotes flourishing generally. It is not something done in order to flourish; it is, in part, what one's flourishing is. It is from this perspective that such dicta as 'Morality provides its own motivation' make sense. It is not that morality ought to be expected to generate motivation out of some motivationally inert substance, for example from rationality as conceived by Hume: how could it? Rather it is that although promoting human flourishing generally may be in one's enlightened self-interest that will not be one's (primary) motivation for promoting flourishing generally when one is oneself actually flourishing. Enlightened self-interest could provide a motivation to promote flourishing generally, but this will be primarily active in humans who are not (yet) flourishing themselves.

An *a posteriori* proof that there are actual cases of human flourishing which partially consists in promoting flourishing generally has certain distinctive features. It does not establish more than an actuality, so it does not eliminate the *possibility* of there being other less socially co-operative forms of flourishing. Thus the proof will not necessarily be reflectively undermining to those who genuinely believe that they should live their lives in some alternative way. (Of course, it *may* be undermining: people who are living frustrating lives, divided in part by their pursuit of inappropriate goals are susceptible to influence by people who are simply exemplifying a flourishing life. Flourishers can thus function as umoved movers.) But that is not the point of the proof. The proof is intended reflectively to reinforce those who are tempted to live this form of flourishing life—to render them less vulnerable to sceptical undermining. It does so in two ways. First, since the proof is *inwardly directed*—aimed at those who are living, almost living, or interested in living this form of flourishing life—it helps to make the agents reflectively aware that this *is* a form of flourishing, and one which it is possible for *them* to live. Second, the strategy of the proof makes it difficult to pose a sceptical challenge and even more difficult to

[50] For a discussion of *a posteriori* proofs, see my *Aristotle and Logical Theory* (Cambridge: Cambridge University Press, 1980), Ch. five.

live a life that could be described as a sceptic living his scepticism. One reason that Callicles is such an interesting figure is that for thousands of years he has been *mocking* anyone who tries to prove that there is no possibility of acting in one's interest other than by acting justly. He stands for the durable exuberant possibility that neither Socrates nor anyone since has been able to eliminate. But a self-consciousness of what constitutes flourishing that is induced by actual example— that does not seek to eliminate every alternative possibility—will not be undermined by the mere construction of a possible alternative. Since *qua* possibility, he is no longer a threat to reflective stability, Callicles is transformed from an (interesting) sceptic into a (boring) dogmatist. Considered solely as someone who is commending a life of swaggering, injustice and 'looking after number one', Callicles is a less than compelling figure. (In this regard, it is worth comparing the devastating nature of Nietzsche's negative critique of Christian morality, with the pathetic positive conception of flourishing, the superman, which he commends.)

To be a sceptic one must threaten reflective stability. One will thus have to be different from Callicles; not even an actual alternative example of flourishing need be undermining. We may, for example, recognize that certain forms of artistic life do pose actual examples of alternative, unco-operative, forms of flourishing. Yet that recognition need not be undermining to those whose flourishing partially consists in promoting flourishing generally—to those not harbouring a desire to set sail for a South Sea isle.[51] To pose a sceptical challenge, one will have to live one's scepticism: embody a genuinely alternative form of flourishing that by its very existence induces self-doubt among those who have, until now, taken flourishing partially to consist in socially beneficial behaviour. By his very existence he would not merely establish an alternative actuality, he would impugn our purported *a posteriori* proof, by casting doubt on whether we had in fact succeeded in picking out an actual case of flourishing. I cannot rule out the possibility of such a sceptic, but *I* am sceptical of his actuality.

It is a commonplace that Aristotle's eudaimonism rests on a metaphysical biology that assumes that man has a definite nature, the fullest exercise of which would consist in worthwhile and noble activity. Since Darwin it has frequently been questioned whether, in fact, man has a nature, and since Freud it has been relatively easy to wonder whether the full exercise of whatever nature man might happen to possess would reveal him to be a conflicted, neurotic, miserable sort of being. Another virtue of an *a posteriori* proof is that is shows that the tie between a moral outlook based on human flourishing and a definite

[51] See Bernard Williams, 'Moral Luck', in *Moral Luck*, op. cit.

metaphysical biology is looser than might have been expected. For if we are convinced of a concrete case that *this* is a form of human flourishing, then *prima facie* we will expect an adequate metaphysical biology to explain how this flourishing is posssible. Again, one cannot rule out the possibility of one's beliefs about flourishing being overruled by discoveries in developmental biology or psychology, but in the face of convincing *a posteriori* demonstration, there is, I think, a strong intellectual requirement that the scientific image of man explain and underwrite, rather than undermine, this manifest image.[52]

This *a posteriori*, eudaimonistic approach to morality poses a grave and unanswered question: how far should our moral concern extend? Any morality which takes the detached perspective as constitutive of the moral standpoint will have an easy answer. Since from a detached perspective one makes no distinctions among human beings, but views them all impartially, it would be irrational to extend our moral concern to only a section of the community. Any such division of the community would, from a detached perspective, look arbitrary. Conversely, if one abandons the detached perspective as important to morality, it becomes unclear why all humans should be equally worthy of our moral concern. I have suggested that the moral standpoint requires seeing oneself as one person among others, but how many others? which others? I have also argued that one has an objective reason to promote human flourishing generally, but how generally? We tend to think that the demands and concern of morality extend universally, but with the abandonment of the detached perspective this belief needs an argument to support it. It is not obviously true. People in fact have a difficult time spreading their moral concern to cover all humanity. Even reflective moral agents are, by and large, most highly motivated to work within their own society. When questioned they tend to admit this and accept it as a personal failing that their moral concern does not extend as far as it should. It would at least be grimly humorous if it turned out that there was no reason for people to spread their moral concern further than they are in fact inclined to do.

I have, of course, no *a priori* or transcendental argument that our moral concerns should extend universally to encompass all humanity, but I would like to argue, if only programmatically, that it is at least theoretically and historically possible that our concern ought to be so extended.[53] First, theoretical links can be forged between promoting flourishing within a particular society and promoting human

---

[52] See Wilfrid Sellars, 'Philosophy and the Scientific Image of Man', in *Science, Perception and Reality* (London: Routledge and Kegan Paul, 1963).

[53] In this essay I shall ignore the important question of whether our moral concern should be even further extended to include other animals.

flourishing generally. If we are promoting *human* flourishing, the good life of man, then even if this is done within the confines of a particular society, with its own peculiar avenues of human realization, then what we are promoting cannot be radically unlike the human flourishing that is promoted in other societies. Cultures differ, and ways of flourishing within them will differ because flourishing is in part a social activity, and the societies offer different routes and contexts for men to express themselves. There is no core activity, flourishing, which can be understood independently of the way men flourish in particular cultures. And yet, as Wittgenstein would say, there must at least be a family resemblance among the various activities that are taken to constitute flourishing within the various cultures. Otherwise the idea that these are diverse ways of flourishing loses content.

Also, Wittgenstein's encompassing form of life depends on more than rationality or pure thought alone. It depends on sharing routes of interest, feelings of naturalness, ways of reacting.[54] This suggests that there is not merely a rational but also an affective link between individuals participating in the societies of which they are part and the larger world of humanity in which those societies are situated. The moral outlook demands that one see oneself as one person among others: the common participation of all humanity in this larger 'whirl of organism' makes it at least possible that one's moral vision encompasses all humanity. One need not view people from a detached perspective, as so many rational consciousnesses, in order to treat them all as objects of moral concern. One can see them in the particular details of their distinct lives and nevertheless count them as part of the others among whom one sees oneself.

Historically speaking, we live in a period in which the societies that inhabit the world are being drawn together by various technological, economic and political developments. The societies of the world are being pushed, as it were, to participate in a larger world-community of societies. They may resist this push—*pace* Marx there is nothing historically inevitable in the development—but it becomes increasingly clear that the cost of such resistance may be the end of human life. If man is a political animal, who can only flourish within a flourishing society, it is conceivable that we have reached a historical period in which the smallest political unit which can guarantee an environment for human flourishing is the world-community of societies. If this is so, then it may *have become true* that one's moral concern should extend to all humanity. It is easy to assume that if there are any moral truths, they must be timelessly true, perhaps because morality tends to present itself

[54] See Stanley Cavell, 'The Availability of the Later Wittgenstein', in *Must We Mean What We Say?* (New York: Scribner's, 1969).

as universalizable. I am suggesting that such presentation may have been until recently misleading—at best an aspiration—but that it has become or is becoming true in the present historical period.[55]

Though the idea that various beliefs about the world may become true with changes in the attitudes and intentions of the agents and the conditions in which the agent must act goes back to Aristotle,[56] it is Hegel who did so much to promote the idea that a society's morality will depend on the historical period in which it is situated. However, Hegel explicitly opposed the idea that a world-community of societies or any morality based on it was a historical possibility.[57] He argued rather lamely instead for the ultimate irreconcilability of nation-states, the limited ability of wills to achieve unity and the necessity of war. It is a shame that he was thus distracted from the idea of a world-community of societies, for it avoids all his really significant criticisms of absolute freedom. What is envisioned is not a single society in which all individuals are treated completely on a par—a blank condition indeed—but a second-level society: a society of societies. The individual societies retain their various personalities—and thus disparate avenues of flourishing are preserved—though, of course, these personalities are to some extent transformed as they are drawn into a larger community. There is, to use Hegelian terms, a unity in difference.

Hegel himself did not see the possibility of this unity in difference. No man, according to Hegel, can see beyond his historical period,[58] and if this is so, then Hegel could not see beyond his. Perhaps Hegel lived at a time when he could not seriously envisage this higher unity, though it is amazing, intellectually speaking, that he did not think through to this possibility. For in the dialectical development of *Geist* the part always takes itself to be more than it is: it claims a wholeness which it does not possess. Why then did Hegel, when he thought he had identified the whole, not seriously wonder whether he might not merely be articulating the part's point of view? This raises a deep question, which I shall only pose: why did Hegel not have a theory of error? For if one takes the idea of historical dialectic seriously, one ought to take seriously the possibility that one's view of reality—even if it includes the belief and plausible arguments to the effect that one is living at the end of this dialectical process—is severely blinkered by the time in which one lives. One would not, on Hegelian principles, be able to step outside one's time and gain a detailed understanding of life at a future

[55] If we think of morality as lacking timeless truths, then we should not be surprised or disappointed at the paucity of transcendental arguments.
[56] See Aristotle, *De Interpretatione* 9.
[57] See e.g. *The Philosophy of Right*, op. cit. §§ 321–324, 329–340.
[58] Ibid. preface.

historical period, but one should be able to sketch out areas of one's own thought that might be wrong. For instance, Hegelian principles of dialectic alone ought to suggest to a Hegelian that Hegel's defence of the nation-state is one more limited vision.[59]

If, however, one does not take dialectic seriously, one abandons the idea that anything is being necessarily manifested in history. One can then view a world-community of societies as a possibility that may or may not be realized due to various factors, including the self-conscious motivation and activity of agents who wish to bring such a society about. Such, I think, should be the position of a neo-Aristotelian: one who wishes to draw from Aristotle's ethical and political writing, but who recognizes that we cannot return to life in the *polis*. Hegel may have been wrong that any adequate ethical system must incorporate Kantian subjectivity, but he was surely correct in claiming that the historical changes in social, political and economic organization as well as related changes in men's consciousness made it impossible simply to return to an ancient ethical theory. If Aristotle's ethics is to be of more than historical interest, it must be adapted to social life as it has developed since the *polis*.

Let us consider how this neo-Aristotelianism might be applied to the special case of the Ik. The Ik seem to have no internal reasons to participate in any activities which could remotely be thought of as flourishing. One cannot generate a real interest in flourishing from their internal reasons, nor can one do so by turning them into empty abstract consciousnesses. Nor is there external reason for them to flourish: motivation for their flourishing cannot be derived from rational deliberation alone. However, it is arguable that there is objective reason for the Ik to flourish: for the Ik may be seen as participating in a larger community of societies that (in better moments) promotes human

---

[59] It is beyond the scope of this paper to probe Hegel's specific arguments in detail, so I will simply note that while I find them extremely variable in quality, none are persuasive. The best argument is to the effect that the self-consciousness of a nation-state requires other autonomous states against which to define itself (cf. *Philosophy of Right*, §§ 321–324). This argument is clearly based on deep metaphysical principles regarding self-consciousness (cf. *Phenomenology of Spirit*, §§ 178–196), but I think that it is arguable that whatever truth there is in this thesis can be honoured by the diversity that would continue to exist within a world-community of societies. For there would not be one single homogeneous society, there would be a community of disparate societies. At worst, Hegel gives an appalling defence of war (cf. the Addition to § 324 of the *Philosophy of Right*) where he illegitimately identifies peace and stagnation. The opposite of stagnation is not war but organic life, and while this may require diversity, there is no argument to show that this diversity must be expressed in war.

flourishing. The Ik need food, they need education, they probably need a bit of coercion. They need at the societal level the analogue of the drunk's cure for alcoholism. But such a cure is a process *they* could undergo. One need not treat them as bloodless abstract consciousnesses in the hope of satisfying the antecedent of some unlikely subjunctive conditional. One needs rather to feed and educate them: to behave paternalistically towards them.

A radical critic may wonder whether there is any justification for behaving paternalistically toward the Ik. He may agree that if they were fed and educated, they would become motivated to flourish, but wonder why they should be so encouraged. He may agree that man is a political animal but wonder why they should be prodded into becoming men: after all, they have at present no motivation to become such. There are, I think, two answers which can be given. First, if a world-community of societies is a genuine historical possibility, then even the Ik cannot live totally removed from it. Already their lives are affected by social, economic and political relations with the Dodos, the Turkana and even with the Ugandan government. And if a world-community is a possibility, then these social relations must be seen as possessing deeper significance than their surface manifestation: they must be seen as part of the social fabric that makes the possibility of a world-community a possibility. The Ik play at the level of this world-community of societies the exactly analogous role that the drunk plays within our society: that of an individual who has no internal reasons to act in any way that promotes human flourishing. In each case, the internal reasons of the society as a whole concerning human flourishing are only objective reasons for the individual. But in each case the individual members of each society will, for the most part, have internal (as well as objective) reasons to promote the flourishing of all members of the society. The motivation may stem from enlightened self-interest—the individuals tend to flourish in a society that is itself flourishing—or from taking the flourishing of society to be worthwhile in itself. At the level of the world-community of societies, the individual members are societies and the internal reasons of a given society will of course either flow from or be reflected in the motivations of its members. So the first answer to the question of why we should behave paternalistically toward the Ik is that we are motivated to do so, and we find that our motivation withstands reflective testing and moral scrutiny.

Second, though our *a posteriori* approach to flourishing allows a looser fit between ethics and biology than Aristotle himself endorsed, it is nevertheless clear that man is capable of flourishing in a way that is forever closed to a chimpanzee or a rabbit. So in acting paternalistically towards the Ik we are not merely altering their behaviour patterns from one neutrally described state to another, we are helping them to realize themselves.

This approach to moral objectivity is of course open to abuse. One shudders at the thought of Edsels and Coca Cola being imposed on the Ik to promote 'human flourishing'. Abuse in the name of paternalism is a serious problem, and there is no foolproof method for avoiding it. There are, however, tests for abuse. First our behaviour toward the Ik and our general conception of flourishing ought to be reflectively acceptable to the Ik, once they have reached a stage where they are capable of reflective moral agency. This reflective acceptance does not constitute human flourishing, as some critical theorists have hoped; it is merely a symptom of flourishing, as we understand it, that humans who are flourishing will find their state reflectively acceptable. Marcuse warned that it is possible so to stultify people with technology—to drown them in Coca Cola and Edsels—that they will find their 'one-dimensional lives' acceptable.[60] This thesis is, I think, false. It may be possible to stultify people with technology, but the evidence suggests that, even while stultified, they will not find their condition acceptable. Witness the fact that Marcuse wrote within the 'one-dimensional society' he set out to criticize and that it had a favourable reception there. His work can be seen not as a correct diagnosis of a society's malaise, but as one (inaccurate) expression of a discontent widespread in the society. There is, in any case, a second test for abuse which technological drowning fails. Our behaviour towards the Ik ought to be reflectively acceptable to ourselves and to the larger community of societies of which we are a part.

Perhaps the most serious challenge to the moral outlook I have been advocating is to explain how it is possible to avoid a deeply complacent conservatism. The short answer is: don't be complacent. If a more comprehensive answer is to be given, it will not, I think, be in an essay or a book but in a life. Aristotle stressed that it was hopeless to try to write down a code or set of rules which would specify how one should act in a particular situation.[61] Moral acts tend to take place in particular and complex circumstances, and no set of rules will be an adequate guide to behaviour. In a similar vein, I do not think that there is much to say about avoiding uncritical conservatism, though there is much to do. By studying other cultures, other moral outlooks, various psychological and sociological theories, by reflectively testing one's own beliefs against each other to see how well they fit, and by becoming aware of the dangers of uncritical conservatism one begins to take on a

[60] Herbert Marcuse, *One Dimensional Man* (London: Routledge and Kegan Paul, 1964).
[61] See *Nicomachean Ethics* II–III.6.

self-critical stance. Perhaps too one should recognize that failure is not inevitable, that there are remarkable examples of active, critical moral consciousnesses to be studied and emulated. And, perhaps most importantly, we should recognize that the consciousness of a reflective moral agent points beyond itself. Aristotle defended slavery, Hegel the supremacy of the nation-state: yet in retrospect it is evident that their thought transcends the limitations that they themselves did not recognize.[62]

[62] I have had the great pleasure of discussing the issues raised in this essay with John Dunn, Cynthia Farrar, Raymond Geuss, Norman Lear, Charles Parkin, Quentin Skinner, Timothy Smiley and Bernard Williams and I have learned from them all. This essay has been much improved by their criticisms of a previous draft. I am especially grateful to Bernard Williams, both for his personal generosity to me and because in contemporary work in this field, he has set the questions and the standards.

Morality, Survival and Nuclear War

SUSAN KHIN ZAW

This paper proceeds from a sense of dissatisfaction with much of current moral argument about defence policy, in particular the role of nuclear weapons. Discussions of the moral issues tend to divide into two distinct kinds of writing: on the one hand, impassioned calls to action based on and allied with equally impassioned moral exhortations; and on the other hand, usually in academic contexts, meticulous analyses and comparisons of aspects of nuclear policy with paradigm cases of acknowledged moral categories or requirements, with the object of showing by analogy with these that the particular aspect of policy under discussion is or is not morally wrong. My unease is caused by the fact that, while it is difficult not to respond to the impassioned style of argument, as one recognizes in it a practical and moral urgency which our situation seems to demand, nevertheless it plainly appeals only to those already convinced of its conclusions. The unconverted tend to regard it with suspicion or disdain, for in contrast to the analytical style, which manifestly seeks to compel the intellect, the impassioned style seems to make its effect by stirring the emotions as much as if not instead of by compelling the intellect. On the other hand the analytical style can seem curiously irrelevant, even trivial, in relation to the issue. For instance, it has been argued that since: nuclear war is a moral disaster; deterrence is threatening or intending to wage nuclear war; it is wrong to threaten or intend to do something wrong; therefore: deterrence is wrong, and should be abandoned. It is hard to believe that defenders of deterrence as the cornerstone of defence policy are going to be persuaded by such an argument to abandon their advocacy of it, if only because the argument totally ignores the *object* of deterrence. Yet surely the point of engaging in discussion of the morality of defence policy is to have some effect on what is done or recommended to be done. Thus the analytical style of argument equally fails to convert the unconverted: a common response of the unconverted to arguments such as the one quoted is to concede the theoretical conclusion but sever the link with action by representing morality as an impossible luxury in this sphere. In this way even if the intellect is compelled, it is compelled to no avail, practically speaking. So one longs for a discussion which will capture and display the moral issues involved in a manner sufficiently compelling both to satisfy the intellect and to connect with action. It seems to me that if people are prepared to say—and they are—that arguments about the morality of defence policy are irrelevant even if correct, because morality has no application here, then something must have gone badly wrong with the arguments: a moral argument which makes morality itself seem irrelevant to a practical issue must be in some way misconceived. *Correct* arguments about the morality of defence policy should serve, not just to rally the faithful, but also to reach the preoccupations of the opposition.

Some have objected that in asking this I am asking too much: rational moral argument should not be expected to bear so heavy a burden. After all, it is not unknown for even acknowledged moral requirements to give way to self-interest in ordinary life; why should one be surprised or disconcerted when moral arguments are ignored or dismissed as utopian in deliberations about defence policy, especially in this dangerous age of nuclear armament and warring ideologies? The calculation of the path of least risk in such a world is sufficiently difficult without complicating things with moral demands; and if the path suggested by moral considerations is not the path of least risk, it is not at all surprising if moral considerations are dismissed, even when supported by impeccable rational argument.

I think this kind of view misrepresents the role morality plays in the conduct of life, and because of that, misidentifies the source of the problem. I take a broad view of morality as encompassing everything belonging to pursuit of one's conception of the non-instrumental objective good; thus morality becomes a parameter of practical life, not just another variable which may on occasion be taken as vanishingly small. (Another such parameter is survival). In contrast, the view I sketched above suggests that, in practice, morality is merely an occasional extra constraint on action when all other things are equal, easily ignored when they are not. But even though we do not always do as we should, this does not mean that when we act immorally, or without having regard to morality, what we do is intelligible without reference to morality. For our notion of the objective good, however dimly or even incoherently conceived, informs our beliefs about both how the world and our life in the world ought to be, and thus shapes the ends in the light of which practical deliberation takes place—whether the deliberator is aware of this or not. Even episodes of setting aside moral considerations take place within a system of values expressing some sense of the objective good, which sets limits to and may determine the scheme of action within which the episodes take place, and without which they cannot be fully understood. A *human* life cannot be understood without reference to some notion of the objective good, i.e. without some reference to morality, because it cannot be *lived* without some such reference. That is why people apparently incapable of moral concepts, as psychopaths are sometimes said to be, tend to be regarded as psychologically deficient in some poorly understood way—that is, as literally less than human. The influence of essentially moral considerations is often overlooked because a *functioning* morality—i.e. one that is in fact determining action—is not felt as a constraint but taken for granted: thus at moments of decision there are any number of alternatives which are simply not considered because they are regarded as bad in themselves and therefore automatically ruled out. This is so even when the action in fact selected is something most people would regard as morally abominable: if there is anyone of whom it is *not* so, he is immediately felt to lack some essentially human characteristic.

It does indeed appear that the most irreconcilable difference between nuclear disarmers and deterrers is above all a difference about morality. For obviously, moral considerations are not left out of account by defenders of nuclear armament. Some even accept that nuclear war would be a moral disaster; but the object of current policy is represented as being to prevent both it and something also seen as a moral disaster—the domination of the world by an evil régime. And the slogan 'Better dead than red' is more obviously the slogan of a *moral* stance than 'Better red than dead'. It is arguable that even if nuclear war is the greater evil, a sufficiently small risk of it is morally preferable to a sufficiently large risk of the lesser evil of universal Soviet hegemony. From this point of view, to prefer the high risk of the lesser evil to the lower risk of the greater evil is not moral rectitude, but culpable failure of nerve, rationalized into claims that deterrence is immoral. What the situation requires is not craven submission to the lesser evil but the resolution to pursue the only path which holds out the hope of avoiding *both* evils. As for moral objections, if killing in self-defence is not a crime, then there can be nothing wrong in matching threats with threats: indeed it is obligatory, for strength is the only language understood by the wicked, and restrains where conciliation would encourage.

This general line of thought is familiar enough. But if it represents at all correctly the view of defenders of the *status quo*, it is rather surprising that excessive idealism and concern with morality should be made a reproach to the opposition, as it often is. This must surely be a confusion, since both parties in fact try to seize the moral high ground, though they may locate the heights in different places. What could be more idealistic than proclaiming 'Better dead than red'? The real reproach against the disarmers must be that their idealism and morality are not so much excessive as spurious—perhaps that the excesses betray the spuriousness. For instance, I detect signs of the charge of spurious morality in Terry Coleman's report of the 22 October CND rally in

London for the *Guardian*. Coleman, while granting that the marchers were in the main well-meaning people, expressed the view that they were motivated not by moral conviction but by fear of death. This was not intended as a compliment; but why on earth should one *not* be motivated by fear of death? When such an imputation is intended as a slur—and it clearly was in this case—there is a strong suggestion that the motivating fear is not rational but infantile, carrying with it a concomitant wish, not to eliminate an eliminable risk—which would be a perfectly respectable aim of policy—but *per impossibile* to live for ever, or to live in a world without the dangers inescapably present in the real world. There is a sub-text accusing members of CND of retreat from reality: of a failure of nerve, of unwillingness to face unpalatable truths. It is thus suggested that the moral claims and demands of CND proceed not from any authentic moral vision, but from the vain wish that things were different—the essential point being that the wish is seen as *vain*. The moral vision is regarded as inauthentic because it is believed that instead of grappling with practical problems of policy it really expresses a kind of nostalgia: the purported moral demands are really demands for something impossible (viz. that nuclear weapons should be uninvented), converted, since that *is* impossible, into the next best thing: that mankind at large should with one voice renounce nuclear weapons, moral superiority being—absurdly—measured by quickness off the mark in renunciation despite the possible evil consequences (such as the triumph of Communism). This disregard for consequences may be mistaken by those who display it for devotion to moral principle; but it is not: it is a sign of retreat from reality prompted by panic.

These accusations tend to be mirrored by markedly similar accusations against deterrers from disarmers: deterrers have retreated from reality and rationality into a paranoid fantasy about the Red Menace, their judgments are conditioned not by objective weighing of the evidence but by the needs of their fantasy, which drives them to a wildly unrealistic, and hence necessarily vain, search for a quite delusory total security. Lured on by this impossible dream, they refuse to face up to either what the nuclear conflict which may well be the outcome of their policy will actually be like, or what are most likely really to be the policy objectives of the Soviets. In other words the moral vision of the deterrers is inauthentic, their moral claims spurious, and their appraisal of technical evidence skewed, because all three are founded on irrational terrors. The evidence for this is the irrationality and moral lunacy of the policy they propose. For it is a gamble which not just they but the whole world cannot afford to lose; yet there is a clear and non-negligible risk of its loss. (For instance, through technical failure.) To accept this risk for the sake of protecting relatively local interests is an act of criminal folly comparable to Hume's example of preferring the destruction of the world to the scratching of my finger: in a sense that is *exactly* what it is. But morality *cannot* command us to destroy the world. To prevent the spread of evil régimes is perhaps a duty, but to prevent it by inviting the destruction of those supposedly being protected must be a moral abomination. Thus one opponent of deterrence has likened it to motor accident prevention by tying babies to car bumpers. Suppose someone seriously proposed such a scheme, on the grounds that it was bound to work because the dreadfulness of the risk would make people take extraordinary care, and claimed that there could be no moral objection from the risk to the babies because the *intention* of the whole thing was that the babies should not get hurt: we would think such a person obviously mad. The policy of deterrence is mad in just this way: it is similarly unrealistic in disregarding possible, even probable consequences, by which means its proposers equip themselves with the necessary moral blindness to the enormity of what they are proposing.

It is very striking that the two sides accuse each other of exactly the same fault—defective moral vision—and see this fault as emerging in exactly the same symptoms: lack of realism and practical irrationality. The manifestations are of course different, but the faults are the same. Fault and symptoms are intimately connected: the defective moral vision sustains and is sustained by the other two. This suggests that whatever else disarmers and deterrers disagree about, they agree in thinking that there are *constraints* on morality in the sense that a morality that does not answer to those constraints is suspect. The constraints are that the demands of morality should be in some sense realistic and rational: they should acknowledge and be responsive to facts about the world and about people—that is, morality should not need to ignore the facts in order to be applicable—so that it can conduct through the world as it actually is people such as we actually are. Perhaps it is just another aspect of this requirement that both sides feel morality should, also, respond to the demands of *survival*: a morality that has scant regard for the preservation of human life is also automatically suspect. The moral importance of threats to life is seen in the way both disarmers and deterrers rely on an assumption of it in defending their moral claims: deterrers ward off moral accusation by appealing to the legitimacy of killing in self-defence, disarmers with the claim that morality cannot demand universal destruction.

I think it is interesting and significant that the two sides should seek to discredit each other by raising doubts about each other's moral perception. It looks like recognition that the difference between them *is* a moral difference, and that it is a deep and ramifying one, not a relatively localized disagreement confined to one specific practical issue. Another sign of this is that we appear to have here a stalemate from which there is no rational exit, since even with regard to matters for which scientific or technical evidence can be offered, each side tends to regard with suspicion the other's arguments from such evidence, as probably specious rationalizations. Thus a radio interviewer recently cast doubt on an engineer's objections to the deployment of cruise missiles on the grounds that they had not been adequately tested, by pointing out that since the engineer was against cruise, he would say that, wouldn't he.[1] And on the moral issue, there seems insufficient agreement about starting-points for rational debate even to get going. Thus the contenders do not even seem to agree about what constitutes evidence for their moral claims; each finds it impossible to see the moral comparisons invoked by the other as even relevant, let alone compelling. Rather they seem to find the comparisons of nuclear deterrence with justifiable homicide or babies on bumpers grotesque. And each can back up this view by pointing out specific ways in which nuclear deterrence differs from these two things. Does this mean that *both* sides are wrong, or that we have reached a bedrock of moral disagreement which rationality cannot penetrate?

I think the answer is the first rather than the second, for it seems to me that in invoking such comparisons both sides err in expecting more of a particular style of argument than it can here deliver. The style is the comparison of a problematic case with a moral paradigm case. Such comparisons, though very familiar in both lay moral debate and practical philosophy, cannot take the strain imposed by this particular issue. In the absence of any other generally accepted form of moral argument, when the method of comparison collapses under the strain it looks as if we have reached the limit of rationality in this sphere. But perhaps this is only because we have not fully understood or explored all the ways in which rationality can be applied to such problems.

To see this, consider what makes deterrence morally problematic. It is surely that this form of deterrence is something *new*: it involves new actions made possible by technological and economic development, in the straightforward sense that the policy of nuclear deterrence is only available to us because it is now possible to do things which simply were not possible before, such as almost instantaneously kill large numbers of people from a very long way off. In this respect the moral problem of deterrence resembles the moral problems created by advances in medical technology which enable us to maintain human beings in states

[1] This is obviously no answer at all to *specific* technical objections, but seems to be regarded as a refutation of them—perhaps on the weak but understandable ground that experts frequently disagree, and since the lay person is in no position to judge who is right on technical matters, he can only rely on his assessment of the character and motivation of the witness.

in which they couldn't previously be maintained. That situation is so new that often we do not even know what to call it: are we keeping people *alive* or not? Are we keeping *persons* alive or not? Similarly, the existence of nuclear weapons and the associated delivery and surveillance systems have created a situation without precedent. The obvious way of coping with anything new is to think of something similar to it which one *does* know how to deal with, either because it is familiar or for some other reason, and treat the new situation in the same way. Thus we call mutual preparations for unprecedently large-scale destruction, 'deterrence', because deterring the other side from starting anything is what we hope the preparations will do, on the analogy of previously successful attempts at deterrence by means of more or less similar preparations, though for lower levels of destruction, in previous more or less similar situations. And in the moral domain, one side compares morally problematic deterrence to the familiar case of one man killing or threatening to kill another in self-defence, the other to the invented but morally uncontroversial case of accident prevention by putting babies on bumpers. And there actually *are* resemblances between deterrence and both of these things. But of course, if something really is new, it will not *exactly* resemble anything familiar; and if it really is problematic, it will not *exactly* resemble anything uncontroversial. Thus deterrence is in very many ways quite unlike previous cases of deterring aggression by military strength, warning a potential assailant that you will shoot to kill, and pursuing accident prevention by putting babies on bumpers. And this will be so *whatever* deterrence is compared with, as long as it is compared with something which is either familiar or uncontroversial. But the *point* of such comparisons is precisely to compare the problematic with the familiar or the uncontroversial. It follows that when the moral problem arises through novelty there will always be a gap between the problematic case and the paradigm invoked to shed light on it; there will always be differences as well as similarities. If the similarities as such are grounds for treating the cases alike, the dissimilarities as such must be grounds for treating them differently. Thus such comparisons on their own are inconclusive at best, and particularly so in the case of deterrence, since *nothing* can be quite like preparing to destroy the world: that really is a one-off job, because there is only one world. At this point, disarmers are liable to feel that even if there is nothing quite like deterrence, this hardly matters, for after all destroying the world can hardly be controversial: there can be no doubt that destroying the world is wrong. (That, no doubt, is what makes the comparison with babies on bumpers attractive: both cases can be seen as teleologically paradoxical, and for that reason, morally very clear.) But of course *that* deterrence is wrong is precisely what is at issue, which means that it is *not* very clear to everyone. Perhaps there is no doubt that destroying the world is wrong. But it is not the same as *preparing* to destroy the world. Hence the argument from the evil of an action to the evil of its intention, which I quoted on behalf of disarmers at the outset. But even if deterrers accepted the description of deterrence as preparing to destroy the world, which they probably would not, this argument too relies on just the sort of comparison I have been discussing, and is inconclusive in just the same way. It seems very clear that individual people do have evil intentions—there *are* such things as evil intentions, in persons at any rate—and that in persons, an evil intention is an intention to do an evil action. But the policy of deterrence is adopted by states or governments, not by individual persons. Here is one difference at least from the paradigm, from which who knows what others follow. It is not at all clear that states and governments can have intentions in the same way as persons, nor, consequently, that the same things can necessarily be said about their intentions. I suspect it is because people are aware of such differences, though they may not immediately be able to point them out, that they do not find the argument compelling, even when they cannot see how to fault the argument from the comparison and thus feel obliged to assent to its conclusion.

Clearly what is needed to reinforce such arguments is some way of showing that the similarities between the cases compared are *relevant* to the moral question and the dissimilarities are not; for this is what is really at issue. Deterrence can be described in many different ways and points of similarity found between it and many different things; the problem is knowing *which* of all these ways of seeing it, or *which* of all the many things which are true of it, is relevant to deciding whether it is the right thing to do. Some philosophical theories of morality provide criteria of moral relevance in the form of a fundamental principle or principles, such as, for instance, the 'greatest happiness' principle of Utilitarianism: if morally right actions are just those which maximize the general happiness, then only those aspects of an action which bear on its propensity to maximize the general happiness will be morally relevant. But even if everyone accepted such a principle, its application to particular cases would remain very often problematic and a matter of dispute; worse still, not everyone does accept such principles as fundamental. Moreover, Utilitarianism is only one of many philosophical theories of morality, and different theories of morality advocate different fundamental principles. Nor do philosophers agree about which philosophical theory of morality is correct, or even the most rationally acceptable. Thus in the current state of the art, philosophy fails at just the point where it is most needed in the practical debate.

In the absence of generally accepted moral theories or criteria of moral relevance, is there any point at all to the sorts of comparisons I have been discussing? I think they have a point *because* there is a gap between the things compared, and they are compared *with the object* of assimilating one to the other. Where there is no gap for assimilation to cross there is no point in the comparison, for the assimilation has already happened: the case is clear; there is no problem. The function of the comparisons is not to *compel* the intellect, but to *invite* it to view the case in a particular way, by reminding it of factors which hitherto may not have been salient. If, once they *are* salient, they strike one as the *relevant* factors, so that the cases compared *are assimilated*, the intellect may well then be compelled to the desired moral conclusion by inferences from that particular description of the case suggested by the assimilation. But it is not *this* compulsion which persuades: it is whatever persuaded the convert to accept the assimilation. But he may *not* be so persuaded, in which case *nothing* compels him to accept either the inferences or the moral conclusion. Thus the same argument will be experienced by one side as both rational and compelling, and by the other side as neither; and this can only deepen the suspicions each side has of the rationality and motivation of the other. That is why the positions of the two sides in this debate look so hopelessly entrenched.

Is there a rational exit from this impasse? If I am right in thinking that what divides the most entrenched factions on the two sides is a deep moral difference, and that this difference is located at or beyond the limits of the current state of the art of philosophy, is there any way that philosophy can usefully contribute to the debate? Well, philosophers can of course arm themselves with their theories and simply pile in on one side or the other; but this is unlikely to be helpful, for dissension among philosophers about practical morality is liable to create the same scepticism about philosophy in the lay public as dissension among economists about economic policy has caused about economics. The trouble is that the stakes in defence policy are even higher than in economic policy; if we cannot afford to be wrong about economics, still less can we afford to be wrong about defence. If it is uncertain where the truth lies one can of course suspend judgment. But unfortunately even in uncertain times one has to *act* (indeed all times are uncertain); though the practice of philosophy can tolerate pluralism with regard to theories about morality, political life cannot. Even when one does not know what to think, one has to decide what to *do*. To decide on a particular course of action in a morally problematic area one has to *make up one's mind* about what is morally relevant, so, if one seeks one's criteria of relevance in a moral theory, for the purposes of that decision one has to adopt one theory and reject the rest. But given the existence of competing theories of which none are capable of outright proof but all have some rational justification, what is *thereafter* the most rational course for the theoretically uncommitted agent? On the one hand consistency may seem to require that he stick with the particular theory that, to his mind, delivered the goods on this occasion; but on the other hand reflections on the state of the art may suggest that philosophical pluralism is the more *practically* rational course, at least to the extent of keeping the whole range of plausible theories in stock against possibly different future needs.

But if this is the attitude to theory, then philosophical theory loses its point. Theories, after all, aim to be *true*; only the truth of a theory could legitimate its use morally to justify a practical decision. If its inapplicability to some other case casts doubt on its truth, then that doubt remains even in those cases where the theory seems most readily applicable. If different and incompatible theories are brought forward by the same person to buttress and justify moral decisions in different cases then philosophy is assisting an exercise in rationalization, not the exercise of rationality. Even if one is personally convinced of the truth of a particular moral theory, in the absence of outright proof—and it is doubtful, to say the least, that the subject is one that admits of outright proof—the mere existence of different theoretical convictions must give one pause. It is always possible that one is wrong, in which case it could be disastrous to let one's theoretical convictions override residual intuitive qualms and determine action. Certainly if one relies on moral intuition alone one may be led into actions which, within the context of a theory, can be represented as morally inconsistent. But the inconsistency may be merely a reflection of the inadequacy of the theory; and in any case there are worse crimes than inconsistency. If no theory can be proved correct but most have something to be said for them—which is what seems to be the case—then it is rational *not* to submit one's practice to a theory, when making the right practical decision matters more than theoretical consistency, as I submit it usually does. I am *not* saying that in morality intuition is our only resource, or that we should not at least attempt to be consistent; obviously one must use one's reason both to try to understand why one has the moral intuitions one does, and to preserve consistency as far as possible. But one may be more consistent than one knows, and one may be rational without becoming the captive of a theory. Philosophical energies tend to be devoted to theory construction and defence, which is *one* expression of rationality, and to philosophers may come to seem its supreme expression; but *practical* rationality demands something rather different.

Nevertheless, people *do* decide what to do, and often display a certain consistency in their choices even without benefit of philosophy; and it may be that what governs practical decision-making is the same *kind* of thing as what governs choice among philosophical theories. Though philosophers rightly pay a great deal of attention to arguments for theories—that, after all, is their *métier*—it seems obvious that the kind of theory one finds attractive or convincing is not determined by the arguments alone, perhaps especially in the case of moral theories. There is a coming together of the arguments and something else which pre-dates them, and which the arguments articulate. Theories grow out of a need. To gain someone's allegiance to a theory, or to convince them that they ought to do something other than they suppose, it may be necessary first to make them perceive the need to which the theory or the new course of action answers. There are of course needs peculiar to individuals which they cannot be argued into or out of; presumably all individuals have *some* needs of this kind. In so far as moral theories or practical choices rest on such needs, they will resist rational deconstruction; here the role of rationality is to exercise quality control on the articulation of the needs in the theories or the choices. But there are collective needs as well as individual needs; and *new* collective needs can be created by new circumstances. The new needs may however he rendered invisible by mental habits produced by previous theoretical allegiance or patterns of practical choice. In such a case rationality may assist in demonstrating the need; thus hunters may be rationally convinced that because of an explosion in the population of hunters and a consequent decline in the population of game, there is a need for limits on hunting if hunting itself is to continue.

But the change we are seeking to bring about is a change in *moral* perceptions, specifically in the perception of what moral values are most important in relation to a particular decision. However, changing needs resulting from changing circumstances affect such perceptions also. Suppose there is a vaccine against a dangerous illness which is ninety per cent effective and is known to result in death or serious brain damage to a small proportion of sensitive people. The government of a country where there was some risk of the disease might reject mass compulsory vaccination on the grounds that such a programme would certainly mean some deaths and disablements, and no government had the right to impose death and damage on the unknown innocents. But if the community was threatened by a major epidemic which could only be contained by a mass compulsory vaccination programme, they might feel that in the circumstances such a programme was morally justified, and indeed that failure to undertake it was a dereliction of duty. But I think the case of deterrence is different again from this. In the vaccination example, there is no problem about the actual values involved; libertarians may object that the government should leave citizens to protect themselves or not with vaccination, as they choose, and authorities may reply that this will inevitably expose many to infection and death who need not be so exposed, and they have a duty to ensure that the environment is infection-free just as they have a duty to ensure that the water supply is pure; but neither side has difficulty in understanding the position of the other. New circumstances have created a new and acute conflict between the rights of the community and the rights of individuals, which different parties may resolve in different ways; but there is no difficulty for either side in seeing what the other side regards as wrong. But with deterrence, the problem seems to be that one side simply cannot see what is wrong with what the other side regards as morally abominable. It is no longer even universally accepted, as it once was, that nuclear war is a moral disaster, or even a disaster of any kind. So it would be a step forward if the views of the antagonists could be made mutually intelligible; mutual understanding may assist negotiation of an agreed policy, and is a prerequisite of any conversion from one side to the other. This conversion would require a much more fundamental shift in moral perspective than is called for in the two examples I have just given; is there any way in which rational leverage can be exerted to encourage the necessary shift?

I think it is possible for the conditions of life to change so drastically that existing values can actually lapse, and new values be created in their place. I think this may be what makes deterrence problematic. And I think one may be able to produce rational grounds for believing that there is a need for such a change as this. I suggested earlier that there is some going conception of constraints on morality which is shared by both disarmers and deterrers; the specific suggestion was that the constraints were reality and survival. If it can be shown that a moral stance oversteps these constraints, this will perhaps amount to the nearest possible thing to a rational case against it.

I want now to offer an example of an actual change in values under the pressure of circumstances. Consider in this light Colin Turnbull's description of the Ik in his book *The Mountain People*. The Ik were a tribe who had to adjust to living in virtually permanent conditions of famine. At the time that Turnbull describes there was not enough food available to support existing numbers; equal sharing of what there was would have meant slow but inexorable universal starvation. However equal sharing was not attempted; individuals (apart from nursing infants) fended for themselves, with the result that food went to the relatively strong within a particular age-group, while the weak and sick starved and died. The strong showed neither compassion nor concern for the weak, not even when these were members of their own family; indeed they laughed at their misfortunes, as for instance when an old woman fell down a ravine. When Turnbull himself tried to succour the weak, he was rebuked for wasting food, water and medicine on those who were going to die anyway (as indeed invariably happened, on his own account; he cites not a single case of a person actually saved by his ministrations; even his own servant died of starvation). What struck Turnbull was that the unfortunate often shared in the laughter at their own expense; the old woman who fell into the ravine laughed too. In general the weak seemed neither to expect help nor to resent the lack of it, but to acquiesce in their fate. When compassionate non-Ik observers rushed to help, though, the dying broke down and wept, and admitted remembering and regretting a time when things were different and people helped each other. Experiencing compassion again when, for very obvious reasons, it had disappeared from their world, made the present unbearable to them: they were no longer capable of the miracles of endurance and objectivity which had hitherto sustained them.

Turnbull himself considers the Ik to have abandoned all morality, but I do not see that we are forced to this conclusion. Perhaps both weak and strong could only bear the world as it was by thinking that, given the food situation, it was *right* that the strong should not help the weak but preserve themselves by eating what there was, leaving the weak to die. Maybe what they did was literally make a virtue of necessity, which is one way of living with necessity. It is possible to make moral sense of their behaviour by seeing both weak and strong as motivated by the thought: It is better for some to live than for all to die. If one takes acknowledgment of the reality of others as part of the core of morals, and if one takes the thought as an expression of this acknowledgment, then action genuinely motivated by the thought may be morally motivated. In that case one can view what was happening as a shift in moral perspective demanded by the exigencies of the time. A collective end, viz. that some should live, has been adopted as objectively good, and is thus an end recommended by morality. But in the prevailing circumstances adjustments have to be made to other moral categories in order to achieve that end. Compassion is no longer a virtue; perhaps it has even become a vice. It is replaced by a new virtue which one may call *acceptance of one's fate*. This virtue is most strikingly evident in the behaviour of the weak; but perhaps it is not altogether absent in the strong, too. Who is to say that it did not cost them to turn out their little children and drive away their old parents? Significantly, one man who did this last had no doubt that everyone (including Turnbull) would think he had acted rightly. He was, of course, wrong about Turnbull: the new guises of virtue were initially incomprehensible to that compassionate observer, who at first was taken up by his horror at the absence of the virtues (such as compassion) with which he was familiar. But he found that practice of these virtues did not work in this world: thus Turnbull describes his own compassion as invariably failing to achieve its object. It did no enduring good, but simply made necessity harder to bear, by making people long once more for what was in fact impossible. Under these pressures Turnbull himself began to doubt that in these circumstances the actions dictated to him by compassion really were virtuous. Thus one may speak of the virtue of compassion being lost from the world of the Ik.

It may be said that it is not that compassion is no longer a virtue, but that the *expression* of compassion has changed; compassion is now expressed in *not* doing the things that Turnbull did. But what is compassion without positive expression? As the old rhyme says, sympathy without relief is like mustard without beef. But in such a world, exercise of active compassion—that is, sympathy *plus* relief—is pointless because the only possible relief is utterly inadequate to the need; the result of those who have giving to those who have not will either merely reverse their positions, or make it more likely that everyone will die, and thus make more likely the *loss of the future*. That, I think, is why it cannot be seen as a good. On the other hand, as long as at least some survive, even those now about to die can still imagine and share in thought a future which makes sense of the present. Seen in this light, it makes sense to forgo compassion, and that is why I see forgoing compassion as a sort of virtue rather than simply as a vice. Similarly, if I am one of the weak, and my death makes it possible for the less weak to live, then my death can be accepted. We both get something out of the bargain; the strong get life; I get sense, which makes my fate endurable. That is why I do not protest at it, why I laugh when I fall down a ravine rather than curse God and die.

Again it may be said that even if active compassion in the sense of offering relief from starvation is ruled out, there was no need for the Ik to be as horrid to each other as they in fact were: they need not have turned out their little children, nor driven away relatives who only came to die under their roof, nor laughed at the misfortunes of others. Nor does starvation debar one from helping someone who has fallen down a ravine. But maybe it does; maybe it exacts husbanding of strength; and maybe compassion cannot be abandoned piecemeal: if compassion is ruled out for some kinds of suffering, maybe human nature requires that the habit of compassion be lost altogether. Those who are suffering can be driven away and laughed at by the formerly compassionate because when it cannot be relieved the sight of suffering is unbearable. (Turnbull, again on his own admission, for a long time contrived not to see it, refusing to believe that the Ik were indeed starving and attributing their emaciation to a naturally bony build.) Or again, Kalahari Bushmen, who unlike the Ik usually strike Western observers as warm and delightful people living in idyllic and loving social harmony, devoted to their children whom they cherish and indulge, do not hesitate to kill at birth infants born in times of drought and scarcity when the community is already living on the edge of disaster.

I do not want to deny that the Ik, as Turnbull describes them, are an unattractive people; one may feel that, even if a change in moral perception was called for, there might have been better solutions to the problem—the Bushman one perhaps. If the abandonment of compassion and the establishment of the new virtue were indeed only achieved at considerable cost to themselves, by doing continual violence to their own previously natural impulses and feelings, then once they saw how high was the price in violence done both to themselves and others in this respect, they could and should have had second thoughts about their new collective end, however objectively good it at first appeared—or at least tried to find another means of achieving it. I think this attributes to the Ik greater moral and social self-consciousness than I intended to attribute to them, but otherwise I would only wish to comment that one can, of course, think what one likes of the Ik: the question is, what does one's inclination to think whatever one does in fact think, show about morality. To follow up this last suggestion: suppose they *were* that self-conscious, and suppose they *did* revise either their ends or their means in response to the way things were working out: would this not be yet another shift in moral perspective in response to changed circumstances? The shift, this time, would be a shift way from the newly acquired moral perspective which was a response to famine, to some as yet unspecified moral position which was a response to their response to famine.

To return to our own case: it is possible to look at the world and see accumulating changes in it whose *future* effects make new virtues necessary *now* (an analogue of the Ik's situation) without those new virtues coming into being because the future effects are not certain or are not generally known or are too far off. Such a perception calls for a form of moral argument which does *not* rely exclusively on appeal to familiar examples but seeks instead to create an appreciation of *new* virtues, which may replace and take precedence over the old ones, and which are what they are because the world is now what it is, and are justified by the world's being as it is, not by making them out to be really the old virtues all along. I suspect that we are now in such a time of virtue-generating change, not just because of the existence of nuclear weapons, but because of the scale of the effects that human activity can now have, through technological and economic advance, on the rest of the world. The actions of relatively small numbers of people small numbers of people (those controlling governments and large or powerful organizations such as multinationals, the IMF, the World Bank, NATO, etc.) can within an ordinary life-span radically affect vast numbers of others not visibly connected with the powerful body, and also the natural world on which in the end we all rely; that is, the material fabric and biosphere of the earth. Nuclear war is only the most dramatic example of the effects of the decisions of the few on the many. Another example is the diminishing of plant and animal species by land development and new methods of farming. Conversely, the majority feels impotent to alter courses of action set by the minority, even though the results may radically alter or even threaten their lives. The majority thus find themselves exposed to in principle preventable evil effects which are yet not prevented, and which may be unintended and unforeseen. Manifest and widespread evils thus appear for which no existing body or individual is entirely responsible and which thus elude control. The speed and scale of such effects has grown to a critical point strikingly epitomized in the advent of nuclear weapons. We are now in the position of the Ik: plausibly, if we go on as we are we shall not survive. This is palpably a new situation for humanity, which requires a shift in perspective if its demands are to be met. Technological power and the new organizational structure of the world have endowed us with new capacities for good and evil, and thus made room for new responsibilities and obligations, new vices and virtues. There is disagreement about the morality of deterrence and nuclear weapons because such considerations have shifted the moral perspective of some but not of others, so that some see moral obligations that are invisible to others. Thus disarmers tend to see the problem of defence policy in a context set by the novel thought that those with the power to destroy the world should acknowledge the dangers they have created and their responsibility to those exposed to those dangers, while deterrers tend to set the context of the problem much more narrowly in terms of responsibilities and dangers arrived at historically: responsibilities of governments to their own people, and dangers from other nations which have proved dangerous in the past.

Can one, however, say there is a *need* to shift from the old perspective to the new? Well, if there really are new dangers, and only the new perspective really caters for them, then one may say there is a need for the new perspective. If it is true that if we go on as we are, we shall not survive, this seems a good enough reason for *not* going on as we are; and the call for the acknowledgment of new responsibilities and the development of new virtues is a suggestion of how we should change our ways. Of course these new ways will bear *some* relation to the old ones; fundamental values are unlikely to change, so that the new virtues will not be totally new, but rather a new expression of continuing values. Thus a possible new virtue such as concern for the preservation of species could be seen as related to the old virtue of thrift (which incidentally seems to have vanished from the spectrum of virtues in a world in which credit-card advertisers urge us to take the waiting out of wanting: possibly because there is less *need* for thrift in a welfare state). And yet conservation isn't quite like thrift; for one thing, it is a virtue primarily incumbent upon institutions—since only they can ensure its effectiveness. Here we encounter another problem: can we attach a clear and concrete sense to the notion of an institution possessing a virtue? Institutions clearly cannot have *characters* in quite the same way as humans; can they then have virtuous characters? Perhaps it is a misleading human analogy which leads to vain attempts to give institutions an analogue of *dispositions*, by such devices as deliberately loose definitions of policy, the slack to be taken up by ministerial discretion. The object seems to be to get the institution to mimic the behaviour of a person of a particular character, in the following sense: what a virtuous character (or a vicious one for that matter) makes possible is a flexibility of response to concrete situations without loss of an essential moral consistency. The decisions of a just man or woman are preferable to (i.e. likely to be more just than) the decisions of the rule-book because a just person can take account of contingencies not covered by the rule-book. But it is not obvious how institutions are to achieve anything similar: the device of ministerial discretion notoriously can lead to arbitrary and unjust anomalies, in other words can produce the exact opposite of the behaviour which, I suggest, it was intended to mimic. As well as these structural differences, there are also differences of content between conservation and thrift. Most conservationists would I think see more that is good in conservation than just the biological prudence of keeping the gene-pool as large as possible; some seem to feel that other species also have a *right* to existence; others that the richness and variety of the world is intrinsically good. I suggest that though there may be nothing new in seeing these things as good, or even as moral goods, it is new to feel that so perceiving them lays any urgent moral demands on us. No doubt men have always marvelled at the richness of the world; but they could feel no obligation to preserve that richness until they realized it was in their power to diminish it. Morality changes when our relation to the world changes, and our knowledge of the world changes our relation to it.

To return to the specific question of deterrence: disarmers are indeed, as Coleman suggests, motivated by the imperative of survival. But it does not follow that they are morally discredited, for if, as I have suggested, the preservation of human life in some sense constrains morality, then concern for survival may be a moral concern. And that is certainly how disarmers see their own concern for survival; perhaps with justice. For *whose* survival is at stake? Presumably the survival of those who would be killed by a nuclear war. It is when we consider these as a body that the imperative of survival seems most compelling. But, I

7

suggest, that is just because the survival up for preservation is *not* primarily one's *own* survival but the survival of a body within which one may or may not be included. For disarmers, it is imperative that 'we' should survive, but 'our' surviving in this sense is perfectly consistent with the individual disarmer *not* surviving—who knows, perhaps because he has been run over by a Russian tank. Somewhat like the Ik, disarmers are motivated by the thought: it is better that most should live than that most should die; and since it is better, most *must* live. This imperative of survival is thus a moral, not a prudential, imperative, despite the identity of its directives to some prudential imperatives. The moral objection to deterrence is that in accepting the threat of nuclear war as an instrument of policy we deny this imperative its proper importance.

In what way, though, is this moral imperative *new*? Has not the mass killing of war always been recognized as a great evil? And have not pacifists always been moved by impersonal concern for the unknown lives to be destroyed by future wars? This is certainly true, but causing large numbers of people to perish horribly is only part of what is seen as wrong with nuclear war. For much more than these may be destroyed: not just the individuals but also the social structures and cultures which supported them and gave their life meaning, and even an unknown part of the natural world on which ultimately all these things depended. Thus what is destroyed is not just the lives but even the *possibility* of such lives. The crime is not just killing people but causing chaos to come again, or rather creating chaos out of order and creating such a chaos that it is uncertain what human order, if any, could emerge from it. Even the destruction of Roman civilization by the barbarian invasions—perhaps the nearest historical parallel—did not achieve this: the civilized world may have been in ruins, but the natural world at least was not threatened. Nuclear war threatens to destroy not just people but the present world, and not just the present but in that also the past which produced this present (by destroying knowledge), and an as yet possible future. The crime is new because it is, so to speak, the destruction of a new entity, which one might characterize as the currently continuing human world.

Perception of this new crime has converted many to a new pacifism. The objection to pacifism has always been that, horrifying as all wars are, some wars are worth fighting, because the alternative is worse than the horrors of war itself. But it is hard to imagine any worse state than the probable state of the world after a nuclear war fought with the current level of armament: nothing could be worth the fighting of such a war. So the destruction would be terrible not just in itself, but terrible also because it was *wanton* destruction, and not only wanton but also paradoxical, because along with everything else it would destroy what it was allegedly undertaken to preserve. Pointless destruction on this scale is an act of such enormity that accepting even the risk of it can seem a crime: hence the moral objection to deterrence, and the feeling that making every effort to avert such destruction is not just a duty, but currently, while the threat is so great, the supreme duty. Before the modern age it would not have made sense to enjoin concern for what is now threatened, because there was no way in which such concern could be expressed. (Similarly in Ik society there was no way for compassion to be expressed.) It is interesting, though, that in former times those who divided the world into two entities somewhat similar to the one now threatened—the Christian and the non-Christian world—and saw the non-Christian world as threatened by the terrible fate of hellfire, *did* see concern for this entity as a duty because that concern could be expression in evangelism and prayer. The possibility of nuclear war has in a sense *created* the new threatened entity by making it thinkable in concrete terms which are the expression of *lack* of concern for it; and we have tried to rise to the moral demands of the occasion by anathematizing deterrence. But what makes us want to do this is that we see deterrence as threatening us with what threatened the Ik: the destruction of everyone (even of those who are not killed) and everything, the loss of the future; not in our case because there will be nothing and no one left after a nuclear war, but because the future after such a war is not one in which we can share, beause it is discontinuous with our present. Those who see themselves in the light of this threat may feel themselves united *only* by this—for the threat cuts across all current political and social groupings. Because of this they are a constituency without a means of political expression in terms of current political structures, a scattered people without a sustaining tribe. One way of seeing the efforts of the anti-nuclear campaigners is as the start of an attempt to create such a sustaining tribe, by getting the scattered people first to think of themselves as a tribe, and then to create the social and political structures necessary to bring the tribe concretely into being and protect its interests. Coleman was right to feel that there is fear in the air: but the fear is for others as well for the individuals themselves, and forming such a tribe is a rational response to a real threat. This is what makes it possible to see the aims of disarmers as realistic, rational and moral, and moral because realistic and rational. It is only preoccupation with old and really obsolete concerns which makes this morality and rationality invisible.

Deterrers have a response to this, however. They would probably dispute the relatively value-free issues, such as the size of the various risks and levels of destruction involved, but let us assume agreement on that and consider the moral issue under that assumption. Deterrers may protest that by blurring the distinction between morality and prudence

189

I have lost sight of morality altogether. Survival is no doubt the most urgent task of prudence, but it has nothing to do with morality. The so-called 'necessities' of survival are necessities only if survival itself is regarded as a necessity. But it is not, and morality has never so regarded it. Maybe the Ik did, as a group, effectively if not consciously choose that the fittest of them should survive, and adjust their morality to suit. But they did not have to choose that. They *could* have chosen to maintain their old system of values governing human relationships and accept the collective death which would have been the price of moral steadfastness. Other societies faced with similar difficulties have not taken the road either of the Ik or of the Kalahari Bushmen: thus it is reported (by Oxfam workers) that some Tuareg communities in the NE African famine did decide on sharing and collective want in preference to selective survival. Isn't this, in fact, the *truly* moral alternative, as acknowledging the supremacy of moral over prudential values? Can't we say this is what the Ik should have done? It is, after all, possible for us to prefer death to dishonour, and we regard those who do as morally admirable. Similarly if someone's moral values crumble in the face of death, we may regard the lapse with charity out of consideration for human weakness, but we still regard it as a lapse: it would have been *better* if the person threatened with death had managed to hold on to his values. In deciding what we think of the Ik we should compare them to, say, someone living under a corrupt régime which makes right living inconsistent with survival. We consider the morally right (though difficult) course for such a person to be to continue to live rightly and accept the death which will be the consequence, rather than to betray his values in order to survive. Just so the Ik should have accepted death rather than betray their original values. Otherwise we end up with the conclusion that whatever is, is right—the antithesis of all morality. Even whole societies can, like individuals, embrace death in defence of their values in preference to a shameful survival: no doubt the Tuaregs hoped they would not actually all die, but the Cubans, for instance, declare themselves ready to fight to the last man or woman rather than submit to the United States. And such behaviour is perfectly intelligible. For there are lives which are not worth living. And the life the Ik preserved for themselves was just such a life. It is sophistry to distinguish between the abandonment of morality and the change of moral values, even in the nuclear age. Our situation may indeed be that, like the Ik, we have to *choose* between morality and assured survival.

I do of course acknowledge that there are things worth dying for, both for individuals and communities. But even if we admire the Tuaregs and the Cubans, I do not think it possible for *us* to say that *other* societies ought to do likewise: though we may endeavour to persuade our *own* society that *it* should. This decision is one that must be left to those actually faced with the choice between death and something else. Even if I may choose death for myself, I may not choose it for others, nor lay down what they must be prepared to die for; because one knows only what one's *own* death means. It is a question of how one's own choice appears to one, of what makes it possible for a death to appear as a good. For though one may rationally and morally choose to die *for* something, one cannot rationally and morally choose *gratuitous* death; death in itself remains an evil. We admire the deaths of political martyrs because we do *not* see them as gratuitous. But what does this mean? Well, we regard the heroic dissident's choice of death as obviously right because we see his acts and choice as taking place within the context of societies (his and our own) for which his choice is *significant*. His choice of death is a comment on the régime. Since societies continue even though the individual doesn't, his death seems worthwhile both to us and to him because there is always the possibility, even the hope, that *someone* will see its significance, will read correctly what it says (even if it is only his killers). Belief in its significance is what makes it worth doing. One may think here of Auden's poem 'In Memory of W. B. Yeats':

> Time, that is intolerant
>
> Of the brave and innocent. . . .
>
> Worships language, and forgives
>
> Everyone by whom it lives.

This suggests that we value such acts because though men die, the word lives. But even the word lives only as long as it is *understood*. Signifiers must *signify to someone*. At the limit the hero's act is bearable for him because it is significant to him. That is what it is for something to be worth doing for its own sake. Nevertheless, even in this case, even at the limit, the individual acts within the context of a community—the community which has made it possible for that act to have that significance for him. If there can be no private language, *a fortiori* there can be no private moral language. Suppose now that the Ik do choose collective death rather than the abandonment of compassion: when they have died their death for the sake of virtue as they conceive it, for whom will this supreme sacrifice be significant? Awareness of a significance-conferring context makes the heroic dissident's sacrifice seem good by allowing him to see it as having a point beyond his own personal concerns, and hence a point he can die for: for though he loses *his* future, there is still *the* future—the future of the context which gives

191

his death significance. The difference with the Ik is that they stand to lose, not just a personal future, but *the* future: in their situation, choosing death means choosing the death not just of individuals but of the tribe. The act itself destroys the context which gives it significance, and thus in its accomplishment becomes a meaningless suicide. Perhaps the significance-conferring context need not be human: religion or a theory of history may supply a view of the world as a hierarchy or series of societies of which the self-sacrificial society is only one transient member. If the Ik have such a religion it is conceivable that collective death could appear to them, in the context of the world as supplied by religion, as morally required. Maybe that was what made the Tuaregs' decision possible. Similarly the Cubans can see their acceptance of death rather than submission as a message both to their enemies and to the socialist world. But without such a context, I do not think collective death can appear as other than pointless suicide: *that* is the link, in such cases, between morality and survival. The morality of an act is inseparable from its significance: if we are uncertain of one, we are uncertain of the other. Consider the difference in our attitude if a man accepted death in a different way, and judging uprightness impossible under the régime committed suicide on his own initiative. We are less certain of the moral standing of this because the message, the significance of the act, is less clear. It might say: men such as myself cannot live under this régime. But this leaves us ignorant of the content of 'such as myself'. Or it could mean: *I* cannot live under this régime. This again leaves it open why not. Even if we fill this in as a reference to the difficulties of living *uprightly* under the régime, the act itself seems to say: death is preferable to living uprightly or attempting to live uprightly under this régime, which may just as well be a sign of weakness as of strength in the individual; and if it is a sign of weakness we will not admire though we may feel for him.

Consider now acceptance of death by a whole society. This, similarly, makes sense and has value only within the context of a larger, persisting society which confers significance and therefore value on it: maybe *we*, after the event, can see the Ik or the Cubans dying *en masse* for what they hold dear as a good thing and an example to us all (indeed a good thing *because* an example to us all) because we see it as a proclamation of our values (mirrored in theirs). But unless the context necessary for this view is available to them, it is meaningless to say that the view is morally required of them. That the hypothetical act seems morally admirable *to us* does not mean that it is morally required *of them*; for without this context, their collective death cannot be seen by them as a moral good. That is what makes it, instead, collective suicide. And morality cannot require this. Morality cannot require nuclear war because engaging in nuclear war is not only collective suicide but also destruction of all the non-religious contexts which give reality to all the values we currently acknowledge. It is possible for some religions to see nuclear war as morally good because they place it in a context of cycles of cosmic destruction and regeneration which transcend merely human history; it requires a context on this scale for destruction on this scale to appear as morally good, and in such a context merely human morality appears both transient and insignificant.

It may be accepted that nuclear war is social suicide, and that it cannot be seen as morally good. But neither of these in themselves show that it is morally *wrong*. For suicide itself is not necessarily wrong. It should be clear by now that I do not think the wrongness of nuclear war is just the wrongness of suicide. Nevertheless, I would claim there is a reason why suicide has seemed both irrational and wrong. I think the reason is that there is self-evidence in the assertion that something is better than nothing. Life is better than death because death is nothing; for even though an actual life *is* not always better than nothing, it always *may* be; thus it is possible for individuals to find value even in suffering. But the possibilities of nothing are nothing. Life thus just is potentially better than death, and so it is both rational and a moral requirement to preserve our own life (our duty is to prefer the good). By the same token, choosing nuclear war is wrong because it is choosing death, and not just individual death, but indefinitely widespread death. But this is not to say that choosing death is *always* wrong, both because an individual life may actually have exhausted possibilities for good, and because one's own life is not the only good. There is perhaps another moral than the nuclear warrior's to be drawn from this, however, If governments should now remember not just their duty to those they govern, but also their duty to threatened humanity, maybe on occasion the interests of this can override the interests of the governed, and make national self-immolation necessary if the alternative looks like being *total* loss of the future (i.e. loss of everyone's future). This may be another of the new moral possibilities new powers have created.

What are the practical implications of my moral claims? Even if everything I have said about the moral structure is right, no particular practical decision immediately follows from that alone: a great deal will depend, also, on what one thinks are the facts about the world. To morally assess practical proposals I am offering nothing more helpful than that they should be measured both against present reality (Are things like this? Will this really work?) and against ourselves (What does this mean to us? Is it really worth it?) rather than against habits of thought derived from the past. This is much harder than it may seem, for of course it is only past habits that make present reality thinkable at all. On the other hand, it is also thoughts that make reality what it is. The chief suggestion of this paper is that in order to cope successfully with our current problems we may need to think more freely than we are used to, for to confront new problems with old perceptions and solutions may be both unrealistic and immoral. If politics is the art of the possible, part of that art is the recognition of unfamiliar possibilities.

The Scope of Reason: An Epistle to the Persians

RENFORD BAMBROUGH

'Does the planetary impact of Western thought allow for a real dialogue among civilizations?' This arresting question was set to the lecturers at the first international symposium of the Iranian Centre for the Study of Civilizations, which took place in Tehran in October 1977. Plans were made for a second symposium to be held in January 1979 under the title 'The Limits of Knowledge According to Different World-views'. The Director's letter of invitation amplified the theme in a series of questions:

> For instance, is the agnosticism which has now extended to a world-wide level the consequence of the destruction of objective reason, namely the universal *logos*, as conceived earlier in the great metaphysical doctrines of the East and the West? Is there any organic link among these: the creation of modern political myths, the individual's fragmentation and the reduction of thought to its mere instrumentality? Is knowledge limited solely to our calculating reason or can it lead to spheres raising us above the limits determined by Kant in his *Critique of Pure Reason*?

I accepted the invitation, notwithstanding an assurance that the Centre was 'concerned not only with the problems of a theoretical-epistemological standpoint but also with the existential implications of the problem as well'. Preparations for the symposium were well advanced, and had included the writing of about two-thirds of my paper, when I received a letter from the Director, dated 7 October 1978, announcing the postponement of the symposium 'in view of recent events in Iran'. The fall of the Shah soon followed, and the postponement is strictly *sine die*. This lecture, apart from this introductory explanation, is closely based on my undelivered epistle to the Persians.

The theme of the second Tehran symposium is well calculated to engage the interest and deserve the attention of a variety of thinkers from a number of widely different traditions, and yet it could equally serve as a theme for discussion between representatives of different schools or tendencies within a particular tradition or civilization. Certainly this is true of the tradition of Western philosophizing, from the ancient Greeks and Hebrews to modern Europeans and Americans, from which I draw my own philosophical sustenance. I am grateful to the Centre for the honour of an invitation to take part in this symposium and for the stimulus and opportunity it gives me to develop some reflections on the scope of reason which bear equally on our present formal theme and on some problems that are internal to the Western tradition itself.

This coincidence is more than a coincidence. I shall be arguing later that there necessarily could not be such a wide divergence of belief and understanding between one tradition and another as is presupposed by some familiar views on East–West relations, some accounts of the differences between one religion and another or one political system and another, and some views of the nature of language, thought and culture. But even if I am wrong in this bolder claim, it is at least clear that the present topic—the limits of knowledge, the scope of reason—is central in Western philosophical thought from the sophists and Socrates to Kant and Wittgenstein, and any European or American scholar interested in the history of thought and in thinking for himself about the problems of philosophy will find it both absorbing and inescapable. That alone makes it a proper object of attention at a conference where there is to be dialogue between the Western tradition and other styles of thought. But there are further and wider reasons for adopting it as the unifying theme of such a conversation. For *any* tradition of thought, however widely it may differ from the Western tradition in other respects, must share with the Western tradition an involvement in this problem from one side or another. There are two separate ways of making this plain to anyone who is inclined to doubt it.

1. Any tradition or any individual thinker who is supposed to differ sharply from the typical Western thinker in *not* being preoccupied with questions about the limits of knowledge, will presumably have reasons, implicit or explicit, for rejecting or neglecting such an approach or preoccupation. It is hard to see any form that these reasons could take that would not itself amount to a more or less direct concern with the problems with which we were supposing such a thinker or tradition *not* to be concerned. For the argument would have to be that the search for a statement of the nature and limits of knowledge was an incoherent enterprise, or in some other way fruitless or misconceived.

2. The second point clarifies and reinforces the first. *Within* the Western tradition, it has often been argued that the search for foundations of knowledge is an incoherent enterprise, or is in some other way misconceived, or, though a coherent possibility for beings more gifted than ourselves, is for us necessarily fruitless and misguided. Those who have argued in these ways, far from being identifiable as isolated rebels, departing from the main roads of Western thought, are

actually among the chief travellers on those roads. What is central to the Western tradition is a *debate* about the nature and limits of knowledge, and all possible sides of the debate have been vocally and articulately represented. To reject the tradition is not to reject a thesis or doctrine but to abandon a question, and even to do that would be to speak for and with some of the voices that belong to the tradition itself.

The same point may be made even more simply by noticing that the individual thinker is always engaged in a dialogue *with himself*: Descartes and the malicious demon, Socrates and the sceptic or cynic, may be represented by separate individuals or groups, but they may equally, as in the *Meditations* or in the Socratic dialogues, serve as the dramatic embodiment of a conflict or hesitation between two or more elements in a single heart or mind. Mr Tom Stoppard has said that he writes dialogue because it is the only respectable way of contradicting oneself.

My emphasis is on the *scope* of reason because I believe that all too much stress has been placed upon the *limits* of reason. With this emphasis goes an aspiration after wholeness or comprehensiveness of view which is often thought to be alien to Western traditions in philosophy, and to be specially characteristic of Eastern thought. The contrast is far too crude and violent to be tolerated. Even if we confine ourselves to philosophers in a relatively narrow sense, and do not include prophets and poets and mystics, we must think of Parmenides and Pythagoras and Plato and Spinoza and Hegel as well as of Locke and Hume and Kant and James and Wittgenstein; and we must not think that the monisms and dualisms of the members of the former group are necessary for, and the pluralisms of the members of the latter group incompatible with, a desire to see things steadily and to see them whole.

Nearly all the contrasts that it is tempting to draw here are too simple to fit the complexities of the actual history of human thought. There is only one human world, and the vast variations within it are as much variations between one time and another in the same place, and between one man and another in the same time and in the same place, as between one place and another at the same time. Western thought has all the variety and range that belong to human thought as a whole, and so has Eastern thought, and the unity of each tradition is largely independent of the influence of the other. The same elements may be differently mixed in different continents and ages and individual human beings, but the elements are bound to be the same, and hence to be recognizable to each of us even when they occur in different proportions and combinations in ages or places which therefore present to us an alien appearance. This is equally true of what is intriguing and refreshing because it is alien as of what is disturbing and menacing because it is alien, and of what is intriguing and refreshing and menacing and disturbing because it is alien.

History and individual experience and observation, biology and psychology and sociology, all alike confirm and presuppose the unity of mankind even when their individual beneficiaries or exponents are most concerned to emphasize human variety. The human species is one animal species, whose members no doubt differ among themselves at least as much as cattle, horses or dogs:

> *First Murderer*:   We are men, my liege.
> *Macbeth*:   Ay, in the catalogue ye go for men;
> As hounds, and greyhounds, mongrels, spaniels, curs,
> Shoughs, water-rugs, and demi-wolves, are clept
> All by the name of dogs. The valued file
> Distinguishes the swift, the slow, the subtle,
> The house-keeper, the hunter, every one
> According to the gift which bounteous nature
> Hath in him clos'd; whereby he does receive
> Particular addition, from the bill
> That writes them all alike; and so of men.

The lesson that is taught by experience can also be learnt *a priori*. We can show by abstract argument that mankind must share a common consciousness, and the argument may take either of two forms. One of them concerns 'the particular fabric and constitution of the human species' and the other applies to 'all rational beings as such'.[1]

The latter version of the argument is simpler, in spite of its wide scope. It depends on the necessary truth that even a *conflict* of opinions can be found only where there is a *community* of understanding. Unless we share some means of expression, some terms of intellectual trade, we cannot recognize ourselves as disagreeing, however deeply, since disagreement presupposes, along with the conflict between what you believe and what I believe, the mutual relevance of something that you believe and something that I believe. The argument has the same force when applied to individuals in conflict or to nations and ages and centuries-long traditions of thought. Nothing could be relevant as a criticism or repudiation of, or as a correction or even as an alternative to a belief or creed or tradition, unless it met with it or bumped into it or passed it by in the same space.

The plaintiff is necessarily conceived as pointing out something to the defendant, and he cannot do this unless he is in contact with him. When we speak of total incomprehension we are not speaking literally. Of course it is possible for two people to fail to communicate: one of

[1] Hume, *Enquiries*, § 134.

them may speak only English, and the other only Chinese. But in that case neither can know except through an interpreter that he is in conflict with the other, and an interpreter reveals shared understanding at the same time as he reveals misunderstanding.

In exchanges between those who are in conflict or disagreement, whether friendly or unfriendly, whether on the scale of the individual or at the international level, there is learning and teaching, movement and change in belief and understanding. The terms of moral and intellectual assessment are the same in both contexts, the same whether the conflict and contact are between individuals or parties or nations or world-wide blocs or ancient religions or political traditions: arrogance, humility, blindness, insight, patience and haste, rigidity and flexibility, prejudice and openness of mind. Some of these terms are more specifically intellectual and others more specifically moral, but they all bestride the untidy boundary that is all that marks, if anything does, the distinction between those supposedly separate territories.

The quarrels between monisms and pluralisms have a bearing on the mapping of these regions. In the theory of knowledge, as in the scientific or religious or metaphysical search for a unified understanding of the world as a whole, there has been confusion about unity and plurality, identity and variety, flexibility and rigidity.

One who believes that there is an objective truth in a certain sphere of enquiry is suspected of wishing to oversimplify the subject-matter of that enquiry. The objectivist in morals and aesthetics is thought to be claiming that there are simple canons of taste, standards of moral conduct, criteria for determining what is right or good or beautiful or sublime. The subjectivitist or relativist is proud of his open-mindedness and flexibility, his freedom from the rigidities that he thinks he would have to endorse if he acknowledged that there is a moral or aesthetic truth. And all too often his opponent shares his belief that objectivity requires inflexibility, and so seems to supply ammunition for the subjectivist's campaign. Yet when they agree on this, the subjectivist and the objectivist are agreeing on a confusion. The range and variety of a subject matter, the complexity of a set of objects or questions, has nothing to do with whether the study of those questions or subjects or objects is logically capable of being rationally and objectively conducted. Number theory and solid state physics and meteorology and molecular biology present complex difficulties to the mathematician or the scientist; history and palaeography and textual criticism call for all the subtlety and circumspection that the scholar can command. The meaning of the Rosetta Stone or Linear B or Virgil's Fourth Eclogue or Blake's Tyger may at one time or to one or many generations of scholars seem unfathomable, but they show by their efforts to fathom it the confidence that they share with the physicist and the meteorologist that a question is a signpost pointing towards an answer.[2] The more complex the questions the more complex the answers, the more varied, the more varied. But nobody supposes that genetics or probability theory is unscientific because it is complex and varied in its problems and procedures, and there is no more reason to fear or hope that ethics or aesthetics or philosophy or religion bursts the bonds of reason.

The metaphor of bondage explains why I speak of hope as well as fear. Some thinkers have supposed that the cogency of an argument is a constraint on liberty of judgment. Hare insists that we are free to form our opinions on moral matters in a stronger sense than that in which we are free to form our opinions on questions of logic or questions of fact.[3] Sartre and other existentialist thinkers have believed that they could not preserve the full autonomy of the moral agent or the full authenticity of his actions and judgments unless they declared that 'man is condemned at every instant to invent man',[4] that there is no human nature as a guide to what is an appropriate life for a human being, that an act must be *gratuitous*, ungoverned by facts, precedents, traditions, or anything else that could count as a *reason*, if it is to be the expression of a free human response to the agent's circumstances. Even the most sympathetic attempt to present this view must lapse into incoherence at this point. By the time this degree of detachment has been achieved, there is nothing that can be recognized as a response or reaction *to* anything. What makes the objectivity or appropriateness of a judgment impossible also makes a judgment impossible. And that in turn reflects on the understanding of action and agency, since to do something is to engage oneself intelligibly and describably in a context of facts and circumstances that has a meaning for oneself as agent and hence a corresponding intelligibility for others who may be affected by one's actions, or who may contemplate and assess the actions with detachment. Unless these possibilities of mutual relevance are provided and recognized, there is no scope at all for anything to be seen as an action or as an attempt or an intention or a judgment.

The motive of the misrepresentation is in any case misguided. Freedom is not infringed by reason. John Stuart Mill argued eloquently for liberty of thought and expression, enquiry and publication, precisely because he recognized that such liberty is necessary for the pursuit of the independent and objective truths that he believed to be

[2]See Wittgenstein, *Philosophical Remarks* (Oxford: Basil Blackwell, 1975), §149.

[3]R. M. Hare, *Freedom and Reason* (Clarendon Press: Oxford University Press, 1963), 2.

[4]Jean-Paul Sarte, *Existentialism and Humanism* (London: Methuen, 1948), 34.

discoverable both in science and in morals. Again the application of the point to non-moral enquiries demonstrates the fallaciousness of the subjectivist or sceptical or existentialist argument about morals and politics and philosophy and religion. The physicist does not see the outcome of his experiments as a limitation on his freedom of thought. The historian or mathematician is not labouring under a tyranny if he sees himself as logically compelled to reach a particular conclusion. On the contrary: to unburden oneself of the constraints of evidence and argument is to make enquiry and research impossible rather than to facilitate the research or liberate the researcher. The laws of logic and the rules of evidence are like the law of the land, which, in the words of Hobbes, is like the fence that the king has set by the roadside: it is not put there to stop travellers in their journey but to keep them in the way.[5]

The subjectivist's misconceived notion of freedom collaborates with his misconception of the significance of variety and complexity to produce an unrecognizable picture of the scene of human thought and enquiry. The oversimplification is on his side, not on ours. It is because he has an oversimple conception of reason that he excludes from it so many of the multifarious phenomena that Wittgenstein's 'natural history' brings within its scope. We can do justice to the concrete detail and its diversities, while still aspiring to achieve a large view, only if we see how one detail leads to another, and what memorable patterns may be traced in the inexhaustible manifold of details. Consider for example the part played in animal and human life by *curiosity*.

Curiosity killed the cat, but only after keeping it alive, according to some authorities, through eight previous emergencies. It keeps human beings alive too, and for them, as for at least some other animals, that is only part of its value. At the beginning of the *Metaphysics* Aristotle makes such a strong statement that the cynical or even the cautious might think he was overdoing it: *pantes anthrōpoi tou eidenai oregontai phusei*: 'All men by nature desire to know'. But when he goes on at once to remark on the delight that we take in the senses, he indicates where we are to look for the support that his claim can be given. It would be pompous as well as misguided to credit all men with the aspiration that people on platforms have in mind when they speak of 'the disinterested pursuit of knowledge'. But much humbler and commoner instances have to be remembered. When there is a fight or a dogfight in the street people stop to see what will happen next. We gossip over the garden fence, crowd to see shows and spectacles, listen to or watch the news and whatever comes on next, are restless at breakfast on the days when

[5]Quoted by Peter Geach, *The Virtues* (Cambridge University Press, 1977), 88.

no newspapers are published. What we are concerned with here goes far beyond the contexts in which the word 'curiosity' or the word 'knowledge' is commonly or naturally used. We like jokes and stories. We dislike being puzzled or deceived or bewildered. We notice what is unfamiliar, are struck by what is startling. (The Cavendish Professor of Physics at Cambridge, it was recently reported in *The Times*, was sceptical about the phenomenon of ball lightning until he and his laboratory were almost literally struck by it.)

William James in *The Principles of Psychology* deals with curiosity by name in a section of the chapter entitled 'Instinct'. But much that has to do with knowledge and understanding, and the desire for knowledge and understanding, has to come into the other sections of the same chapter, whose headings are: Imitation, Emulation, Pugnacity, Sympathy, Hunting instinct, Fear, Acquisitiveness, Constructiveness, Play, Sociability and shyness, Secretiveness, Cleanliness, Shame, Love, Maternal love. And this chapter on 'Instinct' is followed by chapters on 'The Emotions' and on 'The Will' of which the same could be said. Our human understanding pervades our human life.

Philosophers are often too limited in their consideration of a concept because they think primarily or only of the contexts and occasions of the use of the most general word that we have for expressing it. To understand causation is not just to be able to analyse propositions of the form 'A causes B' but to know what we are doing when we speak of cooking, burning, shooting, insulting, disappointing, cutting a cake or a dash or an acquaintance. Aesthetics starts on the wrong foot and probably stays there if we think first of contexts in which we might use the word 'aesthetic' or 'aesthetic' words. An understanding of the subject must include an understanding of how and why we arrange books on a shelf, dishes on a table, food on a plate, plants in a garden, chairs and their occupants at a meeting of the Institute, words and sentences in a paper to be read there. We must also not forget the more dramatic instances that can lead to the more pompous formulations. Schopenhauer has these in mind when he speaks of 'the *enthusiasm* of curiosity'.[6] There is a fairy tale in which a king rewards a service by a couple of his humble subjects with a handsome and well provided house, allowing them to use all its resources except the contents of one dish that stands on the floor in a corner. They are forbidden even to look under its silver cover. When the wife's importunity finally persuades her husband to lift the cover, a mouse runs from the dish into the neighbouring apartments of the king, who returns to pronounce a sentence of banishment on those enthusiasts of curiosity. And the two

[6]Schropenhauer, *Parerga and Paralipomena*, (Clarendon Press: Oxford University Press, 1974), 465f.

peasants are Adam and Eve tasting of the fruit of the tree of knowledge of good and evil, and she is also Pandora opening her box. Oedipus solves the riddle of the Sphinx and gains a crown for the achievement. For his next trick he undertakes to investigate a matter about which he ends up knowing far too much.

What I have offered so far is some sketchy natural history, mainly natural history of human beings. I have done it as a prelude to presenting a philosophical thought, a simple and perhaps platitudinous thought, but if so then a platitude of the kind to which some philosophers can be relied on to reply: 'That is a platitude, and what's more it's false'. (They never quite use that form of words, but it is often a fair summary of their response.) The simple thought is this: there is no curiosity unless there is knowledge. This thought may be more likely to strike you in the way that I hope it will if I set beside it some equally simple thoughts that are parallel to it:

There is no losing unless there is finding.
There is no hunting unless there is catching.
There is no ignorance unless there is knowledge.
There is no perplexity unless there is understanding.
There is no doubt unless there is certainty.

I will also add a thought which I believe to be parallel to the others, but which I know from experience is unlikely to be thought as simple as I think it is:

There is no question where there is no answer.

The case for these simple thoughts, and for the claim that they help us with philosophical problems about knowledge and understanding, must rest on the treatment of examples and therefore needs long discussion. But the nature of the claim can be clarified in fairly general terms and with reference to a small number of examples. Consider again some of the phenomena that I have been referring to: doubt, certainty, puzzlement, seeking, questioning, wondering, expecting. They have three features that are germane to my anti-sceptical anti-relativist purpose:

1. Each of them *is* a natural phenomenon, material for natural history, something that actually occurs as a state or activity of people and/or animals. (The dog is looking for a bone, the child is baffled by the conjuror, the Cavendish Professor is astonished by the lightning.)

2. Each of them has implicit in it—at *least* implicit—some *assessment* in logical or epistemological or other evaluative terms. What is *surprising* is what was *not* to have been expected. What is *doubtful* is not adequately supported by reasons or evidence.

203

3. The terms of assessment, and therefore the phenomena in which they are implicit (or explicit) form *networks*, or perhaps *a* network. I was pointing out some of the interlacings in this network or some of these networks when I presented my simple thoughts.

The description of these natural phenomena, the exploration of the networks, is what epistemology is. The human understanding cannot therefore be captured in a less complicated net. In particular, it cannot be expressed in the linear structures that philosophers build when they leap straight into asking fundamental questions about grounds, criteria, principles, foundations of knowledge and understanding. The alternative that I am commending is to recognize that enquiry and reasoning in general, and particular departments of enquiry and reason, such as physics and morals and aesthetics and history and philosophy—and even gossip—are *going concerns*. It is only by clinging to some of the ropes in the network that we can get near enough to examine others, and if we aspire to examine the whole network, we must do it piecemeal. The examination accordingly cannot result in condemnation of the whole enterprise as radically unsound or ill-founded.

It is because I think that it provides a new point of entry to some familiar problems that I am interested in the natural history and epistemology of curiosity. In particular, I think my simple thoughts about curiosity raise a difficulty for sceptics or relativists which is not new but arises here in a new way. Such thinkers themselves are concerned to correct what they diagnose as *misunderstandings* on the part of their opponents. In expounding and trying to correct such misunderstandings they involve themselves in mankind's thinking. We listen to them because we hope that we may extend our understanding by doing so, and understand them only because they do enter with us into the going concern that we may wish to defend against them. Paradoxically, they often adopt an air of *knowingness* as they seek to expose our benighted dogmatism or ignorance.

So curiosity serves mainly as a representative or sample of the great range of terms which characterize natural states of people and animals and which involve assessment in inescapably logical terms. What I am calling a network is close to what Wittgenstein in *On Certainty* describes as the system from which all my questions and answers derive their intelligibility. In starting at that end—with the concrete and the natural—Wittgenstein is at one with C. S. Peirce, who in a repudiation of the Cartesian programme of systematic doubt says that you cannot start by doubting everything; you can only start where you are, and that means that you can only start 'laden with an immense mass of cognition'[7] of which you could not unburden yourself even if it were desirable to do so. The pragmatism and naturalism of Peirce and Wittgenstein is liable to be accused of the crime of *psychologism*. The question, we are told, is not whether we *do* act or react in certain ways, but whether we are right to do so. Yes: and the short answer to it is another simple thought: that in the states or activities that I have been describing, we are involuntarily committed to something that is either right *or* wrong, either true *or* false; we shall either succeed *or* fail to find the bone, the fallacy, the end of the rainbow. As for curiosity, it will either be *satisfied* or *fail* to be satisfied.

One who sets the bounds of reason as wide as I have drawn them must become inured to charges of excessive optimism. The complaint arises from a confusion between actualities and possibilities. To say that there is a path is not to say that we shall have the skill to trace it and the stamina to follow it as far as it could lead us. To believe that there could be a chart of the unknown territory is not to believe that it will ever be charted. But there is all the same an important connection between the actuality and our view of the possibilities. To deny that there is a path or that there could be a chart is to stifle the efforts and aspirations of oneself and others to undertake the necessary exploration.

Here again there is scope for fear as well as hope. Some thinkers wish the bounds of reason to be narrower because they think that reason is a tyrant over any realm that it governs. The optimism is on the other foot when those who narrow the limits of knowledge hope thereby to escape effort in finding and responsibility for defending their answers to the main questions of philosophy and morals and religion, while those who share my view of the rational determinability of those questions are concerned to emphasize and then to face the difficulty of finding the answers that they believe to be in principle discoverable.

The difficulties are of at least two kinds, corresponding to the divisions, important even if in danger of being seen as wider than they are, between theory and practice, understanding and will, intelligence and character. Some of the difficulties—and some of them are so severe as to amount to practical impossibilities—are due to the limitations of our human powers of understanding, as individuals and as a species. We deserve no discredit for not achieving the impossible. But often, as a species or as individuals, we fall short of achieving what our intellectual powers have equipped us to achieve. We may then speak of ourselves and each other, individually or corporately, as foolish or stupid or ignorant or confused, and be thinking mainly of the limitations of our intellectual powers and efforts. But the word *efforts*, and even some of those terms of appraisal—foolish, stupid—show the ease of the

[7]C. S. Peirce, *Collected Papers*, V (Harvard University Press, 1934), §416.

transition to another sort of difficulty and another sort of failure. To fail in this second dimension is to be weak or irresolute at the best, and at the worst it may amount to wilful self-indulgence or any one of a range of other evil purposes. Here I will give just one illustration of how one may combine the recognition that a certain question is rationally settleable with (a) a firm conviction that one of the possible answers is now known to be correct, and (b) a profound pessimism as to whether that answer will ever come to be universally or even generally accepted among human beings.

It is probable that a majority of the population of the earth has some degree of confidence in the methods and results of astrology, and certain that a belief in astrology will be widespread for many centuries to come. I do not myself believe in astrology at all, but I am pessimistic about the prospect of achieving unanimity on this topic with all the rest of mankind. As this statement itself suggests, I do however regard the question of the validity of astrology as calling for and allowing of rational discussion and determination. I have what I regard as good reasons for my own conclusion on the matter, and I am willing to consider reasons put forward by astrologers and their readers and clients. The question may remain controversial for centuries or for ever, but the controversy is about a matter of fact, and there is a fact of the matter, as both parties at least implicitly recognize.

This example illustrates a distinction overlooked by those who dismiss as 'optimistic' the view that questions in general, or certain paticular classes of highly controversial questions—those of politics or ethics or religion—are capable of being rationally resolved. To hold that a question or a class of questions is in principle settleable by reason is to subscribe to a philosophical opinion about the epistemology of that question or class. That opinion is independent of any expectation about the degree of progress likely to be made in the discussion of such questions. Expectations of progress or lack of progress, whether optimistic or pessimistic, need to be supported by evidence about the intellectual qualifications and degrees of determination of those engaged or likely to be engaged in devoting their minds and energies to the relevant discussions and investigations. I am no more optimistic about the prospect of achieving unanimity on the question of astrology than any philosopher who holds the question to be in principle unamenable to rational resolution. Such a philosopher ought in any case to notice that his own view provides no evidence *against* the possibility or probability that unanimity will be achieved. My objectivist epistemology commits me to a particular kind of explanation of our failure to make progress rather than to a particular degree of optimism or pessimism about the prospects of making it. I may reasonably, and do actually, hold both that every question is capable of rational determination and that there is no ground for optimism about the prospects of reconciling the conflicting parties in disputes about the main issues of religion, politics, philosophy and morals. (I also have some reservations about the suggestion that an expectation of such progress on a large scale would deserve the name of optimism. It is not clear that a life without disagreement would be a human life at all, or that the work of the reason could be done 'without contraries'.)[8]

The catalogue of human stupidity, perversity, indolence and ill-will is just as familiar to me as it is to philosophers who disagree with me about the scope of reason, and I am as fully entitled as they are to treat it as a ground for pessimism about the intellectual and moral future of the human species.

To show that progress in understanding is not impossible in principle is not to show that it will be achieved easily or at all. The arguments for the view that our fundamental disagreements are irresoluble do not establish the conclusion that they are designed to support, but they do show that our intellectual and moral and political tasks are formidable. They do not show that the requirements cannot be met, but they show what complex and varied requirements they are, each rare in itself and so rare in combination that it is tempting to follow the sceptics to the conclusion that they are actually incompatible.

In any sphere of thought or action we need conflicting gifts and experiences, qualities and capacities that it is too much to ask of one and the same man. The statesman or general must be decisive but thoughtful, detached but compassionate. The scientist or philosopher, the author or composer or critic, must have a patient eye for detail and an ambition to grasp the world or the work as a unified whole. The search for international understanding and co-operation is important because it is important to think of the flooded valley of the Ganges. We need to think of the flooded valley because we need to help the village that is sinking into or rising from the mud. When we speak of the village we mean this or that man and woman and child, and each of these is to himself or herself a whole world that has its own distinctions of pattern and detail, tedium and crisis.

The sceptic thinks of himself as the enemy of *credulity*, but his scepticism is itself a form of what he takes himself to be fighting. The suggestion that something is *uncertain* needs to be supported by just as high a standard of evidence as any other view. Whether something is *doubtful* is not a question on which one side can be allowed to award itself a lighter burden of proof than another. Scepticism is a form of credulity, just as cynicism is a form of sentimentality. Cynicism is not usually seen in this light, mainly because we tend to think of a particular

[8] Blake, *The Marriage of Heaven and Hell*.

group of sentiments when we think of sentimentality. On reflection we can see that it is just as easy and just as sentimental to indulge or wallow in one's toughness or realism or brutality as in one's sensibility and compassion. Similarly, it is just as credulous to question the obvious as to decline to question the doubtful or the obviously false. To somebody who does not accept that Moore has two hands we might suitably say—and this is what I say to those who are sceptical or relativist about the scope of reason—'If you disbelieve that you'll believe anything'.

The Scientific and the Ethical[1]

BERNARD WILLIAMS

Discussions of objectivity often start from considerations about disagreement. We might ask why this should be so. It makes it seem as though disagreement were surprising, but there is no reason why that should be so (the earliest thinkers in the Western tradition found conflict at least as obvious a feature of the world as concord). The interest in disagreement comes about, rather, because neither agreement nor disagreement is universal. It is not that disagreement needs explanation and agreement does not, but that in different contexts disagreement requires different sorts of explanation, and so does agreement.

The way in which one understands a given kind of disagreement, and explains it, has important practical effects. It can modify one's attitude to others and one's understanding of one's own outlook. In relation to other people, one needs a view of what is to be opposed, rejected, and so forth, and in what spirit; for oneself, disagreement can raise a warning that one may be wrong, and if truth or correctness is what one is after, one may need to reform one's strategies.

Disagreement does not necessarily have to be overcome. It may remain an important and constitutive feature of one's relations to others, and also be seen as something that is merely to be expected in the light of the best explanations that we have of how such disagreement arises. There can be tension involved here, if one at once feels that the disagreement is about very important matters, and that there is a good explanation of why the disagreement is only to be expected. The tension is specially acute when the disagreement is not only important, but expresses itself in judgments that seem to demand assent from others.

Among types of disagreement, and the lessons that can be learned from them, there is a well-known polarity. At one extreme there is the

[1] The lecture that I gave to the Royal Institute of Philosophy on this subject was subsequently much revised, and has become Chapter 8 ('Knowledge, Science, Convergence') of a book, *Ethics and the Limits of Philosophy*, to be published in the Fontana Masterguides Series early in 1985. It seemed more sensible not to go back to an earlier version of the text, and what appears here (wiith the agreement of Fontana Books) is a slightly abbreviated version of that chapter.

situation of two children wanting one bun, or two heroes wanting one slave girl. The disagreement is practical and it is entirely explicable, and the explanation of it is not going to cast much doubt on the cognitive powers of the people involved. It may be said that this kind of case is so primitively practical that it hardly even introduces any judgment over which there is disagreement. Even at the most primitive level, of course, there is disagreement about *what is to be done*, but this is so near to desire and action that no one is going to think that the disagreement shows any failure of knowledge or understanding on anyone's part. It is simply that two people want incompatible things. But the conflict may well not remain as blank as that, and if the parties want to settle it by ordered speech rather than by violence, they will invoke more substantive judgments, usually of justice, and the children will talk about fairness, or the heroes about precedence.

In their most basic form, at least, these disagreements need not make anyone think that someone has failed to recognize or understand something, or that they cannot speak the language. At the opposite pole of the traditional contrast are disagreements that do make one think that. What these typically are depends on the theory of knowledge favoured by the commentator, but they often involve the observation under standard conditions of what J. L. Austin used to call 'middle-sized dry goods'. A feature of these examples that will be important later in the discussion is that the parties are assumed to share the same concepts, and to be trained in the recognition of furniture, pens, pennies or whatever it may be.

Around these paradigms there have been formed various oppositions: between practical and theoretical, or value and fact, or *ought* and *is*. Each of these has been thought to represent a fundamental difference in what disagreement means, and they are often taken to suggest contrasting hopes for resolving it. However, it is a mistake to suppose that these oppositions are different ways of representing just one distinction. Indeed, the two paradigm examples that I have mentioned significantly fail to correspond to the two ends of any one of these contrasts. The quarrel about the allocation of a good is certainly an example of the practical, but until one gets to the stage of taking seriously the claims of justice, it is not yet a disagreement about value. A disagreement in the perception of furniture is without doubt a disagreement about a matter of fact, but is not yet a disagreement about what is most often contrasted with the practical, namely the theoretical. To assemble these kinds of example into some one contrast requires more work to be done. It has been done, characteristically, by reducing the evaluative to the practical, and extending the factual to the theoretical. Both these manoeuvres are of positivist inspiration, and they are both suspect. It is not surprising that some philosophers now doubt whether there is any basic distinction at all that can be constructed to the traditional pattern.

I accept that there is no one distinction that is in question here. I also accept that the more positivistic formulations that have gone into defining each side of such a distinction are misguided. However, I believe that in relation to ethics there is a genuine and profound difference to be found, and also—it is a further point—that the difference is enough to motivate some version of the feeling (itself recurrent, if not exactly traditional) that science has some chance of being more or less what it seems, a systematized theoretical account of how the world really is, while ethical thought has no chance of being everything that it seems. The tradition is right, moreover, not only in thinking that there is such a distinction, but also in thinking that we can come to understand what it is through understanding disagreement. However, it is not a question of how much disagreement there is, nor even of what methods we have to settle disagreement, though that of course provides many relevant considerations. The basic difference lies rather in our reflective understanding of the best hopes that we could coherently entertain for eliminating disagreement in the two areas. It is a matter of what, under the most favourable conditions, would be the best explanation of disagreement being removed: the explanation—as I shall say from now on—of convergence.

The two 'areas', as I have called them, are the *scientific* and the *ethical*. I hope to explain why one end should be labelled the 'scientific', rather than, say, the 'factual'. It can be explained quite briefly why the other end, the ethical, is not called by any of several other familiar names. It is not called 'the evaluative', because that additionally covers at least the area of aesthetic judgment, and that raises many questions of its own. It is not called 'the normative', which covers only part of the interest of the ethical (roughly, the part concerned with rules), and also naturally extends to such things as the law, which again raise different questions. Last, it is not called 'the practical', because that would displace a large part of the problem. It is not hard to concede that there is a distinction between the practical and (let us say) the non-practical. There is clearly such a thing as practical reasoning or deliberation, and that is not the same as thinking about how things are. It is *obviously* not the same, and that is why positivism thought that it had validated the traditional distinction by reducing the evaluative to the practical. But that reduction is mistaken, and it makes the whole problem look easier than it is.[2]

[2] See David Wiggins, 'Truth, Invention and the Meaning of Life', *British Academy Lecture* (1976); and 'Deliberation and Practical Reason', in *Essays on Aristotle's Ethics*, Amélie Rorty (ed.) (California, California University Press, 1980).

The basic idea behind the distinction between the scientific and the ethical, expressed in terms of convergence, is very simple. In a scientific enquiry there should ideally be convergence on an answer, where the best explanation of that convergence involves the idea that the answer represents how things are, whereas in the area of the ethical, at least at a high level of generality (the issue of generality is one that we shall come back to), there is no such coherent hope. The distinction does not turn on any difference in whether convergence will actually occur, and it is important that this is not what the argument is about. It might well turn out that there will be convergence in ethical outlook, at least among human beings. The point of the contrast is that even if that happens, it will not be correct to think that it has come about because convergence has been guided by how things actually are, whereas convergence in the sciences might be explained in that way if it does happen. This means, among other things, that we understand differently in the two cases the existence of convergence or, alternatively, its failure to come about.

I shall come back to ways in which we might understand ethical convergence. First, however, we must face certain arguments which suggest that there is really nothing at all in the distinction, expressed in these terms. There are two different directions from which that objection can come. In one version, it says that the notion of a convergence that comes about because of how things are is an empty notion. In the other, it says that the notion of such a convergence is not empty, but that it is available as much in ethical cases as in scientific—that is to say, the notion has some content, but it does nothing to help the distinction.

I have already said that the point of the distinction and of its explanation in terms of convergence does not turn on the question whether convergence as a matter of fact occurs. On the scientific side, however, it would be unrealistic to disconnect these ideas totally from the ways in which the history of Western science since the seventeenth century is to be understood. For one thing, any aspiration for the convergence of science that conceded at the same time that it had not occurred up to now might well seem merely Utopian and only fit to obscure the real issues, like the once fashionable hopes for a Galileo of the social sciences. More importantly, the conception of scientific progress in terms of convergence cannot be divorced from the history of Western science because it is the history of Western science that has done most to encourage it.

It is quite hard to deny that that history displays a considerable degree of convergence. What has been claimed is that this appearance has no real significance, because it is a cultural artefact, a product of the way in which we choose to narrate the history of science. Richard Rorty has written:[3]

> It is less paradoxical . . . to stick to the classical notion of 'better describing what was already there' for physics. This is not because of deep epistemological or metaphysical considerations, but simply because, when we tell our Whiggish stories about how our ancestors gradually crawled up the mountain on whose (possibly false) summit we stand, we need to keep some things constant throughout the story . . . Physics is the paradigm of 'finding' simply because it is hard (at least in the West) to tell a story of changing universes against the background of an unchanging moral law or poetic canon, but very easy to tell the reverse sort of story.

There are two notable faults in such a description of scientific success and what that success means. One is its attitude to the fact that it is easy to tell one kind of story and hard to tell the other. *Why* is the picture of 'the world already there', helping to control our descriptions of it, so compelling? This seems to require some explanation on Rorty's account, but it does not get one. If the reference to 'the West' implies a cultural or anthropological explanation, it is totally unclear what it would be: totally unclear, indeed, what it could be, if it is not going itself to assume an already existing physical world in which human beings come into existence and develop their cultures, and by which they are affected in various ways.

The point that an assumption of that kind is going to lie behind any explanations of what we do leads directly to the second fault in Rorty's account, that it is self-defeating. If the story that he tells were true, then there would be no perspective from which he could express it in this way. If it is overwhelmingly convenient to say that science describes what is already there, and if there are no deep metaphysical or epistemological issues here, but only a question of what is convenient (it is 'simply because' of that that we speak as we do), then what everyone should be saying, including Rorty, is that science describes a world that is already there. But Rorty urges us not to say that, and in doing so, and in insisting, *as opposed to that*, on our talking of what it is convenient to say, he is trying to reoccupy the transcendental standpoint outside human speech and activity which is precisely what he wants us to renounce.[4]

[3] *Philosophy and the Mirror of Nature* (Princeton, Princeton University Press, 1980), 344–345. I have discussed Rorty's views in some detail in a review of his *Consequences of Pragmatism* (Minneapolis, 1982): *New York Review* **XXX**, No. 7 (28 April 1983).

[4] There is a confusion between what might be called empirical and transcendental pragmatism. Some similar problems arise with the later work of

A more effective level of objection lies in a negative claim that Rorty and others make, that no convergence of science, past or future, could possibly be explained in any contentful way by reference to the way that the world is, because there is an insoluble difficulty with the notion of 'the world' as determining belief. It comes out as a dilemma. On the one hand, 'the world' may be characterized in terms of our current beliefs about what it contains; it is a world of stars, people, grass, tables and so forth. When 'the world' is taken in this way, we can of course say that our beliefs about the world are affected by the world, in the sense that for instance our beliefs about grass are affected by grass, but there is nothing illuminating or contentful in this—our conception of the world as the object of our beliefs can do no better than repeat the beliefs that we take to represent it. If, on the other hand, we try to form some idea of a world that is prior to any description of it, the world that all systems of belief and representation are trying to represent, then we have a quite empty notion of something completely unspecified and unspecifiable.[5] So either way we fail to have a notion of 'the world' that will do what is required of it.

Each side of this dilemma takes all our representations of the world together, in the one case putting them all in, and in the other leaving them all out. But there is a third and more helpful possibility, that we should form a conception of the world that is 'already there' in terms of some but not all of our representations, our beliefs and theories. In reflecting on the world that is there *anyway*, independent of our experience, we must concentrate not in the first instance on what our beliefs are about, but on how they represent what they are about. We can select among our beliefs and features of our world-picture some which we can reasonably claim to represent the world in a way that is to the maximum degree independent of our perspective and its peculiarities. The resultant picture of things, if we can carry through this task, can be called the 'absolute conception' of the world.[6] In terms

---

Wittgenstein: see 'Wittgenstein and Idealism', in *Understanding Wittgenstein*, Royal Institute of Philosophy Lectures Volume 7 (London, Macmillan, 1974), and reprinted in *Moral Luck* (Cambridge, Cambridge University Press, 1981); and Jonathan Lear, 'Leaving the World Alone', *Journal of Philosophy* **79** (1982).

[5] Rorty, 'The World Well Lost', in *Consequences of Pragmatism*, 14. See also Donald Davidson, 'The Very Idea of a Conceptual Scheme', *Proceedings and Addresses of the American Philosophical Association* **67** (1973/4).

[6] Cf. *Descartes: The Project of Pure Enquiry* (Harmondsworth, Penguin Books, 1978). See also N. Jardine, 'The Possibility of Absolutism', in *Science, Belief, and Behaviour: Essays in Honour of R. B. Braithwaite*, D. H. Mellor (ed.) (Cambridge, Cambridge University Press, 1980); and Colin McGinn, *The Subjective View* (Oxford, Clarendon Press, 1983).

of that conception, we may hope to explain the possibility of our attaining that conception itself, and also the possibility of other, more perspectival, representations.

This notion of an absolute conception can serve to *make effective* a distinction between 'the world as it is independently of our experience' and 'the world as it seems to us'. It does that by understanding 'the world as it seems to us' as 'the world as it seems peculiarly to us'; the absolute conception will, correspondingly, be that conception of the world that might be arrived at by any investigators, even if they were very different from us. What counts as a relevant difference from us, and indeed what for various levels of description will count as 'us', will itself be explained on the basis of that conception itself; we shall be able to explain, for instance, why one kind of observer can make observations that another kind cannot make. It is centrally important that these ideas relate to science, not to all kinds of knowledge. We can *know* things, the content of which is perspectival: we can know that grass is green, for instance, though *green*, for certain, and probably *grass*, are concepts that would not be available to every competent observer of the world, and would not figure in the absolute conception. (As we shall see very soon, people can know things even more locally perspectival than that.) The point is not to give an account of knowledge, and the opposition that we are discussing is not to be expressed in terms of knowedge, but of science. The aim is to outline the possibility of a convergence characteristic of science, one that could contentfully be said to be a convergence on how things (anyway) are.

That possibility, as I have explained it, depends heavily on notions of explanation. The substance of the absolute conception (as opposed to those vacuous or vanishing ideas of 'the world' that were offered before) lies in the idea that it could non-vacuously explain how it itself, and the various perspectival views of the world, should be possible. It is an important feature of modern science that it contributes to explaining how creatures who have the origins and characteristics that we have can understand a world which has the properties that this same science ascribes to the world. The achievements of evolutionary biology and the neurological sciences are substantive in these respects, and the notions of explanation involved are not vacuous. It is true, however, that such explanations cannot themselves operate entirely at the level of the absolute conception, because what they have to explain are psychological and social phenomena, such as beliefs and theories and conceptions of the world, and there may be little reason to suppose that they, in turn, could be adequately characterized in non-perspectival terms. How far this may be so is a central philosophical question. But even if we allow that the explanations of such things must remain to some degree perspectival, this does not mean that we cannot operate the

215

notion of the absolute conception. It will be a conception consisting of non-perspectival materials which will be available to any adequate investigator, of whatever constitution, and it will also help to explain to us, though not necessarily to those alien investigators, such things as our capacity to grasp that conception. Perhaps more than that will turn out to be available, but no more is necessary, in order to give substance to the idea of 'the world' and to defeat the first line of objection to the distinction, in terms of possible convergence, between the scientific and the ethical.

The opposite line of objection urges that the idea of 'converging on how things are' is available, to some adequate degree, in the ethical case as well. The place where this is to be seen is above all with those 'thick' ethical concepts that possess a lot of substantive content. Many exotic examples of these can be drawn from other cultures, but there are enough left in our own: *coward, lie, brutality, gratitude*, and so forth. They are characteristically related to reasons for action. If a concept of this kind applies, this often provides someone with a reason for action, though that reason need not be a decisive one, and may be outweighed by other reasons. Of course, exactly what reason for action is provided, and to whom, depends on the situation, in ways that may well be governed by this and by other ethical concepts, but the general connection with action is clear enough. We may say, summarily, that such concepts are 'action-guiding'.

At the same time, their application is guided by the world. A concept of this sort may be rightly or wrongly applied, and people who have acquired it can agree that it applies or fails to apply to some new situation. In many cases that agreement will be spontaneous, while in other cases there is room for judgment and comparison. Some disagreement at the margin may be irresoluble, but that does not mean that the use of the concept is not controlled by the facts or by the users' perception of the world. (As with other concepts that are not totally precise, marginal disagreements can indeed help to show how their use *is* controlled by the facts.) We can say, then, that the application of these concepts is at the same time world-guided and action-guiding. How can it be both of these at once?

Prescriptivism gave a very simple answer to that question. According to prescriptivism, any such concept can be analysed into a descriptive and a prescriptive element: it is guided round the world by its descriptive content, but has a prescriptive flag attached to it. It is the first feature that allows it to be world-guided, while the second makes it action-guiding. Some of the difficulties with this picture concern the prescriptive element, and how that is supposed to guide action in the relevant sense (telling yourself to do something is not an obvious model for recognizing that one has a reason to do it). But the most significant objection, for this discussion, applies to the other half of the analysis. Prescriptivism claims that what governs the application of the concept to the world is the descriptive element, and that the evaluative interest of the concept plays no part in this. All the input into its use is descriptive, just as all the evaluative aspect is output. It follows that for any concept of this sort, one could produce another which picked out just the same features of the world, but which worked simply as a descriptive concept, lacking any prescriptive or evaluative force.

Against this, critics[7] have made the effective point that there is no reason to believe that a descriptive equivalent will necessarily be available. How we 'go on' from one application of a concept to another is a function of the kind of interest that the concept represents, and one should not assume that one could see how people 'go on' in their use of a concept of this sort, if one did not share the evaluative perspective in which the concept has its point. An insightful observer can indeed come to understand and anticipate the use of the concept without actually sharing the values of the people who use it: that is an important point, and we shall come back to it. But in imaginatively anticipating the use of the concept, he also has to grasp imaginatively its evaluative point. He cannot stand quite outside the evaluative interests of the community he is observing, and pick up the concept simply as a device for dividing up in a rather strange way certain neutral features of the world.

This seems a very plausible account, and certainly a possible one, of what is involved in mastering concepts of this kind and understanding their use. It needs, in fact, to be not much more than possible to play an important part in this argument, by reminding moral philosophy of what the demands made by an adequate philosophy of language or by the philosophy of social explanation may turn out to be. If it is not only

[7]Notably John McDowell, 'Are Moral Requirements Hypothetical Imperatives?', *Proceedings of the Aristotelian Society* Supplementary Volume 52 (1978); 'Virtue and Reason', *Monist* **62** (1979). McDowell is above all concerned with the state of mind and motivations of a virtuous person, but I understand his view to have the more general implications discussed in the text. The idea that it might be impossible to pick up an evaluative concept unless one shared its evaluative interest I take to be basically a Wittgensteinian idea. I first heard it expressed by Philippa Foot and Iris Murdoch in a seminar in the 1950s. For the application of ideas from Wittgenstein's later philosophy to ethics, see e.g. Hanna F. Pitkin, *Wittgenstein and Justice* (California, California University Press, 1972), and Sabina Lovibond, *Realism and Imagination in Ethics* (Oxford, Blackwell, 1983). McDowell himself draws important consequences in the philosophy of mind, rejecting the 'belief and desire' model of rational action. I do not accept these consequences, but I shall not try to argue the question here. Some considerations later in this paper, about the differences between ethical belief and sense perception, bear closely on it.

possible but plausible, moral philosophy will be well advised to consider what needs to be said if it is true.

The sympathetic observer can follow the practice of the people he is observing; he can report, anticipate, and even take part in discussions of the use that they make of their concept. But, as with some other concepts of theirs, relating to religion, for instance, or to witchcraft, he is not ultimately identified with the use of this concept: it is not really his.[8] This possibility, of the insightful but not totally identified observer, bears on an important question, whether those who use ethical concepts of this kind can have ethical knowledge in virtue of properly applying those concepts. Let us assume, artificially, that we are dealing with a society that is maximally homogeneous and minimally given to general reflection; its members simply, all of them, use certain ethical concepts of this sort. (We may call it the 'hypertraditional' society.) What would be involved in their having ethical knowledge? According to the best available accounts of propositional knowledge,[9] they would have to believe the judgments which they made; those judgments would have to be true; and their judgments would have to satisfy a further condition, which has been extensively discussed in the philosophy of knowledge, but which can be summarized by saying that those first two conditions must be non-accidentally linked: granted the way that the people have gone about their enquiries, it must be no accident that the belief they have acquired is a true one, and if the truth on the subject had been otherwise, they would have acquired a different belief, true in those different circumstances. Thus I may know, by looking at it, that the dice has come up 6, and that (roughly[10]) involves the claim that if it had come up 4, I would have come to believe, by looking at it, that it had

[8] McDowell ('Virtue and Reason') allows for this possibility, but he draws no consequences from it, and ignores intercultural conflict altogether. He traces scepticism about objectivity in ethics, revealingly, to what he calls a 'philistine scientism', on the one hand, and to a philosopical pathology on the other, of vertigo in the face of unsupported practices. Leaving aside his attitude to the sciences, McDowell seems rather unconcerned even about history, and says nothing about differences in outlook over time. It is significant that in a discussion of the virtues that mostly relates to Aristotle, he takes as an example kindness, which is not an Aristotelian virtue.

[9] The most subtle and ingenious discussion of propositional knowledge I know is that of Robert Nozick in Chapter 3 of his *Philosophical Explanations* (Cambridge, Mass., Harvard University Press, 1981). Some central features of Nozick's account, notably its use of subjunctive conditionals, had been anticipated by Fred Dretske, as Nozick acknowledges in his note 53 to that chapter (op. cit. 630), which gives references.

[10] How rough? Perhaps he cannot read four dots as 4, though he can read six dots as 6. What if he can only read six dots as 6, and everything else as not 6?

218

come up 4 (the alternative situations to be considered have to be restricted to those moderately like the actual one.) Taking a phrase from Robert Nozick, we can say that the third requirement—it involves a good deal more elaboration than I have suggested—is that one's belief should 'track the truth'.

The members of the hypertraditional society apply their 'thick' concepts, and in doing so they make various judgments. If any of those judgments can ever properly be said to be true, then their beliefs, in those respects, can track the truth, since they can withdraw judgments of this sort if the circumstances turn out not to be what was supposed, can make an alternative judgment if it would be more appropriate, and so on. They have, each, mastered these concepts, and they can perceive the personal and social happenings to which the concepts apply. If there is truth here, their beliefs can track it. The question left is whether any of these judgments can be true.

An objection can be made to saying that they are. If they are true, then the observer can correctly say that they are; letting 'F' stand in for one of their concepts, he can say for instance, 'The headman's statement, *That is F*, is true'. But then (the objection goes) he should be able to invoke a very basic principle about truth, the *disquotation principle*,[11] and say, in his own person, *that is F*. But he is not prepared to do that, since F is not one of his concepts.

How strong is this objection? It relies on the following principle: A cannot correctly say that B speaks truly in uttering S unless A could say something tantamount to S himself. (A lot of work has to be done to spell out what counts as something 'tantamount' to S, if this is not going to run into merely technical difficulties, but let us suppose all such problems solved.) Imagine then a certain school slang, which uses special names for various objects, places and institutions in the school. It is a rule that these words are appropriately used only by someone who is a member of the school, and this rule is accepted and understood by a group wider than the members of the school themselves (it would have to be, if it is to be *that* rule at all). People know that if they use these

[11] A. Tarski, 'The Concept of Truth in Formalized Languages', in *Logic, Semantics, Meta-Mathematics* (Oxford, Oxford University Press, 1956). On the present issue, cf. David Wiggins, 'What Would be a Substantial Theory of Truth?', in *Philosophical Subjects: Essays Presented to P. F. Strawson*, Z. van Straaten (ed.) (Oxford, Blackwell, 1980). Wiggins' discussion raises a further issue, whether the observer could even understand what the sentences mean, unless he could apply a disquotational truth formula to them. (In this he is influenced by Donald Davidson, 'Truth and Meaning', *Synthese* **17** (1967). The fact that there can be a sympathetic but non-identified observer shows that it cannot be impossible to understand something although one is unwilling to assert it oneself.

terms in their own person they will be taken for members of the school, or else criticized, and so forth. This provides an exception to the principle, since observers cannot use these terms, but they can correctly say that members of the school, on various occasions, have spoken truly in using them.

In this simple case, it is of course true that the observers have other terms that refer to just the same things as the slang-terms, and that is not so, we are supposing, with the local ethical terms. That makes a difference, since in the school case the observer can clearly factor out what makes a given slang statement true, and what, as contrasted with that, makes it appropriate for a particular person to make it. But we can see the use of the ethical concept as a deeper example of the same thing. In both cases, there is a condition that has to be satisfied if one is to speak in that way, a condition that is satisfied by the local and not by the observer. In both cases, it is a matter of belonging to a certain culture. In the school case it is, so far as the example goes, only a variance of speech, while in the ethical case there is a deeper variance which means that the observer has no term which picks out exactly the same things as their term picks out, and is independent of theirs. He has, of course, an expression such as 'what they call "F"', and the fact that he can use that, although it is not independent of their term, is important: his intelligent use of it shows that he can indeed understand their use of their term, although he cannot use it himself.

We can understand in these circumstances why disquotation is not possible, and the fact that it is not gives us no more reason, it seems to me, than it does in the school case to deny that the locals can speak truly in using their own language. However, there is a different, and stronger, objection to saying, in the ethical case, that that is what they do. In the school case, the observer did not think that the locals' use of their terms implied anything that he actually believed to be false. In other cases, however, an observer may see local statements as false in this way. I am not referring to statements which the locals might equally have seen as false, those that are mistaken even in local terms. I mean the case in which the observer sees some whole segment of their discourse as involving a mistake. It is a complex question in social theory, in what cases that might be so. Social anthropologists have discussed whether ritual and magical conceptions should be seen as mistaken in our terms, or rather as operating at a different level, not commensurable with our scientific ideas. Whatever may be said more generally, it is quite hard to deny that magic, at least, is a causal conception, with implications that overlap with scientific conceptions of causality.[12] To the extent that that is so, magical conceptions can be

[12] See John Skorupski, *Symbol and Theory* (Cambridge, Cambridge University Press, 1976).

seen from the outside as false, and then no one will have known to be true any statements claiming magical influence, even though they may have correctly used all the local criteria for claiming a given piece of magical influence. Those criteria do not reach to everything that, on this view of the matter, is involved in such claims. In cases of this sort, the problem with conceding truth to the locals' claims is the opposite of the one just discussed. It is not that their notions are different from the observer's, so that he cannot assert what they assert. The problem is that their statements imply notions that are similar enough to some of his, for him to deny what they assert.

One may see the local ethical statements in a way that raises that difficulty. On this reading, the locals' statements imply something that can be put in the observer's terms, and which he rejects: that it is *right*, or *all right*, to do things that he thinks it is not right, or all right, to do. Prescriptivism sees things in this way. The local statements entail, together with their descriptive content, an all-purpose *ought*. We have rejected the descriptive half of that analysis; is there any reason to accept the other half?

Of course, there is a quite minimal sense in which the locals think it 'all right' to act as they do, and they do not merely imply this, but reveal it, in the practice under which they use these concepts and live accordingly. To say that they 'think it all right' merely at this level is not to mention any further and disputable judgment of theirs, but merely to record their practice. Must we agree that there is a judgment, to be expressed by using some universal moral notion, which they accept and the observer may, very well, reject?

I do not think that we have to accept that idea. More precisely, I do not think that we can decide whether to accept it until we have a more general picture of the whole question; this is not an issue that by itself can force more general conclusions on us. The basic question is how we are to understand the relations between practice and reflection. The very general kind of judgment that is in question here—a judgment, that is to say, using a very general concept—is essentially a product of reflection, and it comes into question when someone stands back from the practices of the society and its use of these concepts and asks whether this is the right way to go on, whether these are good ways in which to assess actions, whether the kinds of character that are admired are good kinds of character to admire. Of course, in many traditional societies some degree of reflective questioning and criticism exists, and that itself is an important fact. It is for the sake of the argument, to separate the issues, that I have been using the idea of the hypertraditional society, where there is no reflection.

In relation to that society, the question now is this: does the practice of that society, in particular the judgments that members of the society make, imply answers to reflective questions about that practice, questions which they have never raised? Some judgments made by members of a society do have implications at a more general or theoretical level which they have never considered. That may be true of their magical judgments, if those are taken as causal claims, and it is true of their mathematical judgments, and of their judgments about the stars. We may be at some liberty whether to construe what they were saying as expressing mathematical judgments or opinions about the stars, but if we do interpret them as making those judgments and expressing those opinions, they will have those implications. If what a statement expresses is an opinion about the stars, one thing that follows is that it can be contradicted by another opinion about the stars.

There are two different ways in which we can see the activities of the hypertraditional society, which depend on different models of ethical practice. (They are in fact mere sketches or shells, rather than models: they still need their content to be supplied. But they can already have an effect.) One of them can be called an 'objectivist' model. According to this, we shall see the members of the society as trying, in their local and limited way, to find out the truth about values, an activity in which we and other human beings, and perhaps creatures who are not human beings, are all engaged. We shall then see their judgments as having these implications, rather as we see primitive statements about the stars as having implications which can be contradicted by more sophisticated statements about the stars. On the other, contrasted, model we shall see their judgments rather as part of their way of living, a cultural artefact that they have come to inhabit (though they have not consciously built it). On this, non-objectivist, model, we shall take a different view of the relations between that practice and critical reflection. We shall not be disposed to see the level of reflection as, implicitly, already there, and we shall not want to say that their judgments have, just as they stand, these implications.

The choice between these two different ways of looking at their activities will determine whether we say that the people in the hypertraditional society have ethical knowledge or not. It is important to be quite clear what ethical knowledge is in question. It is knowledge involved in their making judgments in which they use their 'thick' concepts. We are not considering whether they display knowledge *in using those concepts rather than some others*: that would be an issue at the reflective level. The question 'does that society possess ethical knowledge?' is seriously ambiguous in that way. The collective reference to the society invites one to take the perspective in which their ethical representations are compared with other societies' ethical representations, and that is the reflective level, at which they certainly do not possess knowledge. There is another sense of the question in which it asks whether members of the society could, in exercising their concepts, express knowledge about the world to which they apply them, and the answer to that might be 'yes'.

The interesting result of this discussion is that the answer will be 'yes' if we take the non-objectivist view of their ethical activities: on that view, various members of the society will have knowledge, when they deploy their concepts carefully, use the appropriate criteria, and so on. But on the objectivist view, they do not have knowledge, or at least, it is immensely unlikely that they do, since their judgments have (on that view) extensive implications at the reflective level which they have never considered, and we have every reason to believe that when those implications are considered, the traditional use of ethical concepts will be seriously affected.

The objectivist view, while it denies knowledge to the unreflective society, may seem to promise knowledge at the reflective level. Indeed, it is characteristic of it to expect that it would be at that level that the demands of knowledge would for the first time be properly met. But there is no reason to think that, at least as things are, there is knowledge at the reflective level which is not either common to all ethical systems and has not much content ('one has to have a special reason to kill someone'), or else has simply survived from the unreflective level. The objectivist view sees the practice of the hypertraditional society, and the conclusions that we might reach at the reflective level, equally in terms of beliefs, and its idea is that we shall have a better hold on the truth about the ethical, and will be in a position to replace belief with knowledge, precisely in virtue of the processes of reflection. I see no reason to think that the demands of knowledge at this level, at least as things are, have been met. At the end of this paper I shall suggest that, so far as propositional knowledge of ethical truths is concerned, this is not simply a matter of how things now are. Rather, at a high level of reflective generality there could not be any ethical knowledge of this sort—or, at most, just one piece.

If we accept that there can be knowledge at the hypertraditional or unreflective level; and if we accept the obvious truth that reflection characteristically disturbs, unseats or replaces those traditional concepts; and if we agree that, at least as things are, the reflective level is not in a position to give us knowledge that we did not have before; then we reach the notably unSocratic conclusion that in ethics, *reflection can destroy knowledge*.

Another consequence, if we allow knowledge at the unreflective level, will be that not all propositional knowledge is additive. Not all pieces of knowledge can be combined into a larger body of knowledge. We may well have to accept that conclusion anyway from other contexts that involve perspectival views of the world. A part of the physical world may present itself as one colour to one kind of observer, and another to another; to another, it may not exactly be a colour that is presented at all. Call those qualities perceived by each kind of observer 'A'. 'B', 'C'. Then a skilled observer of one kind can know that the surface is A, of another kind that it is B, and so on, but there is no knowledge that it is A and B and C. This result would disappear if what 'A', 'B', etc., meant were something relational; if, when observers said 'that is A' they meant 'A to observers like us'. It is very doubtful that this is the correct account.[13] If it is not, the coherence of those pieces of knowledge is secured at a different level, when those various perceived qualities are related to the absolute conception. Their relation to that conception is also what makes it clear that the capacities that produce these various pieces of knowledge are all forms of *perception*. Of course, we have good reason to believe this before we possess any such theoretical conception, and certainly before we possess its details, as we still do not. That is because our everyday experience, unsurprisingly, reveals a good deal of what we are and how we are related to the world, and in that way itself leads us towards that theoretical conception.[14]

Some think of the knowledge given by applying ethical concepts as something like perception; but we can now see a vital asymmetry between the case of the ethical concepts, and the perspectival experience of secondary qualities. It lies in the fact that in the case of secondary qualities, what explains also justifies, but in the ethical case, this is not so. The psychological capacities that underly our perceiving the world in terms of certain secondary qualities have evolved so that the physical world will present itself to us in reliable and useful ways. Coming to know that these qualities constitute our form of perceptual engagement with the world, and how this mode of presentation works, will not unsettle the system.[15] In the ethical case, we have an analogy to the perceptual just to this extent, that there is local convergence under these concepts—the judgments of those who use them are indeed, as I put it before, world-guided. That is certainly enough to refute the simplest oppositions of fact and value. But if this is to mean anything for

[13] Cf. Wiggins, 'Truth, Invention and the Meaning of Life'; Colin McGinn, *The Subjective View* (Oxford, Oxford University Press, 1983), 9–10, 119–120.

[14] A formulation of the distinction between primary and secondary qualities is very nearly as old in the Western tradition as the self-conscious use of a principle of sufficient reason.

[15] I have taken two sentences here from an article, 'Ethics and the Fabric of the World', to appear in *Morality and Objectivity*, Ted Honderich (ed.) (London, Routledge, forthcoming), a volume of essays in memory of John Mackie; it discusses Mackie' views on these subjects, and in particular his idea that perceptual and moral experience each involve a comparable error. See also McGinn, op. cit., especially Ch. 7.

a wider objectivity, everything depends on what is to be said *next*. With secondary qualities, it is the explanation of the perspectival perceptions that enables us, when we come to reflect on them, to place them in relation to the perceptions of other people and other creatures; and, as we have just noticed, that leaves everything more or less where it was, so far as our perceptual judgments are concerned. The question is whether we can find an ethical analogy to that. Here we have to go outside the local, perspectival judgments, to a reflective or second-order account of them, and there the analogy gives out.

There is, first, a problem of what the second-order account is to be. An *explanation* of those local judgments and of the conceptual differences between societies will presumably have to come from the social sciences: cultural differences are what are in question. Perhaps no existing explanation of such things goes very deep, and we are not too clear how deep an explanation might go. But we do know that it will not look much like explanations of secondary quality perception. The capacities it will invoke will be those involved in finding our way around in a social world, not merely the physical world, and that, crucially, will mean *in some social world or other*, since it is certain both that human beings cannot live without some culture or other, and that there are many different cultures in which they can live, differing in their local perspectival concepts.

In any case, an explanatory theory is not enough to deal with the problems of objectivity raised by the local ethical concepts. In the case of secondary qualities, the explanation also justified, because it could show how the perceptions are related to physical reality, and how they can give knowledge of that reality, which is what they purport to do. The question with them is: is this a method of finding one's way around the physical world? The theoretical account explains how it is. In the ethical case, that is not the kind of question raised by reflection. If one asked the question 'Is this a method of finding one's way around the social world?', one would have to be asking whether it was a method of finding one's way around some social world or other, and the answer to that must obviously be 'Yes', unless the society were extremely disordered, which is not what we were supposing. The question raised is rather 'Is this a good, acceptable, way of living compared with others?'; or, to put it another way, 'Is this the best kind of social world?'

When these are seen to be the questions, the reflective account that we require turns out to involve reflective *ethical* considerations. Some believe that these considerations should take the form of an ethical theory. These reflective considerations will have to take up the job of justifying or unjustifying the local concepts once those have come to be questioned. If a wider objectivity were to come from all this, then the reflective ethical considerations would have themselves to be objective.

225

This brings us back to the question that we touched on just now, whether the reflective level might generate its own ethical knowledge. If this is understood as our coming to have propositional knowledge of ethical truths, then we need some account of what 'tracking the truth' will be. The idea that our beliefs can track the truth at this level must at least imply that a range of investigators could rationally, reasonably and unconstrainedly come to converge on a determinate set of ethical conclusions. What are the hopes for such a process? I do not mean of its actually happening, but rather of our forming a coherent picture of how it might happen. If it is construed as convergence on a body of ethical truths which is brought about and explained by the fact that they are truths—that would be the strict analogy to scientific objectivity—then I see no hope for it. In particular, there is no hope of extending to this level the kind of world-guidedness that we have been considering in the case of the 'thick' ethical concepts. Discussions at the reflective level, if they are to have the ambition of considering all ethical experience and arriving at the truth about the ethical, will necessarily use the most general and abstract ethical concepts such as 'right', and those concepts do not display that world-guidedness (which is why they were selected by prescriptivism in its attempt to find a pure evaluative element from which it could *detach* world-guidedness).

I cannot see any convincing theory of knowledge for the convergence of reflective ethical thought 'on ethical reality' in even distant analogy to the scientific case. Nor is there a convincing analogy with mathematics, a case in which the notion of an independent reality is at least problematical. Every non-contradictory piece of mathematics is part of mathematics, though it may be left aside as too trivial or unilluminating or useless, but not every non-contradictory structure of ethical reflection can be part of one such subject, since they conflict with one another in ways that not only lack the kind of explanation that could form a credible theory of error, but have too many credible explanations of other kinds.

I do not believe, then, that we can understand the reflective level through a model in which we can come to know ethical propositions at that level, while in less reflective states we aim to possess that truth, but can at best arrive at beliefs. We must reject the objectivist view of ethical life as, in that way, a pursuit of ethical truth. But that does not rule out all forms of objectivism. There is a different project, of trying to give an objective grounding or foundation to ethical life, by showing that a certain kind of ethical life was the best for human beings, was most likely to meet their needs. The question asked by this approach is: granted that human beings need, in general, to share a social world, is there anything to be known about their needs and their most basic motivations that will show us what that world should best be?

I cannot argue the question here, but I doubt that there will turn out to be a very satisfying answer to that question. It is probable that any such considerations will radically under-determine the ethical options even in a given social situation (we must remember that what we take the situation to be is itself, in part, a function of what ethical options we can see). They may under-determine it in several different dimensions. Any ethical life is going to contain restraints on such things as killing, injury and lying, but those restraints can take very different forms. Again, with respect to the virtues, which is the most natural and promising field for this kind of enquiry, we only have to compare Aristotle's catalogue of the virtues with any that might be produced now to see how pictures of life that can be recognized as equally appropriate to human beings may differ very much in their spirit and in the actions and institutions that they would call for. We also have the idea that there are many and various forms of human excellence that will not all fit together into a one harmonious whole. On that view, any determinate ethical outlook is going to represent some kind of specialization of human possibilities. That idea is deeply entrenched in any naturalistic or, again, historical conception of human nature—that is to say, in any adequate conception of it —and I find it hard to believe that that will be overcome by an objective enquiry, or that human beings could turn out to have a much more determinate nature than is suggested by what we already know, one that timelessly demanded a life of a particular kind.

The project of giving to ethical life, in any very determinate form, an objective grounding in considerations about human nature is not, in my view, very likely to succeed. But it is at any rate a comprehensible project, and I believe that it represents the only form of ethical objectivity at the reflective level that is intelligible. For that reason, it is worth asking what would be involved in its succeeding. If it succeeded, that would not simply be a matter of agreement on a theory of human nature. The convergence itself would be partly on scientific matters, in a very broad social and psychological sense, but what would matter would be a convergence to which these scientific conclusions would provide only part of the means. Nor, on the other hand, would there be a convergence directly on to ethical truths, as in the other objectivist model. There would be one ethical belief which might perhaps be said to be in its own right an object of knowledge at the reflective level, to the effect that a certain kind of life was best for human beings. But that will not yield other ethical truths directly. The reason for this, to put it summarily, is that the excellence or satisfactoriness of a life does not stand to the beliefs involved in that life as premise to conclusion. Rather, an agent's (excellent or satisfactory) life is characterized by *having* those beliefs, and most of the beliefs will not be about that agent's dispositions or life, or about other people's dispositions, but

227

about the social world. That life will involve, for instance, the agent's using some 'thick' concepts rather than others. Reflection on the excellence of the life does not itself establish the truth of judgments using those concepts, or of the agent's other ethical judgments. It rather shows that there is good reason (granted a commitment to an ethical life at all) to live a life that involves those concepts and those beliefs.

The convergence that signalled the success of this project would be a convergence of practical reason, by which people came to lead the best kind of life and to have the desires that belonged to that; convergence in ethical belief would largely be a part and consequence of that process. One very general ethical belief would, indeed, be an object of knowledge at that level. Many particular ethical judgments, involving the favoured 'thick' concepts, could be known to be true, but then judgments of that sort (I have argued) can very often to be known to be true anyway, even when they occur, as they always have occurred, in a life that is not grounded at the objective level. The objective grounding would not bring it about that judgments using those concepts were true or could be known: that was so already. But it would enable us to recognize that certain of them were the best or most appropriate 'thick' concepts to use. Between the two extremes of the one very general proposition, and the many quite concrete ones, other ethical beliefs would be true only in the oblique sense that they were the beliefs that would help us to find our way around in a social world which—on this optimistic programme—would have been shown to be the best social world for human beings.

That would be a structure very different from that of the objectivity of science. There is, then, a radical difference between ethics and science. Even if ethics were objective in the only way in which it could intelligibly be objective, its objectivity would be quite different from that of science. In addition, it is probably not objective in that way. However, that does not mean that there is a clear distinction between (any) fact and (any) value; nor does it mean that there is no ethical knowledge. There is some, and in the less reflective past there has been more.

A Sociological Theory of Objectivity[1]

DAVID BLOOR

(i) The Theory Stated

I want to propose to you a theory about the nature of objectivity—a theory which will tell us something about its causes, its intrinsic character, and its sources of variation. The theory in question is very simple. Indeed, it is so simple that I fear you will reject it out of hand. Here is the theory: it is that *objectivity is social*. What I mean by saying that objectivity is social is that the *impersonal* and *stable* character that attaches to some of our beliefs, and the sense of reality that attaches to their reference, derives from these beliefs being *social institutions*.

I am taking it that a belief that is objective is one that does not belong to any individual. It does not fluctuate like a subjective state or a personal preference. It is not mine or yours, but can be shared. It has an external, thing-like aspect to it. You will have noticed that I have made no mention of truth. For the sake of simplicity I shall treat the true/false distinction as different from the objective/subjective distinction. Ordinary English usage is not clear cut on this point, but just as it is often useful to distinguish rational beliefs from true beliefs, I shall distinguish objective beliefs from true beliefs. A theory about objectivity must primarily address the object-like stability of the things we believe in, and the external, compelling character of the standards, rules and procedures that we use. A good theory should be able to illuminate the objectivity of specific beliefs, say, beliefs in the existence of atoms, or gods or tables, as well as the objectivity of mathematics and of moral principles.

It may be easier to grasp the claim behind the slogan that 'objectivity is social' if we think of the theory resulting from two distinct steps. The first step is to lay out the specifications that something must meet in order to merit the title 'objective'. My claim is that these specifications are met by social institutions. The taken-for-granted practices sanctioned by a group have just this quality of being external to the individual. They have a stability far greater than the individual's changing desires. They are the common ground where individuals meet. They are shared. So institutions satisfy the general conditions for

[1] With the exception of section (v), which has been considerably expanded, what follows is the text of the lecture given to the Royal Institute of Philosophy on 22 October 1982.

David Bloor

objectivity. The second step is to seize the opportunity presented by this interesting fact, and to *identify* the objective with the social. The second step does not, of course, *follow* from the first step. It is an act of theory formation: a conjecture, not a deduction. Its justification, as I hope to show, comes from its suggestive power, and its problem-solving capacity. It provides us with a simple and useful tool with which to investigate an otherwise elusive property of beliefs. That we badly need such help is shown by obscurity that so often attends discussions of objectivity—I am thinking, of course, of the strong Platonizing tendencies that have accompanied some of the more notable attempts to do justice to the objectivity of knowledge.

(ii) Popper's Theory Re-interpreted

Before I put the social theory of objectivity to work, I shall try to make my approach more acceptable. One way to do this is to compare it with other treatments of the same subject. Sir Karl Popper is amongst the leading champions of objectivity, and one of the sharpest critics of subjectivism, so his theory is an obvious point of reference for work in this field. You will recall that in his book *Objective Knowledge*, Popper distinguishes three 'worlds'.[2] World *one* is the world of material objects and processes. World *two* is the world of psychological states and processes. And world *three* is the world of objective knowledge. This is populated by propositions (both true and false), by theories and conjectures, and also poems and works of art. In short, it is the realm of *intelligibles*.[3]

One way in which I could try to exploit this comparison is by highlighting the obscurity of Popper's ontology, or by emphasizing the difficulties in reconciling the man-made and developing character of his world three with what he calls its 'relative autonomy'.[4] In other words, I could try to bolster the credibility of the social theory by discrediting the opposition. Like some of the defenders of democracy I could say: if you think this is bad, wait till you see the rest. In fact, I shan't use this

[2] K. R. Popper, *Objective Knowledge. An Evolutionary Approach*, (Oxford: Clarendon Press, 1972), 154 (hereafter abbreviated to *O.K.*).

[3] *O.K.* 154, 166.

[4] According to the Lewis principles, for all formulae *a* and *b*, *a* tautologically implies *b* if *a* is a counter-tautology. This might be taken to mean that if world three contains contradictory propositions it contains *all* propositions, and so all further evolution and development of its content will be impossible. It will, so to speak, be full and complete and hence static. This objection has been put forward by J. Cohen, review of *The Self and its Brain* by K. Popper and J. Eccles, *Mind* **88** (1979), 301–304, 302.

method. It is too negative. What I shall try to do is to bring out the strengths of Popper's theory and then try to explain these strengths by means of my own theory. I shall, incidentally, point out some important weaknesses, but I shall try to do this in a way that is constructive and cumulative and that helps us improve on what Popper says.[5]

What I want to argue, of course, is that Popper's 'third world' is really the social world. If the social theory of objectivity is correct, then when Popper is articulating the structure and content of world three, and its interactions with worlds one and two, what he is really describing is the status and character of a social institution. This, I want to say, is the *real reference* of his talk, but his metaphysical terminology obscures this fact.[6] So I do not want to reject Popper's theory outright; but nor do I want to accept it as it stands. I want to transform it; or decode it; or—to put it bluntly, to demystify it. I think that Popper's theory of objectivity has not provoked the response it deserves. It has either been accepted too uncritically; or it has been rejected too completely. What we should be doing is trying to get a better grasp of what he is talking about. This, I suggest, can be done with a social theory.

First, take the basic structure of Popper's theory. He is a pluralist. His universe has three parts to it—three 'worlds', though, rightly, he does not want us to take the word 'world' too seriously. In the same way a social theory can be usefully (and provisionally) formulated in terms of three levels. But instead of the individual mind being poised between world one and world three, it is poised between the material and the social world. As individuals we have both an animal side and a social side. We belong to both nature and culture—our 'second nature'. So

---

[5] For a fuller statement of the following arguments see: D. Bloor, 'Popper's Mystification of Objective Knowledge', *Science Studies,* **4** (1974), 65–76. This is an essay review of *Objective Knowledge*. For critical reaction to this line of interpretation, see the discussions by R. Dolby, H. Meynell and D. Wojick, *Science Studies*, **4** (1974), 187–195; L. De Witt, *Social Studies of Science*, **5** (1975), 201–209; and J. Grove, 'Popper "Demystified". The Curious Ideas of Bloor (and some others) about World 3', *Philosophy of the Social Sciences*, **10** (1980), 173–180. In what follows I address a few of the more important objections. I should emphasize at the outset that my reading of Popper's theory is not meant to be true to Popper's *intentions*. Indeed, it directly cuts across those intentions. It is amusing to find references to these subjective intentions used as an argument against my reading by Popper's objectivist defenders.

[6] I am pleased to find that I am not alone in giving a sociological reading to what Popper says. Quinton, for example, says: 'Objective knowledge in this sense is just one more social institution . . .' Unfortunately he does not develop this passing remark. A. Quinton, 'Sir Karl Popper: Knowledge as an Institution', *Encounter* **41**, No. 6 (1973), 33–36.

substituting 'social world' for 'third world' preserves the basic three-fold structure of the picture.

Next take the causal and feedback relations between Popper's three worlds. He tells us that:

> The three worlds are so related that the first two can interact, and that the last two can interact. Thus the second world, the world of subjective or personal experiences, interacts with each of the other two worlds. The first world and the third world cannot interact, save through the intervention of the second world . . .[7]

As I read this, it says that while society can be said to act on its individual members, collective purposes can only impinge on physical nature through the agency of individuals. The knowledge of how to improve the workings of a steam engine, for instance, can only be realized by flesh and blood individuals, bending pipes and fixing rivets. Society as such cannot act directly on nature.

Although I have some reservations about Popper's overall picture of the feedback relations between the three worlds, I can appreciate that for many purposes it provides a useful shorthand. For example, when he says that the third world is a human product, but acts back on the individuals who created it, we can see that social arrangements are likewise a human product, but can be spoken of as things which constrain us. This is a slightly reified way of speaking, but it can be harmless enough. So, if we are not too pedantic, we may say that not only is the three-fold structure of Popper's theory preserved under my transformation, but so are the connections between the three parts.

What are we to make of Popper's claim that objective knowledge is, as he puts it, 'knowledge without a knowing subject'? This too transforms without difficulty. If the third world is the social world, then objective knowledge refers to something like the *state of a discipline*, or the state of culture, at any given time.[8] We would never say that physics—the *discipline* of physics—refers to what this or that individual physicist knows. The word 'physics' refers to the entire corpus of standards, conventions, paradigms, accepted results and procedures, to which the group known as 'physicists' subscribe. It is the property of the *collectivity* and the *role*. Since the class of physicists is not itself a physicist, and has no kind of personality or super-individual self, it is not a knowing subject. So we can deduce from a social theory the very conclusion on which Popper insists: that objective knowledge is knowledge without a knowing subject.

---

[7]*O.K.* 155.

[8]Examination of Popper's examples on p. 110 of *O.K.* bears out this interpretation.

We can in fact transform Popper's theory almost mechanically—going through his book *Objective Knowledge* substituting 'social world' for 'third world'. Thus: Popper tells us that 'the activity of understanding consists, essentially, in operating with third-world objects'.[9] This becomes the claim that our intellectual operations proceed by the use of socially given categories and socially shared meanings. He says, interestingly, that our subjective life is 'anchored in the third world'.[10] This becomes the claim that subjective life is anchored in the social world and tends to consist of responses to social events and their meanings. Popper also says that our very humanity comes from our relation to the third world.[11] This, of course, transforms into the plausible claim that our humanity comes from our participation in society and culture. But I do not want to pile example on example. You can see that, when we transform them, we do not lose the *sense* of Popper's claims. We also preserve their truth value, and at the same time make them more accessible and intelligible. This all supports my thesis that what Popper is really talking about is the social world.

But of course, if Popper's talk of world three were precisely equivalent to my talk of society and institutions, if we could always move smoothly back and forth from one idiom to the other, then the two theories would be equivalent. The choice between them would be no more than a terminological preference. So we must focus on the points where the transformation *breaks down*, and where the theories begin to *diverge*. This is where we might find a basis for preferring one to the other.

(iii) Meaning and Implication

Let me go straight to the main point of divergence. A defender of Popper's theory would, I suspect, say that there is one vitally important feature of our knowledge—and a feature that is central to its objectivity—that no social theory could ever explain. This is the fact that our beliefs and assertions have *logical implications*. Furthermore, these implications might not be known at certain stages in the growth of our knowledge. (Indeed, most of them might never be known.) A believer in world three would insist that we *discover* the logical implications of our premises; so, in some sense, they must exist already. They must come into existence as soon as we formulate our premises,

[9] *O.K.* 164.
[10] *O.K.* 163.
[11] *O.K.* 121.

and then lie in wait for us. It is in order to capture facts of this kind that we seem forced to postulate a quasi-autonomous world of objective knowledge—and one which cannot be equated with the social world. For how can the social world be a repository for the pre-existing but undiscovered consequences of our beliefs?

At this point I could resort to purely negative arguments, and launch a counter-attack. I could say that the theory of world three does not really *explain* this fact about implications either. It just records it. It helps itself to the fact without saying how the trick is done. I could invoke some of the standard arguments against Platonism. Here the argument would be that postulating a realm of entities like logical consequences or mathematical truths, does not help explain how we actually *draw* our conclusions. If the answer exists in advance, how does that help me *now*? Certainly, all that Popper has to offer is a feeble metaphor: just as the eye can literally see a physical object, he says, so the mind can similarly 'see' intellectual objects.[12] How we know that we are seeing the *right* object, however, remains obscure.[13]

But I promised that I would not depend on negative arguments, and I won't. What we need is a radical alternative to the whole picture offered by the Popperian and the Platonist. I would suggest that it is in fact a virtue of the social theory of objectivity that it helps to make our usual talk about implications and consequences look problematic. A social theory would have to be built on the idea that our talk about 'discovering' the implications of our assertions really covers up an act of *creation*. It would have to start fom the idea that there were no logical necessities, or no logical necessities of the kind that we have formally supposed. (If we can get rid of the causal nexus, why not the logical nexus?) We would have to say that, really, logical implications do not pre-exist: we construct them as we go along, depending on nothing but the dispositions that we possess naturally or have been given in the course of our training. This will have to be the reason why we agree to the extent that we do on such matters as the implications of our premises. Our tendency to *say* that the consequences of our premises pre-exist then becomes a facet of our behaviour that calls for special explanation. The explanation might be that certain feelings attend our drawing of inferences—say, feelings of compulsion. Or the explanation might be that this way of talking is a way of trying to justify our (really unjustifiable) tendency to say one thing rather than another. It is our

[12] *O.K.* 155.
[13] I am, of course, paraphrasing Wittgenstein's attack on Platonism as presupposing the very competence that it is meant to explain. See L. Wittgenstein, *Remarks on the Foundation of Mathematics*, (Oxford: Blackwell, 1964), Part I, section 3.

way of creating a continuity between our current and our past verbal practices.

To keep this large and difficult issue within bounds let me try to concentrate it into a single example: that of following a *rule*. We use words to formulate a rule; the rule means what it does because the words used to formulate it mean what they do. We then proceed to behave in certain ways and intend that our behaviour should be *in accord* with the rule. We put ourselves under the guidance of the rule and set ourselves to trace out its consequences. Let us imagine a case most favourable to the Platonist and suppose that we are talking about a rule-bound piece of mathematical activity—doing addition with integers, or developing an infinite sequence.

Now let me bring in the issue of objectivity. If the rule is to be called 'objective', then not any piece of behaviour can be said to be in accord with the rule. If there were no difference between obeying the rule and not obeying it, there would be no point in talking about a rule. The objectivity of the rule is that property of it which makes it independent of this kind of subjective whim, and which makes some behaviour accord with it and some deviate from it. So what does the objectivity of the rule reside in? The tempting answer is that it is the *meaning* of the rule that justifies the subsequent discrimination between obeying it and deviating from it.[14] So the question then resolves itself into one about the nature of meaning and the link between what we mean at one time and what we do at another time, e.g. what we mean when we formulate a rule, and what we do later when we follow it. If anyone thinks that meanings can determine action, or that meanings can in some way be projected into the future and determine their own application, then they will feel comfortable with a Popperian and a broadly Platonist theory of objectivity. For this is their secret premise. They help themselves to a certain picture of rules and meanings. If on the other hand you feel the problematic nature of meaning, then you will have every reason to be sympathetic to a social theory of objectivity.

And, of course, meaning *is* a profoundly problematic notion. Explanations of meaning must always come to an end. At some point we must just *act* in certain ways. Ultimately it is action which determines meaning, not meaning which determines action. Meaning is not created

---

[14] This theory often takes the form of the claim that meaning (e.g. the meaning of the logical constants) is the source of *validity*. For a devastating, though often misunderstood, attack on this claim see A. N. Prior, 'The Runabout Inference Ticket', *Analysis* **21** (1960), 38–39. For a further discussion, including a discussion of the misunderstandings, see B. Barnes and D. Bloor, 'Relativism, Rationalism and the Sociology of Knowledge', *Rationality and Relativism*, M. Hollis and S. Lukes (eds) (Oxford; Blackwell, 1982), 21–47, cf. especially 40–46.

once and for all; it is continually created and recreated. It has to be sustained from one moment of use to the next. In particular we cannot make provision for all non-standard interpretations of a rule. If we explain the rule in words we cannot make provision for all non-standard interpretations of our words. If we try to explain our words, we must use *other* words, and *these* can be given a non-standard interpretation. In the end we come down to nothing but our brute dispositions and our socialization into the accepted practices of a group. This is the ultimate basis of our discrimination between obeying the rule and not obeying it. In a word, what makes the rule objective is a *convention*. What counts as obeying a rule, being in accord with it and the intention behind it, is a matter of convention. That is: its objectivity has a social nature.[15]

What looks like the great weakness of a social theory of objectivity—the problem of coping with logical implication—may yet turn out to be its strongest point and its greatest source of interest. At least, anyone who feels tempted to explore a social theory of objectivity knows that he has some potent resources at his disposal. He has the whole of Wittgenstein's analysis of meaning and rule-following. The rock upon which his opponent's theory will founder is Wittgenstein's famous observation that 'no course of action could be determined by a rule, because every course of action can be made to accord with the rule'.[16]

(iv) Styles of Objectivity

I now want to look at how our ideas about objectivity might vary. The question itself can be difficult to bring into focus. Suppose the tribe on this side of the river worships one god, and the tribe on the other side of the river worships another god. If the worship of the gods is a stable feature of tribal practice, if they are spoken of routinely, if courses of action are justified by reference to them, then I would say both beliefs are objective. But, as yet, this leaves untouched the issue of whether their objectivity is of the same kind or not. Talking about variations in the category of objectivity itself is not always, or exactly, the same as talking about variations in the things believed. It is more like talking

[15] I should emphasize that by a 'convention' I do not mean a verbal maxim or rule but a non-verbal and pre-verbal pattern of behaviour and judgment.

[16] L. Wittgenstein, *Philosophical Investigations* (Oxford: Blackwell, 1967), Part I, section 201. The sociological importance of this is brought out in S. Kripke, 'Wittgenstein on Rules and Private Language: An Elementary Exposition', *Perspectives on Wittgenstein*, I. Block (ed.) (Oxford: Blackwell, 1982), 238–312; and in D. Bloor, *Wittgenstein: A Social Theory of Knowledge* (London: Macmillan, 1983).

about variations in the *manner* in which a belief is held—though not even that quite conveys what I want.

I could imagine that, to some people, the very idea that objectivity is a variable property of a body of belief will sound wrong. Is not objectivity, in itself, one and unchanging? If, like the Kantian, we refer the objectivity of knowledge to the unchanging structure of the mind or, like the Popperian, to its occupying the unique realm called the third world, then my question will not make much sense. What I am trying to do is to articulate and make plausible an alternative framework, and in this framework I think we *can* attach meaning to the question. What, then, would count as a variation within the category of objectivity itself? Go back to our two tribes and our two gods. Suppose one god was close and intimate. Each person has direct access to him. God speaks directly to the believer and is immediately present in his heart to guide and inform him. The other god is distant. All contact with him is via complex ritual and is mediated by an authoritative priesthood. This god cares little for inner states but automatically rewards proper displays of outward piety and formal obedience—and punishes deviation. Here we have a difference in belief, but a difference that might be related to the category of objectivity.

What is my reason for saying that we are now touching on variations in objectivity? It is that the two belief systems have different ways of synthesizing information and experience. They dispose of it in different ways, and place the accent of reality in different places. They provide different *a priori* frameworks for experience. In one case truth and knowledge are simple and immediate and direct; in the other case, knowledge is dependent on tradition and, ultimately, it is only vouchsafed to experts and elite groups. Where, as in this case, different aspects of knowledge are singled out for special protection, or accorded a special authority, there I suggest, we may reasonably speak of different *kinds* of objectivity.

What are the factors that need to be attended to? What gives us the clue that a particular choice has been made about where objectivity is to be located? What we must look for are things like this: Is knowledge represented as easy or difficult? Is reality visible to the eye or only to the trained intellect? Is knowledge a promise for the future or is it located in the past? Is reality ultimately mysterious or can its causal machinery be finally grasped? How are activity and passivity distributed between different parts of reality? Where are the risks and dangers located? A particularly important issue to check in this connection is whether the system of classifications in a body of knowledge has rigid or fluid boundaries. Are the different categories of thing kept strictly apart or can they be mixed and combined without anxiety or danger? Let me dramatize this point by one last appeal to my two imaginary tribes.

David Bloor

Suppose that in one of our tribes it was blasphemy to characterize god as having a body, and absurd and offensive to ask whether he took food or had a stomach or excreted. In the other tribe, god not only had a body, he had the body of a man and the head of a bird. Here I suggest we are looking at a very fundamental difference in belief that is a symptom of quite different organizational principles. In one case categories are kept apart, spirit and matter are quite separate; in the other, categories are happily mixed.

How do differences of the kind I have just described relate to differences in social organization? If I am going to maintain that something is objective in virtue of it being a social institution, then variations in objectivity ought to be locatable as variations in the institutions that embody knowledge. A group who locate knowledge in the future should have a different organization from one that locates it in some present accomplishment; a group that works with a short time span should be recognizably different from one that works with a long time span; groups who happily mix categories should be different from those that keep them pure, and so on. Furthermore, these differences in social organization ought to be intelligibly connected with the differences in how knowledge is organized, so that we can see how the one gives rise to the other. That such intelligible connections can be discovered is something that I shall now try to demonstrate by examples. For the sake of brevity I will begin by using imaginary or hypothetical cases, rather like my tribes, but then I will go on to take a quick look at some empirical material and real-life examples.

Consider, for example, how scientists might react if the predicted results of an experiment do not occur. One policy that might be adopted is never to allow a failed prediction to falsify the theory. Anomalous results would always be interpreted in the light of the theory, and the theory preserved by adjusting its subsidiary assumptions. In this case the object-like stability of a specific achievement will be preserved. The reality of which it speaks will be sustained. Yes, there really *is* such a thing as phlogiston; no, the surprising fact that the calx weighs more than the metal *does not* falsify it. We have just discovered that water creeps into it and that is why it weighs more than we had expected, and so on.[17]

[17] The policy of sustaining a theory in the face of repeated difficulties, rather than treating the difficulties as refuting instances is, of course, commonplace in science. The classic account of science based around this idea is in T.S. Kuhn, *The Structure of Scientific Revolutions* (Chicago, Chicago University Press, 1962). The particular example that I have used is described, though not very sympathetically, in *Harvard Case Histories in Experimental Science*, I, J. Conant and L. Nash (eds), (Cambridge, Massachusetts: Harvard University Press, 1966), 67–115.

A policy like this requires a consensus.[18] A stable conception of reality focused on a specific theory, whether it be phlogiston or oxygen, requires a stable pattern of behaviour. This means that the real or perceived benefits of deviation must be kept low, or temptation kept out of sight. One way of doing this, at least for a while, is to have a small, intensely interacting group who will keep one another in line by the threat and dangers of expulsion.

What we are talking about is something like the conditions for a *monopoly*. Where patterns of group dependence, or systems of patronage, break down, and power becomes diffused and atomized, then it will no longer be possible to know reality in quite this way. Nobody can be stopped from innovating or experimenting with new ideas. Now the response to novel experimental results will be quite different. They will not be assessed in terms of their conformity to existing knowledge. They will not be received anxiously and with suspicion because of the potential threat that they pose. They now represent opportunities. They will be embraced, and eagerly scanned—and then just as rapidly discarded if they are no use.

No particular vision of reality can now retain a privileged position. We cannot feel we have finally grasped its workings. The truth that now confronts us with the force of self-evidence is the endless complexity of reality. In itself it is mysterious, except for the promise that it holds out for endless progress. Now, knowledge can only make claim to objectivity if it keeps changing. Objectivity belongs, not to some past result, but to some indefinite future. All that is objective is the competitive activity of knowing, the rules of the game, and the method of scoring successes over one's competitors.

If I am right, these two locations for the objectivity of knowledge—one in a specific picture of reality; the other in the methodology of research itself—are explained by the forms of social life of the groups creating the knowledge. And what is more, the connection between the stable features of the social system and the stable features of the knowledge is perfectly clear cut. One is not an arbitrary correlate of the other. As we arrange the conventional pattern of our relations to one another we are, at the same time, arranging the framework upon

---

[18] Lakatos calls this the policy of 'monster barring'. See I. Lakatos, *Proofs and Refutations* (Cambridge, Cambridge University Press, 1976). For a sociological reading of Lakatos's work see D. Bloor, 'Polyhedra and the Abomination of Leviticus: Cognitive Styles in Mathematics', *Essays in the Sociology of Perception*, M. Douglas (ed.), (London: Routledge & Kegan Paul, 1982), 191–218.

David Bloor

which our cognition must depend.[19] This should occasion no surprise once we realize that we do not have a choice between arranging our beliefs according to reality, and arranging them according to social convention. We know reality *with* our conventions, not in spite of them. Our conventions represent an unavoidable condition for, and vehicle of, knowledge. To yearn after a reality unmediated by convention is like wanting to see better by getting our organs of vision out of the way.

(v) The Research Programme

The theory of objectivity that I have described is by no means novel. In its essentials it is to be found in the writings of Durkheim, though as I have indicated, it may be deepened by appeal to Wittgenstein's later work. But, whatever its origin, perhaps the most important fact about the theory is that it is related to a programme of empirical enquiry that has been actively and fruitfully pursued for a number of years. (Of course, not all those who have, objectively, contributed to the programme have been, subjectively, aware of the fact.) Connecting cognitive variation with social variation, and explaining the former by the latter, has long been routine practice in large areas of anthropology, sociology and history. What I shall now try to do is to indicate the *kind* of empirical study that has helped us to deepen our understanding of objectivity.

Perhaps the most obvious body of empirical work to choose for this purpose would be the Durkheimean tradition in anthropology. Here, both as a guide and as an exemplar I could cite the investigations of the anthropologist Mary Douglas. She has studied ideas of purity and danger, and the varying response to anomaly, in a variety of cultural contexts.[20] But to make things easier I will take my examples from close to home: from the history of our own tribal practices. I shall select just one theme—the idea that objectivity resides in experience and that objective knowledge can be had 'directly' and 'immediately'. I want to

[19]'Apprehending a general patttern of what is right and necessary in social relations is the basis of society: this apprehension generates whatever *a priori* or set of necessary causes is going to be found in nature.' M.Douglas, *Implicit Meanings. Essays in Anthropology* (London; Routledge & Kegan Paul, 1975), 281.
[20]As well as *Implicit Meanings* (above) see, for example, M. Douglas, *Purity and Danger: An Analysis of Concepts of Pollution and Taboo* (London, Routledge, 1963); *Natural Symbols: Explorations in Cosmology* (Harmondsworth; Penguin, 1973); *Cultural Bias*, Occasional Paper No.34 (Royal Anthropological Institute of Great Britain and Ireland, 1978).

look at *who* has believed that reality is directly given in experience, and *why* they have believed it.

Consider the radical protestant sectaries of the seventeenth century—the Diggers, Ranters and Quakers. Christopher Hill's book, *The World Turned Upside Down*, documents in some detail, not only who they were, but their activities, their predicament and their political and theological doctrines.[21] After the Civil War the agencies of social control were in disarray. The growing number of 'masterless men', and the remnants of Cromwell's army, took the opportunity to order their lives in a new way and run their affairs as they saw fit. They organized themselves into groups and communes. They wanted land, the redistribution of property, the end of church tithes, democracy, the end of the power of the priest and the right to preach their own sermons. These actions and policies were accompanied by a set of justifications. The sectaries formulated an account of reality and experience couched, of course, in the language of theology. They said that God was immanent not transcendent. He dwelt *within* his creation. He was present *in* his creation and did not dwell outside it. Nature itself was therefore divine, so God could be seen with the eyes of flesh and felt immediately within. So each individual was divine and was moved directly by divinity—and so was the world around him.

Although it sounds paradoxical, we may say that the idea of immediate revelation embraced so enthusiastically by the sectaries locates objectivity within the very centre of subjectivity itself—that is, within the direct experience of the individual. The oddity is resolved as soon as we realize what the sectaries were able to do with the idea. It justified them in 'short-circuiting' the whole of the social hierarchy. It rendered priests and all the traditional mediators between man and god totally unnecessary. All reality and morality was located where the sectaries themselves could grasp it. In other words, they had arranged the whole cosmos so that it underwote their claims to autonomy. The interior of the self, to which they appealed as the locus of their superlative mode of experience, was really itself a socially constructed thing. That is why their intensely personal sources of knowledge all delivered remarkably similar messages. The divine voice within spoke of (and, indeed, was the voice of) the interests of their group.[22]

So if we want to explain why objectivity was placed where it was, there are two ideas that may be deployed. These are: first, the basic idea

---

[21] C. Hill, *The World Turned Upside Down: Radical Ideas During the English Revolution* (Harmondsworth; Penguin, 1975).

[22] The idea that to worship god is to worship one's own social collectivity, and that the soul is really the social self is, of course, straight out of E. Durkheim, *The Elementary Forms of the Religious Life*, J. Swain (trans.) (New York: Collier Books, 1961, first French edn, 1912).

of *group interests*, and second, the idea of reality being put to *social use*.[23] We can understand why a particular vision of the world has been constructed by looking at how it is put to use. We must think of it as being actively employed, and then try to grasp the goals and purposes of its users as they operate within a specific, historical context.

How can we test the theory that objectivity is made to reside in experience because it justifies the bid for autonomy? There are two sorts of test we can apply. The first is to look at those who (for very down-to-earth reasons) opposed the sectaries, and see if they also contrived to diverge from them on the ideological plane. If the sectaries justified themselves by making reality immediately accessible, we should expect their opponents to try to put reality out of their reach—locating it in a place where *they* could define and manipulate it. If the sectaries symbolized their autonomy by a theology which made nature itself divine and active, we should expect their enemies to portray nature as the very opposite of divine and active—a something lowly, brute, passive, chaotic and irrational.

This is exactly what happened. Those who were alarmed by the sectaries and who wanted to see the organs of Church and State re-establish their control, elaborated rival theories of objectivity and built rival cosmologies. One of the best known rival accounts of objectivity was the idea of painstaking experiment. This was to be the curb for inspiration, and the time-consuming substitute for immediacy. One of the best known cosmologies built to oppose the sectaries was the corpuscular philosophy of Boyle and the Newtonians.[24] The vital, animated nature of the sectaries was replaced by a world of inanimate, dead matter. Incapable of organizing itself, this material world was controlled directly by God, or by non-material, active principles which were in turn controlled by God. (These were the 'forces' of Newton.) The laws that matter obeyed under this guidance could not be known with immediacy and ease. Care and caution and restraint were to be the

[23] See B. Barnes, *Interests and the Growth of Knowledge*, (London: Routledge, 1977) and S. Shapin, 'Social Uses of Science', *The Ferment of Knowledge: Studies in the Historiography of Eighteenth-century Science*, G. S. Rousseau and R. Porter (eds), (Cambridge: Cambridge University Press, 1980), 93–139. For a valuable survey and bibliography which will serve as an ideal introduction to the present state of scholarship in the sociology of knowledge, see S. Shapin, 'History of Science and its Sociological Reconstructions', *History of Science* xx (1982), 157–211.

[24] See, for example, J. R. Jacob, 'Boyle's Atomism and the Restoration Assault on Pagan Naturalism', *Social Studies of Science* 8 (1978), 211–233. M. C. Jacob, *The Newtonians and the English Revolution, 1689–1720* (Ithaca: Cornell University Press, 1976). For a fuller bibliography see Shapin, 1982, above.

hallmarks of knowledge. We might take this to be self-evident, but if we do we would be wrong. It is not the inevitable expression of our rationality, but a particular cultural stance that we cherish because we have inherited it, and forgotten the contingencies that shaped its growth.

The second way to test the kind of explanation that I have outlined for the sectaries is to see whether other groups, similarly positioned and with similar aims, generate a similar account of objectivity. Rather than scanning the evidence from other sectarian groupings, I shall select a particularly important test-case from within science itself. The tradition that had at one time been defined by its opposition to the claims of immediate revelation came, at a certain point in its history, to contain influential groups who embraced a remarkably similar theory. Of course, it was not *called* 'revelation'. The idiom had changed, and it was called the doctrine of immediate experience, or empiricism, or positivism; but the point behind it was the same—to justify autonomy. The move towards autonomy that I am referring to has been called the 'professionalization' of science. Under the leadership of men such as Huxley, Clifford, Tyndale and Galton, natural philosophers in Britain began to oust the clerical amateurs from the Royal Society and to trumpet their claims to special expertise and competence in organizing the affairs of society. They, in Galton's words, were to be the new priesthood; they were no longer going to be subordinate to the authority of the Church, nor was their knowledge going to be deemed subordinate or secondary in its status. Scientific knowledge, the knowledge gained by experiment, was to be all. One way of ensuring that it was to be all was to deny any reality over and above that revealed by 'experience'—where 'experience' was defined to mean just those things on which the scientific expert can pronounce. This was why the mathematician W. K. Clifford, for example, was so keen to portray geometry as an *empirical* science, and why he was so keen to press the case for non-Euclidean geometry.[25] To adopt the standard view—that Euclidean geometry was *a priori* knowledge of reality—was to open the flood-gates to all manner of claims and, in particular, to the *a priori* claim of the established Church. So once again the idea that objective reality is immediately accessible is used to bring it within a group's control, and to undermine established and authoritative interpretations of the world. The same two explanatory principles therefore apply:

[25] J. Richards, 'The Reception of a Mathematical Theory: Non-Euclidean Geometry in England, 1868–1883', *Natural Order: Historical Studies of Scientific Culture*, B. Barnes and S. Shapin (eds) (London: Sage, 1979), 143–166.

namely, the social use of nature, and the idea of group interests. Empiricism functioned as the ideology of scientific professionalism.[26]

I have, of course, only been able to sketch the application of these explanatory principles. Much more needs to be said, and in the discussion of these and other cases by the historians whose work I have been citing, much more *is* said. Naturally, there will be counter-examples with which to challenge the ideas I have just put forward. These should be welcomed. They will help to deepen and refine the explanations, or perhaps even modify them more profoundly. But counter-examples will only be useful if they are formulated with care. Superficial claims about 'the same' theory serving quite different purposes, or being generated in quite different circumstances, will only serve to distract attention from more important matters. It is no use, for example, saying that 'atomism' was developed by the seventeenth-century corpuscular philosophers, and 'the same' theory was developed by the Greeks, so the sociology of knowledge is wrong. QED. The corpuscular philosophers wrought very specific modifications on their intellectual heritage when they fashioned atomism anew for their special purposes. They were critics of pagan atomism, as well as exploiters of it. In the eyes of Robert Boyle, for example, the pagan atomists made the great mistake of endowing their atoms with the capacity to move themselves—their nature was self-moving. And that was the very idea he was trying to oppose: this was why he modified the ancient atomism. The two theories were therefore *not* the same, but we can only become sensitive to this fact by treating the theories in the context of their use. Theories, like meanings, are made over and over again in each new context of employment.

As well as counter-examples I also anticipate another, more radical, line of objection. I suspect that some philosophers who declare an interest in objectivity will say that they can do their work of analysis without having to bother with the complications and details of historical case-studies. Even if they do not make claim to a purely *a priori* method and subject matter, they may still feel that all the relevant facts are of a highly general character, and can be discovered by a little intelligent reflection. It is easy to see the attractions of this position. It makes life easier and keeps the issue conveniently within departmental boundaries. But if we really want to investigate that particular property of belief to which the concept of 'objectivity' refers, then we must examine the factors on which it depends and the relations of cause and effect that

[26] See, for example, F. M. Turner, 'The Victorian Conflict between Science and Religion: a Professional Dimension', *Isis* **lxix** (1978), 356–376; L. S. Jacyna, *Scientific Naturalism in Victorian Britain: An Essay in the Social History of Ideas*, unpubl. Ph.D. thesis, University of Edinburgh (1980).

bear upon it. Our concept or idea of objectivity will then be as rich and as complex as our understanding of what it refers to. My claim is that no 'analysis' of the concept can pass muster unless it shows a proper awareness of the role of 'interests' and the significance of what I have called the 'social use' of nature.

(vi) Conclusion

I began by saying that a theory of objectivity should tell us about its causes, its intrinsic nature and its sources of variation. I have now formulated replies to these questions. The causes of objectivity are social and reside in the necessity we are all under to establish a coherent form of social life. The nature of objectivity—its mode of being—is social, because to be objective is to be a social institution. The causes of variation in objectivity are social, for they are whatever move men to try to alter their institutions. The manner and character of its variation are, accordingly, defined and limited by the range of options that we have in organizing our social life. If these are endless, then the forms of knowledge will be endless. If they are limited and revolve around a small range of basic possibilities, then so will the forms of objectivity. These are matters for further study.

I do not hope to have convinced you of the truth of the social theory of objectivity, but I would be sorry if I had not convinced you that there was promise and utility in the ideas behind it. I offer it as a basis for interesting future work, and as a counterbalance to superficial or purely polemical accounts of a most intriguing phenomenon. If, on hearing that sentiment, you immediately detect within it a particular bias about the nature of objective thinking, then I will not have failed totally in my efforts.[27]

[27] The discussion after the lecture drew to a close with a philosopher expressing the following sentiment: there might be things wrong with Platonism, but at least it does justice to the fact that when we formulate a proposition there is such a thing as getting it right or getting it wrong FULL STOP. The theory I am proposing says that the termination of dispute and doubt is itself a social process. We have, so to speak, the institution of the FULL STOP. This idea is central to Wittgenstein's late work: that doubt and justification alike come to an end with conventions and a form of life. It is also the idea that is central to the work of the ethnomethodologists. They express the point by saying that the job of repairing indexicality can never be completed. In the idiom of philosophy the point may be re-expressed by saying that all knowledge claims are 'philosophical', i.e. open to dispute. There are only sceptical solutions to sceptical doubts. When we have discovered how we live with the permanent possibility of scepticism, and how and why the possibility is sometimes exploited and sometimes overridden, then we will have understood the social nature of objectivity.

Tractatus Sociologico-Philosophicus

ERNEST GELLNER

I

Men make themselves radically different pictures of reality.

The crucial word in this assertion is 'radically'. Its full force is not often appreciated. But 'picture' also requires some elucidation. The term suggests, like the word 'vision', something relatively static. A 'vision of reality', a style of thought, a culture, is in fact an ongoing process, and one which contains internal options, alternatives, disagreements. There is no language in which one cannot both affirm and deny. Even, or perhaps especially, a culture which maintains that the big issues have been finally settled within it, can yet conceive of the alternatives which are being denied and eliminated. It must give some reasons, however dogmatic, for selecting that which it does select and for excluding that which it excludes, and thus in a way it concedes that things could be otherwise.

This brings us back to one of the ways, perhaps the most important way, in which visions do differ *radically*. They differ in the criteria, and in particular in the terminal criteria, which they employ for the settling of internal disputes, for adjudicating one option to be superior to its rival or rivals.

There is disagreement concerning just how much radical divergence of these kinds there really is in the world. On the one hand, partisans of the fashionable 'incommensurateness' thesis maintain that divergences really are both common and profound, and even conclude that translations from one vision to another are either impossible, or occur only as the result of an accidental, 'fluky', partial overlap between two visions.

On the other hand, anthropologists, who can claim that the noting and documenting of such differences in vision is part of their professional task, are not always convinced that the differences really are so profound or pervasive.[1] They may insist that the oddity or eccentricity of a 'vision' is more in the mode of utterance than in what is

---

[1] Cf. for instance the celebrated work of the late Sir Edward Evans-Pritchard on *Nuer Religion* (Oxford: Clarendon Press, 1956) or C. Lévi-Strauss' *Pensée Sauvage* (Paris, 1962; English translation, Weidenfield and Nicolson, 1966), or more recently, the arguments of Dr Maurice Bloch, in his Malinowski Memorial Lecture, *Man* (N.S.) **12** (1977), 278–292.

actually meant; and that the incommensurateness is consequently in the eye or pen of the translator, who translates literally and does not allow for the shorthand, the elipsis which he takes for granted in his own language or 'vision'. On these lines, it can be claimed that the documentation of 'odd', radically different (from our viewpoint) visions relies overly on solemn, ritual, ceremonial statements and disregards their more humdrum, day-to-day companions in the culture in question, and that the interpretation does not allow sufficiently for what may be called Ritual Licence.

As against this, it can be urged that the comforting view that 'basically all conceptual systems are similar in their basic traits', may itself be an artefact of rules of translation, a projection of conceptual charity, a determination to 'make sense' of alien utterance or conduct, come what may.

This issue is open, and no doubt the questions which make it up could be refined further. But for present purposes, this question need not be settled. There is no doubt whatever about the existence of rival decision-procedures, of terminal courts of appeal, in various styles of thought. In this sense, visions do differ radically.

Once this is admitted, it follows that there is and can be no formal solution of the problem of relativism. If there are two rival visions A and B, and each contains as part of itself the claim that the final court of appeal for cognitive disputes is a' and b', and the application of procedure a' endorses most of A and damns most of B, and vice versa, then there is no *logical* way of converting an adherent of A to B, or B to A.

II

The important carriers of rival visions are collectivities, and these are neither stable nor discrete.

The situation recorded in this statement is easily confirmed by the straightforward observation of simple matters of fact, the commonplaces of history. Diverse visions are carried by various communities and subcommunities; these change, split and fuse, and their visions are transformed with them.

Perhaps radically distinct visions are also on occasion carried by single individuals, or even by temporary or partial moods of single individuals. Recently, an argument was fashionable which purported to show that a 'private language', a system of notions in the exclusive possession of a single individual, was impossible. One point of the argument was that, if valid, it overcame and refuted solipsism, or any form of relativism pushed to the point of insisting on the incommensurateness—and hence incommunicability—of individual visions of single persons. If language or concepts were essentially public parts of a shared linguistic or conceptual community, then individuals were prevented from the very start from imposing solitary conceptual confinement on themselves. The very act of speaking or thinking forced gregariousness on to them. Man was doomed to be a political animal from sheer conceptual need. If a private vision, distinct from all others, can indeed be carried by an individual, or even by a temporary mood of an individual, then the argument which we shall apply to collectively carried visions can easily be extended to such individuals and moods. What is not in dispute is that communities can carry, so to speak, collectively private views. But in a mobile world of overlapping communities, the diversity of communal visions is a problem, not a solution. It is in fact *the* problem under consideration.

It is interesting to note that, on this issue of relativism, two recently fashionable doctrines point in quite opposite directions. The denial of the possibility of private languages and hence of private worlds which, if cogent, condemns us all, whether we wish it or not, to share the public world projected by a public language, bans all conceptual Robin-sonades, and thus (if valid) overcomes individual relativism: the very act of speech, it would seem, establishes a shared public world with shared criteria of validity. At the same time, the just as fashionable doctrine of the incommensurateness of diverse conceptual systems makes relativism not merely respectable but virtually mandatory. If conceptual systems A and B are incommensurate, and if there is no superior and neutral system C in terms of which they could be compared, no rational choice between A and B is possible. If there is no exchange rate between two currencies and no international currency, gold standard or what not, in terms of which they could both be expressed, then there is no possible rational way of assessing their relative cognitive purchasing power.

III

There are two main ways of assessing the relative merit of visions: by Cosmic Exile, or by assessing the Moral Excellence of the contestants.

Cosmic Exile (the phrase is Professor Quine's, and denotes a philosophic aspiration which he denigrates) is a philosophical strategy initiated above all by René Descartes, and brought to a high degree of refinement by the entire epistemological tradition of modern thought, notably—but not exclusively—by the empiricists. The underlying idea is simple, attractive and tempting. It is this: if there exists rival, total, internally coherent (not to say circular and self-maintaining), but externally incompatible visions of the world, as indeed they do, would it not be best to stand outside the world, or rather, outside all these rival available *worlds*, and judge their respective merits from such an extraneous, and hence hopefully impartial, uncontaminated, viewpoint? Arbitrators are normally recruited from outside the dispute, from amongst people equally unconnected, or only symmetrically connected with the disputing parties. When it comes to choosing a *world*, should one not do the same?

And how does one attain this Cosmic Exile? How does one stand outside the world, or all rival worlds? A much favoured recipe for attaining this is the following: clear your mind of all the conceptions, or rather preconceptions, which your education, culture, background, what-have-you, have instilled in you, and which evidently carry their bias with them. Instead, attend carefully only to that which is inescapably *given*, that which imposes itself on you whether you wish it or not, whether it fits in with your preconceptions or not. This purified residue, independent of your will, wishes, prejudices and training, constitutes the raw data of this world, as they would appear to a newly arrived Visitor from Outside. We were not born yesterday. We are not such new arrivals, but we can simulate such an innocent, conceptually original state of mind; and that which will be or remain before us when we have done so, is untainted by prejudice, and can be used to judge the rival, radically distinct and opposed visions. This, in simple terms, is the programme.

Assessment by Moral Excellence is quite a different strategy.

The underlying argument or image is something as follows: the world abounds in rival and incompatible visions, each with its own internal standards of validation, and all of them endorse and fortify their carriers and damn and castigate their rivals. Sometimes, no doubt, there are partial overlaps; which enable the debate or dialogue to go on with a semblance of reason, of appeal to shared ground.

But the chaos, the inward-turned approval and the outward-turned condemnation, are not complete. If we investigate the pattern of rivalry and succession, we do find, precisely, a pattern and an order. For one thing, some of these rival worlds are carried by communities much more attractive than others. By their fruits thou shalt know them: is not the blessedness of the carrier some indication of the soundness of the message carried? Moreover, the overlap in criteria, which enables us on occasion to judge worlds which are neighbours in time or space, by norms which both parties accept in some measure—that overlap itself is part of a series, of a grand pattern, with other such overlaps. To take an oft-invoked example, diverse moral worlds sometimes share the same assessment of a given kind of conduct, and differ only in the range of people to whom the obligation, or prohibition, is to apply.

Neighbouring communities may share the same reaction to the kind of behaviour in question, but one of them may be more generous, more extensive in the application of the principle in question. We may then discern, under the diversity of values, some kind of linear progression, a cumulation, which may in turn be related to other important traits of the social carrier—the complexity of social organization, or the power of its technology, or what not. By identifying this underlying principle, we learn a kind of cosmic grading of the options or visions found *in* the world. Global history itself evaluates the options found within itself. *Weltgeschichte ist Weltgericht.*

These two overall strategies are the most important themes in modern thought; their intertwining *is* the history of modern thought.

The weaknesses of each of the two strategies are well known. Indeed each side is often forcefully reminded of them by its rivals.

Against the idea of Cosmic Exile, it is urged that the operation it engages is quite impossible, and that the claims that it has been done are simply exercises in self-deception. It is not possible for us to carry out a total conceptual strip-tease and face bare data in total nudity. We cannot, as Marx put it, divide society in two halves, endowing one with the capacity to judge the other. We can only exchange one set of assumptions or interpretations for another.

An alternative criticism does not insist that the exercise cannot be carried out, but contents itself with pointing out that if or when carried out, it will not get us anywhere. Pure data are not a world, and they not merely fail to generate a world, they fail even to eliminate any of the rival worlds. The general 'underdetermination of theories by facts', as the phrase goes, makes sure of that, When the neutral, extraneous arbitrator is brought in, it transpires that he is too feeble to pass any judgment. The scanty data at his disposal permit neither theoretical nor moral nor any other choices or decisions. As a cosmic judge, the Pure Visitor lacks sufficient evidence, and is a failure.

The weaknesses of the method of Assessment by Moral Excellence are equally blatant. Where Cosmic Exile presupposed a heroic exercise which is beyond our powers, this method commends an operation which is perfectly feasible—but alas childishly circular. Of course, it is possible to evaluate rival worlds in terms of merit—if you have already granted yourself one world, namely your own, complete with its own values and standards of assessment, in terms of which you can then please yourself and graciously award good conduct marks to the other rival worlds, seen through the prism of your own. If this curious if not comic enterprise ends in your granting the palm to yourself—no wonder! The subtler variant of this argument, which invokes the pattern of differences between various visions, is not less circular, even if the circularity is slightly better camouflaged. If your own value is, for stance, universality or non-discrimination, no doubt you can arrange the historically existing value systems in terms of the closeness of their aproximation to that ideal. You can then pretend, if you wish, that the ideal somehow emanates from the historical or sociological pattern. But the truth is, of course, the other way round: the pattern was generated by measuring societies against the tacitly (or overtly) *assumed* ideal.

IV

Each of these two grand strategies casts its shadow, and the shadow, in each case, is a particular style of viewing the world, a philosophy.

Strictly speaking, the argument now requires that we distinguish, a little pedantically, between two kinds of social 'vision': the primary, unrefined, raw-material ones, and philosophically distilled, smelted, processed ones. *Any* vision within which a community lives can fall into the former class. The second class is more restrictive, and includes only those which have been not merely systematized, but systematized in the face of doubt, the awareness of the problem of diversity of visions and the need to justify one's choice between them. The distinction is not a sharp one, but is an important one. The two visions or styles now under consideration belong to the latter class. They are visions which have passed through the Valley of Doubt and they are identified by the *way* in which they have done it.

To a significant degree, belief systems in our society fall into the refined class. They have been refined in the light of considerations such as have been sketched out above. The manner in which they endeavour to fortify themselves, to justify confidence, and to by-pass doubt, in the main involves using one of the two major strategies as described. These two strategies in turn have profound effect on the world-views which have passed, so to speak, through their sieve. The visions which prevail, at any rate at the intellectually more sophisticated levels of our society, tend to be impregnated with these two general criteria and with their effects.

These criteria cast their shadow: each of them tends to produce rather distinctive *kinds* of world. Let us use the terms 'positivistic' and 'Hegelian', without prejudice, as shorthand code terms for the two strategies—for the attempt, on the one hand, to evaluate rival visions by matching them against pure data, as recorded by a simulated new arrival to the universe, and, on the other hand, for the attempt to evaluate visions by assessing the merit and historic role of their social carriers.

The positivist strategy generates a world which is granular; where the grains, as in well-cooked rice, are discrete from each other, and easily separable; they have a quality of givenness or hardness, of simply being there for no general reason and without thought of anything outside themselves; the theories which cover or describe them are indeed but summaries of the patterns of those grains. They have no more intimate or intuitively plausible or compelling connection with them, which gives the data a brutish, self-contained, uncommunicative air; the theories are drawn from a reservoir containing an infinity of such possible patterns, and nothing other than the contingent constellation of facts can select one of them in preference to others; so the game is, ultimately, random, and 'meaningless'. Over and above their lack of inner necessity, the theories may well be formulated in technical language and be counter-intuitive or unintelligible; they are morally indifferent, passing no implicit judgment on the conduct of men or societies; they are also so to speak identity-indifferent; holding or rejecting any one of them seldom makes any difference to the identity, to the self-definition, of the person holding them. And, by and large, they find their home in the natural sciences, and in the social sciences only when these deliberately endeavour to emulate the natural sciences.

By contrast, the Hegelian strategy tends to leave one with worlds which are not granular/atomic but, on the contrary, intimately intertwined, suffused with a sense of unity—but also, pervaded by 'meaning': the interconnected elements have meaning for each other in that they play roles in each other's fates and in the wider plans of which they are part. Elements in the pattern, such as actions, are what they are in virtue of what they *mean* to the agents who perform them, rather than in virtue of merely external traits. 'Meaning' enters at least twice over, as the significance conferred by participants, and that conferred by the observer. Each is legitimate and, moreover, connected with the other. The relationship of theory to fact is more personal. The theory confers life and legitimacy and vigour on fact. It is not alien to it, and is not merely a shorthand summary for it. It animates the patterns, it does not just abbreviate and codify them. The data revel in the place they occupy in the theoretical pattern. Available theories are not technical nor drawn from the same infinite reservoir: they are intelligible to the actors, they are finite in number and figure on the list of dramatis personae, their confrontations and compromises are an essential part of the plot. They are anything rather than morally neutral, and the attitude which a human character adopts towards them profoundly modifies his identity: the choice of theory is but an aspect of a choice of self and life-style. The home territory of this kind of vision is, of course, history and society.

This, then, is the familiar overall confrontation: a granular, cold, technical and naturalistic world confronts a holistic, meaning-saturated, identity-conferring, social-humanistic one. Occasionally they raid each other's territory and even attempt to occupy large parts of it permanently. Much of the so-called social sciences is a dogged attempt to handle and interpret human affairs in the image of natural science. Conversely, *naturphilosophie* attempts to do the opposite. There are, of course, doctrines which endeavour to combine the appeal of both approaches. Marxism contains both a *naturphilosophie* and a naturalistic, reductive sociology and it tells a moral global tale which reveals the true identity of all characters, and yet also claims impartial, scientific status. Psycho-analysis owes its appeal to the fact that it is simultaneously, through medicine, a part of science, and yet also maintains, nay reinforces, the importance of the intimately personal and immediate, the significance and meaning for the participant. Its theories/interpretations partake all at once of the technical esotericism of science and of the lusty immediacy of one's most personal experience. In brief, the ideological vigour and intense appeal of doctrines which live on this particular borderline, testify eloquently to the importance of that grand opposition in our intellectual life.

But let us leave the hybrid border population and return to the grand positivist/Hegelian opposition. How is one to assess the rival merits of these two great contestants?

Is the world icy and atomic, or warm and intertwined? Which of these two grand meta-visions is the correct one? At this point I shall refrain from making any definitive pronouncements and settling the ultimate nature of reality. Instead, I wish to stress the following interesting point: the two great visions are not only (perhaps not at all) reports on *how things are*; they are reflections, echoes of the two strategies initially adopted for choosing from amongst primary, unrefined visions.

The generation of these meta-visions works as follows: if you are determined to judge things by confronting them with pure, unsullied, unprejudiced data, you will naturally try to break up data into their constituent parts, if possible relenting in this effort of 'analysis' only when ultimate constituent atoms are located. The granularity or atomicity of the world is not so much in the data but in the way of handling the world. The separation will be both lateral and qualitative: 'lateral' in space and time, isolating experience into blobs and sounds and instants, and 'qualitative' in separating all features which can be separated in thought. The various atomic metaphysics (with sensory, material or logical 'atoms') are the eventual consequences, the shadows or projections of this kind of operation. The same is true for the other familiar traits of the positivistic vision.

And, of course, there are very good reasons for proceeding in this atomizing manner. The commonest, most familiar ploy employed by primary visions for imposing their authority on men, is to present themselves as an integral package-deal, not available for separate, part-by-part examination. These visions generally insist on being swallowed whole. To dissect them, they say, is to travesty them, to miss the point; and if they can get away with it, they declare any such granular examination to be blasphemous. And, indeed, as long as they can only be examined as 'totalities', they are generally safe. The well of truth is within the ramparts; it feeds those within and is withheld from the enemies outside.

So the positivistic vision is in some measure the shadow of a cognitive strategy; but the same is also true of its great rival. Is the world a unity, suffused with meanings, meanings which form a system with their rivals, such that their interplay clicks into a pattern, like a well-constructed play, in which later scenes illuminate the significance of what had passed before, and where in the end everything fuses so as to point a moral of it all? One may well doubt it. But if the Hegelian-type strategy is to work, if the choice of final resting-vision is to be made without standing outside, but rather by evaluating the characters and their messages from within the play—well, if all that is to be possible, then something like this must be the case, and those celebrated categories, or slogans, of totality, mediation, dialectic, had better apply to the world . . . otherwise, it all simply won't work. There must be reasonably coherent characters; they must interact, and their cumulative interaction must add up to a decent plot.

Thus, there are good reasons for seeing the world in both the granular and in the holistic manner. To me, the most persuasive argument for atomism in epistemology is that unless it is forcibly imposed, *any* belief system can, through its internal organization, make itself invulnerable. A strong argument for holism is that systems such as language, in the sense of the capacity to generate and understand an infinite range of messages, cannot function as a consequence of a mere accumulation of grains, but presuppose an underlying mechanism, for reasons which Chomsky has made familiar. Functioning systems, such as organisms or languages, certainly are not mere assemblages of independent atoms.

V

God is not garrulous.

This is no trite assertion. It contradicts both the Old Testament and Hegel. The contrary idea—that God *is* garrulous—is plausible, well-diffused and, if true, would be an important element in answering the question as to how we select a valid vision.

Ernest Gellner

By divine garrulousness I mean here the idea that the true verdict is indicated by historical *repetition*. Repetition, Kierkgaard insisted in a different context, is a religious category. It is certainly a mode of persuasion. If you insist long enough and often enough you finally succeed in persuading.

The curious thing was that when loss of faith and the scientific revolution eroded religion in Western society, there was no need to abandon at the same time the belief in the garrulousness of revelation, in the demonstration of ultimate truth by crescendo and repetition. Though the specific *content* apparently had to change, the reiterative intensifying *form* could remain. Indeed, it could remain not in one but in two media. Two great intellectual events occurred, one towards the end of the eighteenth century, one in the nineteenth: the crystallization of the belief in *progress,* which gave sense to human striving and made up for human misery, constituted a new and effective secular theodicy; and secondly, the formulation and acceptance of the idea of biological evolution affirmed much the same, but on an even larger, indeed incomparably larger, canvas.

It was not surprising that a society, accustomed to an old religious tradition to confirm its faith by Cumulative Repetition, should seize on historical progress or on biological evolution as new sources of grand garrulous repetition to confirm a vision and its values. This is what the then fashionable philosophies of progress and/or evolution really said: the thinker discerns the message—say the movement forward to greater complexity and differentiation, to more freedom, more consciousness, more happiness, or what have you—and reminds us of how insistently history, whether biological or human, has repeated and confirmed its truth for us. It sounded plausible, and the West was certainly ready to accept this message, to a large extent did accept it, thus retaining Revelation by Repetition, substituting a new revealed message for the old one.

Alas, it was all false. What differentiates that modern cognitive style, which made possible sustained growth of knowledge and a technology of unprecedented power, is not simply one further repeat performance, at most on a somewhat larger scale than its predecessors, of a style already anticipated in the Stone Age or by the amoeba. No: it was a new style altogether.

So epistemic atomism, whether or not it is a correct report on the ultimate constitution of things, is a device forced upon the honest inquirer by the most common, and perhaps the most important ploy employed by adherent- and loyalty-seeking belief-systems, i.e. the package deal. Package-dealing was so often conflated with what I have called Divine Garrulousness, that the intellectual image called forth by the term 'Hegelianism' tends to conjure up *both* these views. Yet they are logically quite separable, and the time has now come when it is essential to separate them. God is *not* garrulous; history does not cumulatively reiterate the same message for the benefit of the faithful; but another ingredient of 'Hegelianism', the evaluation of vision by the evaluation of its carrier, may still have some life left in it.

VI

Positivists are right, for Hegelian reasons. This the essence of our situation.

Viewed as two self-sustaining visions, or metavisions, positivism and Hegelianism are, each of them, both attractive and haunted by difficulties: but as each of them confirms itself—each is a fort with its own well or truth, sustaining its garrison and inaccessible to outsiders—there is no reason to expect a 'logical' resolution of their dispute, i.e. a formal demonstration, from shared and neutral premises, that one of them is superior to the other.

In fact, the choice is made, and can only be made, in the 'Hegelian' manner, in the sense initially defined in this context—that is, by considering, generically, the merits of the carriers of the two doctrines.

It seems to me fairly obvious that intellectual traditions inspired by the Cartesian-empiricist virtues, aspiring to atomism, to the breaking up of questions, to abstention from intellectual package deals, to the separation of truth from identity, fact and value, are, by and large, traditions which have not only been markedly more successful in their cognitive endeavours, but have also been associated with social orders more attractive and acceptable than their rivals, judging by the manner most of mankind votes 'with its feet', by its concrete choices. Notoriously, they also pay a certain price for their achievements: an atomized, cognitively unstable world, which does not underwrite the identities and values of those who dwell in it, is neither comfortable nor romantic. No purpose is served by pretending that this price does not need to be paid; and no doubt there will be many reluctant to pay it, or at least willing to pretend that they will not pay it (whether or not they would seriously forgo the benefits of industrial—scientific civilization, or merely encourage others to do so); and there will be others still who believe, mistakenly in my view, that the price need not be paid at all, that one can both have one's romantic cake and scientifically eat it.

The irony of the situation, if my account of it is correct, is manifest. The positivistic atomic/empirical vision is to be preferred, but the reasoning which alone can clinch this choice is characteristically Hegelian. It consists of looking at the total complex, at the rival carriers of the opposed visions, and chooses in terms of their merits as totalities. But this procedure does not receive any additional and comforting reinforcement from being one of a long series of similar choices; God is not garrulous, so it is *not* Hegelian any longer in the sense of being inserted into a global series, as one of the successive *pronunciamentos* of one garrulous cosmic authority.

The situation is deeply paradoxical. The atomistic vision is chosen as a totality, holistically, because, as a tradition, it erodes all others, and creates a society with cumulative knowledge, increasing technological power, with at least a tendency towards liberty. Atomism itself is bought as a package deal.

The double confirmation of our vision—by model-plausibility and by historic success—is, philosophically, profoundly inelegant. It is also indispensable. The inelegance flows from the fact that the spirit of the two confirmations is so much in a different style, that their juxtaposition really constitutes a stylistic solecism. The very tone and texture of either one of them is calculated to reduce the effects of the other one to bathos. . . . Yet, none the less, this is our ideological fate.

Validation by assessing the merits of the social carriers is rather grand and imposing, but in quite a different and rather messy way. We are no longer at the very limits of the world, where petty, specific historical facts are ignored, and where only the most general, formal features of reality are admitted. We are *inside* the world (hence the notorious circularity of 'Hegelian' assessment procedures). Here we look at the tangled, complex social/historical reality of the last few centuries, and attempt as best we can to extract the basic options. On balance, one option—a society with cognitive growth based on a roughly atomistic strategy—seems to us superior, for various reasons, which are assembled without elegance; this kind of society alone can keep alive the large numbers to which humanity has grown, and thereby avoid a really ferocious struggle for survival among us; it alone can keep us at the standard to which we are becoming accustomed; it, more than its predecessors, *probably* favours a liberal and tolerant social organization (because affluence makes brutal exploitation and suppression unnecessary, and because it requires a wide diffusion of complex skills and occupational mobility which in turn engender a taste for both liberty and equality). This type of society also has many unattractive traits, and its virtues are open to doubt. On balance, and with misgivings, we opt for it; but there is no question of an elegant, clear-cut choice. We are half pressurized by necessity (fear of famine, etc.), half persuaded by a promise of liberal affluence (which we do not fully trust). There it is: lacking better reasons we will have to make do with these.

And yet, the elegance of Terminal Atomism, radical empiricism which makes the data base sovereign, so to speak, would not on its own convince us (the rival picture was about as good); while, without that Atomism (or positivism, or mechanistic empiricism, or whatever you wish to call it), a purely sociological account of industrial–scientific society and its ethos, would hang in the air. Empiricist-materialist philosophy, with its pretensions to terminality, does make it intellectually a bit more appealing and respectable.

This incongruous double vindication is not an altogether comfortable and satisfying situation, but no better one is available.

VII

He who understands me need not disavow the assertions by which he has reached this perception, but may and should continue to use the ladder by which he has ascended.[2]

---

[2] A longer and slightly different version of this paper is also to be published in *Comparative Social Dynamics: Essays in Honor of S. N. Eisenstadt*, Erick Cohen, Moshe Lissak and Uri Almagor (eds) (Boulder, Colorado: Westview Press, forthcoming).

Index of Names

Select Index of Subjects

belief, 11

critical theory, 156ff.
cultural divergence, 1f., 21, 61f., 97, 106f., 108f., 165
culture, 97ff.
culture, autonomy of, 21, 93, 102f., 120–132

disagreement, 209ff.

ethnocentricity, 1ff., 7ff., 20, 55
eugenics, 114f.

freedom, 81ff.
functionalism, 6f.

human nature, 21, 95ff., 117, 227f.

ideology, 8f., 18f., 20, 112, 150, 245f.
Institutional theory of art, 47ff.

objectivity, 60, 94, 206f., 209, 214f., 229ff., 235ff., 244ff.
objectivity of ethics, 95, 116, 135–170 *passim,* 211, 218n
see ethnocentricity

positivism, 211, 252f., 257f.

relativism, 15, 21, 23ff., 43ff., 105, 106f., 159, 248f.
see also under ethnocentricity

science, 57f., 211ff., 245ff., 256
Social Darwinism, 88, 93, 112
sociology, 41, 90f., 93–110, 111–132 *passim*
sociology of knowledge, 94, 246
structuralism, 9f.